Issues in Microanalysis

The Analysis of Educational Productivity

Volume I: Issues in Microanalysis

Edited by

Robert Dreeben
J. Alan Thomas

Ballinger Publishing Company • Cambridge, Massachusetts
A Subsidiary of Harper & Row, Publishers, Inc.

This book is printed on recycled paper.

This project has been funded at least in part with Federal funds from the Department of Health, Education, and Welfare under contract number 400-77-0094. The contents of this publication do not necessarily reflect the views or policies of the Department of Health, Education, and Welfare, nor does mention of trade names, commercial products, or organizations imply endorsement by the U.S. Government. The Department of Health, Education, and Welfare holds a royalty-free, non-exclusive and irrevocable right to reproduce, publish, or otherwise use and to authorize others to use this work for government purposes.

International Standard Book Number: ISBN 0-88410-191-6

Library of Congress Catalog Card Number: 79-26118

Printed in the United States of America

BT 8491-80   5-30-80

Library of Congress Cataloging in Publication Data

Main entry under title:

Issues in microanalysis.

(The Analysis of educational productivity; v. 1)
"Papers . . . originally presented at a two-day conference held at the Department of Educational [University of Chicago] in June, 1978."
Bibliography: p.
Includes index.
1. Educational tests and measurements—United States. 2. Ability—Testing—Congresses. 3. Education—Economic aspects—United States—Congresses. I. Dreeben, Robert. II. Thomas, James Alan. III. Series: Analysis of educational productivity;
v. 1.
LA132.A53 vol. 1   [LB3051]   370s   [371.2'6]   79-26118
ISBN 0-88410-191-6

Contents

✳

List of Tables

❋

List of Figures

xi

✳

Acknowledgments

The papers published in this volume and in its companion volume were written under the auspices of the Educational Finance and Productivity Center, Department of Education, University of Chicago. The Center was generously supported by the National Institute of Education (Contract No. 400-77-0094) and benefited particularly from the efforts of Michael Cohen and Virginia Koehler.

The papers were originally presented at a two day conference held at the Department of Education in June 1978. We are most grateful to the authors themselves as discussants of each others' papers; to Professor Jacob Michaelsen, University of California, Santa Cruz; and to members of the Advisory Board of the Center: Professor John E. Coons, University of California, Berkeley; Professor Robert M. Hauser, University of Wisconsin–Madison; Professor Luvern L. Cunningham, Ohio State University; and Professor W. Lee Hansen, University of Wisconsin–Madison.

We are especially indebted to Ruth Melville for editing the manuscripts for both volumes and to Sharon Rosen for taking administrative responsibility for the entire enterprise.

We wish to thank the following members of the staff in the Department of Education for their valuable assistance: Robyn Beatty, Aimee B. Collier, Yvette Courtade, Martha Harris, Karol Noble, and Nancy Ward.

※

Introduction

Robert Dreeben and J. Alan Thomas
University of Chicago

The papers presented in this collection represent, we believe, the emerging second generation of investigations on educational effects. While they are not themselves empirical works, they reexamine the existing empirical and conceptual literature in ways that set a new agenda for understanding how educational institutions operate.

The first generation of investigations consisted of three basic types. The first are those commonly considered to be "production function" studies—in a loose and metaphorical sense of that term—of which the Coleman Report (Coleman et al., 1966) is surely the most widely known and is also perhaps prototypical. The Coleman Report is a school effects study that compares the characteristics of schools and treats the relationship between variation in those characteristics and variation in educational outcomes (aggregate levels of achievement). Schools are characterized by the composition of the teaching force, of the student body, and of the community; and these three elements are treated as stocks of resources representing factors of educational production. While the Coleman Report concerns itself with schools, other investigations treat school districts or classrooms as centers of production. All of these investigations seek to identify educational resources whose variations will account for differences in educational achievement.

The second type are commonly known as "status attainment" studies, some of which show how aspects of schooling influence levels of and changes in achievement of individuals in schools, while others show how they influence the life chances of individuals during their postsecondary and posttertiary school years. At issue here are such matters as school track, teacher quality, years of schooling (examined in combination with family and peer influences), and school attendance or nonattendance. Studies of status attainment do not deal with schools as productive agencies, but with education as it contributes to an individual's level of school achievement and adult occupational status and earnings. The impact of schooling in this context must not be confused with school or educational effects in the previous context.

Finally, there are studies of variations in adult knowledge and moral conviction that are attributable to different amounts of schooling during youth. This approach treats only the long-term products and by-products of length of schooling among individuals; it does not inquire into the nature of education or into the productivity of schools. All three types of study concern educational effects, but in different ways; only the first concerns problems related to the nature and workings of educational organizations that affect educational productivity.

Early in the development of production function formulations of education, investigators were aware of the fact that productive activities varied within schools as well as between them. Averaging individual variations to achieve school level measures and ignoring processes occurring internal to schools had the consequence of regarding student bodies as homogeneous. But it was contrary to common sense that all students within schools and within classrooms were treated alike or that they all received comparable amounts of material resources and instructional attention. While very few investigators addressed these problems, many more treated within school problems as if they were status attainment problems. A case in point are the studies of "tracking," which are not actually studies of tracks, but of students identified by track membership. Nevertheless, the issues of within school variation were on the agenda, although few people were addressing that agenda.

It should be recognized, moreover, that for many years psychologists of various hues and stripes, interested in classroom instruction, investigated relationships between teaching and learning. However, even though the research was done in schools, it reflected no particular interest in schools. Most psychological investigators treated teachers in isolation from their surroundings: they looked at teacher traits and activities as they related to learning outcomes among students. And despite a closer perspective on students (compared with production function studies of schools), this work, relying on the notions of teacher style and classroom climate, also regarded students in classrooms as being treated alike. (A notable exception to this statement is the work on aptitude-treatment interaction.)

The second generation of educational effects studies addresses a variety of questions left unexamined by the first generation, and it is to these questions that the authors of the works included in this collection speak most centrally. As we indicated earlier, no one who was knowledgeable about schools seriously believed that all students in a class or a school were actually treated alike. However, because of artifacts related to high levels of aggregation, students within schools were treated statistically alike. It is one thing to say that they should not have been so treated; it is another to think conceptually and empirically about how they should be treated differently. Some of these papers address the latter point.

To understand educational effects, one needs to discover directly what kinds and amounts of instructional resources are made available both to groups of students within schools and within classes and to individual students. One needs to know whether certain categories of students receive different allocations of resources according to their aptitudes, race, sex, or social class, for example. While internal variations in student characteristics, related to variable allocations of resources, have been an acknowledged but unaddressed problem, other problems have scarcely been acknowledged until very recently. First generation research was preoccupied with stocks of resources; it did not address itself explicitly to their allocation and utilization. If a school buys books, but the books stay on a shelf unread, the number of books measures school wealth, not resources brought to bear for instruction. Moreover, resources are not simply particles that can be assigned homogeneously or heterogeneously to different sorts of students. The allocation of resources can be understood in terms of the patterns of instructional groups, of different educational activities, of different kinds of learning materials, and of different formats (whole class and small group instruction, seatwork, and various combinations). These facilities and arrangements constitute processes of resource allocation. They constitute the categories of educational production. In short, the papers included in this volume indicate that educational production is comprised of various processes and forms of resource allocation. They deal with one or another aspect of educational technology and to that extent supplant a perspective on school operation that views it rather narrowly and statically in terms of resource availability.

Much of the first generation work on educational production was constrained by the fact that usually only one measure of outcome (or one at a time) was considered. It was also constrained by the fact that cross-sectional surveys made it impossible to think about schooling as a value-added phenomenon occurring over time. While these limitations and their remedies are obvious in principle, the remedies are not so easy to effect. To study multiple outcomes means understanding both the relationships among the outcomes and those between several outcomes and multiple inputs. And longitudinal research raises some baffling problems of just how to measure change. Second generation research, then, confronts not just minor variations on familiar themes, but a new array of complex and stubborn methodological and conceptual issues.

Finally, there is an explicit recognition in these papers that educational effects are not necessarily understood most appropriately as distinct district effects, school effects, classroom effects, and the like. Obviously there are some issues that are most properly studied at one particular level. Yet ordinary observation tells us that classrooms exist in schools, that schools exist in districts, and that finer gradations of organizational structure can be placed in a many-layered, nested structure. Much closer observation tells us that each level of organization provides certain constraints upon what can happen above and below it; likewise, each level provides certain opportunities for adjacent levels. To understand educational production, then, we need to know the connections between the various levels of educational organizations and how events at each level influence what can and does occur at other levels. To put this idea in more familiar though less precise terms, the relationships among administration, teaching, and learning need to be understood.

The work of the contributors to this collection is clearly second generational in character. Assumptions characterizing first generational work are both explicitly and implicitly called into question, and some of the papers propose remedies for first generational problems. In the preceding pages we have tried to provide a general context for the work of these contributors. None of them deals with the whole picture; all of them, however, concern themselves with significant portions of it.

Below we discuss commonalities among the approaches of the authors in this volume, as well as some of the unique insights each offers. Despite differences in approach, all deal primarily with microprocesses. This emphasis reflects the tendency in much second generational research to regard the classroom as the level where the effects of schooling can be most precisely specified and observed. The chapters deal with the key aspects of the study of school effects—namely, (1) conceptualizing and measuring outcomes, (2) identifying and measuring those school characteristics that affect learning, and (3) examining the processes by which school character-istics are brought to bear on the learning of students. Since these topics are not mutually exclusive, some themes will recur in the following pages.

THE MEASUREMENT
OF EDUCATIONAL OUTCOMES

Few of the first generational researchers were trained in the com-plex field of psychometrics, and it is not surprising that much of their work is vulnerable to criticism on the grounds that outputs are improperly conceptualized and somewhat naively measured. The authors in this volume who deal with this issue are especially con-cerned with the validity of test instruments, the measurement of gains in performance, and the conceptualizing of situations in which multiple outputs are jointly produced.

In the case of large-scale studies using aggregated data, validity issues are relatively unimportant. Since achievement tests are val-idated on the basis of large populations, that no particular class-room teaches the precise content of the tests is relatively unimportant. (In fact, one danger in the use of these tests for evaluative purposes is that some educators may provide instruction based on the precise content of the tests, thus violating assumptions about the distribu-tion of scores.) However, if standardized tests are used as a method of evaluating the effectiveness of specific classroom procedures, the problem of content validity assumes considerable importance, since such tests do not reflect the content taught by any particular teacher. David Berliner points out that there is wide variation among class-rooms in the amount of time devoted to specific aspects of the cur-riculum, and he suggests that these variations will probably lead to differences in performance in achievement test items that reflect these content areas. Therefore, while standardized achievement tests may be highly reliable, they lack, in Berliner's terms, "content validity at the classroom level."

This issue poses severe problems for the second generation re-searcher who is concerned with classroom effects. One solution may be to conduct experimental studies using criterion-referenced tests that are specifically designed to measure the skills included in the ex-periments. However, researchers who prefer naturalistic to experi-mental settings are faced with the problems that (1) existing achieve-ment tests do not reflect what is taught in a cross-section of classrooms and hence cannot be used to measure the effects of classroom processes and (2) no single criterion-referenced test can encompass the content taught in a variety of classrooms, especially if they are purposely chosen to reflect the diversity that exists among school systems.

Even more problematic than the issue of content validity is that second generational school effects studies must deal with the relationship between school processes and learning gains. Previous studies that relied on cross-sectional data ignored this issue; however, identifying the effects of specific classroom procedures or curricula necessitates measuring the performance increment associated with these alternatives.

Again, in a single-classroom experimental study, criterion-referenced tests might provide an adequate measure of gains in learning. In nonexperimental multiclassroom situations where problems of content validity prohibit the use of such instruments, researchers have been forced to use increments in achievement test scores as measures of performance gain; however, it is not clear that an increment of x points in one part of the scale represents the "same amount of learning" as an increment of x points elsewhere in the scale. The problem may be, as Barbara Heyns suggests, that "the single most important item on the educational agenda is constructing and validating tests that can measure learning reliably; there are substantial reasons to doubt that those available can do so."

While issues of content validity and the measurement of achievement gain cannot readily be resolved, second generation researchers of school effects cannot ignore them. An additional problem in the conceptualization and measurement of schooling outcomes is that schools produce many outcomes simultaneously. Jointness in production implies that a single set of inputs may be used in the production of multiple outcomes and that the use of a given input for the production of one output does not subtract from its availability for the production of others. Some aspects of educative services are therefore analogous to the economist's concept of "public goods." One aspect of jointness is that a lecture or discussion conducted by the teacher provides services that are not separable among students; the fact that one student benefits from a lecture does not subtract from the benefits received by classmates. Also, more than one type of skill may be developed at one and the same time: for example, a social studies teacher may teach silent reading and geographic or historical skills and knowledge simultaneously; similarly, the home economics teacher may teach fractions while helping students learn to cook. Finally, there are even more subtle examples of jointness: an open classroom may be implicitly developing decisionmaking skills, while a so-called traditional classroom may be helping students become socialized to fill their future roles as members of the nation's productive system. Jointness refers in part to Berliner's concept of the adjunct curriculum, but it is generalizable to a wider range of schooling outcomes than the term adjunct curriculum implies.

Teachers or schools may therefore be consciously or unconsciously interested in a wide variety of goals, not all of which are measured by standard achievement test batteries. Furthermore, school resources are being utilized to produce several kinds of learning at a given time. Unless this complexity is recognized, classrooms or schools may appear to be more or less efficient than they in fact are.

Chapter 1 (Heyns), Chapter 2 (Brown and Saks), and Chapter 4 (Berliner), deal in greater or lesser degree with issues of educational measurement. They highlight a number of complexities that have not, for the most part, been explicitly recognized by first generational research on educational production. We turn now to a discussion of the issues in the measurement and conceptualization of those school characteristics believed to affect learning.

IDENTIFYING AND MEASURING SCHOOL CHARACTERISTICS

The clearest difference between first and second generational studies of the effects of schooling lies in the conceptualization of relevant school characteristics. First generational studies dealt primarily with stocks of resources such as the number of books in the library, while the second generational emphasis is on resource flows to students, the behavior of teachers rather than their demographic characteristics, and microlevel processes. Furthermore, second generational studies are almost unanimous in regarding students' time as an important input in schooling.

Some of the reasons for this shift are almost self-evident. For example, such characteristics of teachers as their age, length of experience, and college degree have no logical relationship with their classroom performance. Furthermore, there are dangers of misdefining the direction of causality. If, as seems likely, the assignment of teachers to schools and to classrooms is, to a degree, a result of administrators' and communities' matching the characteristics of teachers with those of students, students' learning could determine teacher characteristics rather than the reverse. The strongest reason for including such variables as the number of books in the school library, the experience and training of teachers, and class size as school effect variables is that all these measures affect cost and are therefore directly related to issues in resource allocation; but recent research is dedicated to determining more precisely the relationship between resource allocation and student learning and therefore concentrates on the manner in which resource inputs become embedded in classroom processes, instructional formats, and classroom organizational procedures.

As Harnischfeger and Wiley point out, however, there is a resource allocation dimension to teachers' behavior in classrooms. The manner in which educational expenditures are apportioned among students in a class is partially dependent on teaching strategies such as whole class instruction, instruction in large or small groups, or individual tutoring. The options available to the teacher depend in part on the availability of other persons such as teachers' aides and volunteers. Teachers' decisions about strategies result from their own preferences and from their perceptions of the effectiveness, for their students, of the various strategies being considered.

Obviously some organizing principles are needed to make classrooms understandable, and Brown and Saks propose that one such principle consists of the values and preferences of teachers. According to this point of view, teachers have their own unique preference functions that reflect the values they place on the various outputs of educational systems, including curricular outcomes, and their preferences for the distribution of educational benefits among students. Thus, some teachers may wish to maximize the class mean in a relevant area of achievement while others may want to minimize variance in any given subject area. Teachers' values are therefore important in determining classroom activities because they affect the manner in which resources are distributed among students. And as Harnischfeger and Wiley suggest, teachers may prefer a particular educational strategy. Some, for example, may prefer to teach the entire class as a single unit, while others prefer to individualize instruction. These differences also have distributive implications, since individualization enhances opportunities for teachers to allocate resources among students according to their own judgments and values.

Thus, one major emphasis of second generational studies of school effects is on what teachers do rather than on their demographic characteristics. A second major emphasis, on the input side of the equation, is on how students spend their time. The surge of interest in the effect on learning of the amount of time devoted to it stems in part from the work of Benjamin Bloom and John Carroll, as well as that of several of Bloom's students. Wiley's recent findings that the amount of time devoted to learning varies among schools and is apparently related to mean achievement scores received widespread attention. Ethnographic studies of schools have also focused interest on the manner in which students spend their time as well as on the wide difference between the amount of time made available to students and the time during which they are actually engaged in educational activities.

While Wiley's (1976) earlier study was based on the length of the school day, Berliner points to wide differences among classrooms in the amount of time devoted within the day to specific content areas in reading and mathematics. For example, in a period of about ninety days, one class devoted 400 minutes to linear measurement while another class spent only 29 minutes on this topic. Similarly, one class spent 573 minutes on creative writing, and another class spent only 56 minutes on this topic. Berliner infers that these differences in time allocation will result in differences in average attainment in these topics. He also points out that these differences set limits on the usefulness of standardized tests, because "using standardized tests as outcome measures cannot be defended unless natural variation in choice of content and time allocated to content areas of the curriculum are experimentally controlled."

Harnischfeger and Wiley have developed an accounting system for categorizing the various uses of students' time. They begin by pointing out that a student's active learning time is less than the nominal quantity of time made available by states and school districts, because the former is affected by loss of time due to illnesses and to school closings because of strikes and adverse weather. Active learning time is the quantity of time available for a particular student: this time is divided among various activities such as whole class time, teacher-supervised subgroup time, transition time, and so on. They conclude that studying the time allocations to various learning settings within the total curriculum provides a framework within which pupil learning, teacher effectiveness, and resource allocation may be studied.

Brown and Saks make an interesting contribution to the examination of the complexities of the allocation, within classrooms, of time and other resources. They suggest that classroom technologies are analogous, not to the assembly line, but to the job shop in which various kinds and quantities of both inputs and outputs are used and in which the process of transforming inputs into outputs differs for each unit of output. The relationship of students' time to learning various subjects differs in terms of individual abilities and the nature of each content area. Students are influenced in their allocation of time and effort by the incentives made available to them. Brown and Saks give substantial attention to the manner in which specific types of incentives can be expected to influence students who possess different characteristics.

To summarize, Chapter 2 (Brown and Saks), Chapter 4 (Berliner), and Chapter 5 (Harnischfeger and Wiley) treat questions of the actual allocation of resources in the production of education. They give special attention to the behavior of teachers and not merely, as is typical of first generational researchers, to the characteristics of teachers. All three also deal with the manner in which students' time is utilized in the production of learning. The next section deals with those aspects of the essays that are devoted to an analysis of what goes on in classrooms during the transformation of inputs into outputs, as well as to the implications of this analysis for the statistical treatment of data.

THE ANALYSIS
OF CLASSROOM PROCESSES

All five chapters in this volume emphasize the implications for research of the complexity of outputs, inputs, and the manner in which resources flow to individual students in classrooms. This section summarizes discussions of resource flows and also of the conceptual and methodological problems connected to models that recognize that decisions that affect learning are made at more than one level and that these levels are interrelated.

Harnischfeger and Wiley present a model that permits the analyst to trace personnel resources to individual students. They examine the amount of teachers' time used for direct instruction and for monitoring, managerial, and transitional activities. They then assign costs to individual students by dividing the hourly cost of teachers' time by the number of students in each instructional group.

However, not all the complexities of assigning costs to individual students are adequately dealt with in the Harnischfeger-Wiley analysis. In particular, the study does not treat the issues raised by Brown and Saks, who argue that jointness in production must be considered when teachers' time is assigned among students in instructional groups. Jointness in educational production incorporates the view that when teachers allocate efforts to a group of students through lecturing or discussion formats, all students may receive the results of the instruction more or less equally, since teaching has some of the attributes of a "public good." Hence, to the degree that jointness in production is an accurate description of how resources flow from teachers to students, the size of the group receiving instruction is immaterial to the question of differences among students in the costs of instruction. The alternative assumption proposed by Brown and Saks is that the cost of teachers' time can be allocated to students such that the resources received from one student subtract from those available to others. This "separability" model is closer to the assumptions made by Harnischfeger and Wiley and leads to the notion that group size is a major determinant of the costs that can be allocated to individual students.

Another issue is that material as well as human resources are involved in the production of learning. Although the hourly costs of such resources as books, individualized instructional materials, audiovisual equipment, and even space are low compared with the cost of teachers' services, the use of these materials is important in the consideration of alternative teaching strategies. While the virtual impossibility of comparing the marginal product of human and material resources precludes determining the marginal effect of various input combinations on specific outputs, it is possible that various inputs have specific and unique effects on learning. For example, the ability of students to substitute material resources for human resources may be a function of students' learning ability: high ability students may be more able than those of lesser ability to substitute, for example, books for teachers' services in the production of learning. In this case, the relegation by Harnischfeger and Wiley of "monitoring" to a relatively minor role may be unjustified, since with some students and some content areas, teachers may accomplish their task equally well by managing students' use of materials as by utilizing verbal behavior to produce learning; hence, a high reliance on lecturing and discussion as the main mode of instruction may, for some students, be less efficient than utilizing a variety of methods that include the use of books and prepared seatwork. This may be especially true if a goal of instruction is to develop the student's ability to produce learning independently of adult help.

An important characteristic of second generational studies of school effects is the new awareness that schooling is a multilevel process, involving individual students, classrooms, schools, school districts, and higher levels of government. Earlier studies often attempted to predict individual level performance on the basis of macrolevel data. A prime example of this type of error is making inferences about the distribution of educational outcomes on the basis of knowledge about district level expenditures per pupil; However, expenditures differ across school districts, across schools within districts, across classrooms within schools, and across students within classrooms.

It is widely accepted that the learning of individual students is affected by their own characteristics, the structural characteristics of the classroom and school in which they are located, and the characteristics of their peers. In addition, the amount of money made available at the district level provides resources that in turn represent opportunities to learn, while also setting constraints on learning. A student's learning may be affected by his relative standing within his classroom or within a specific set of peers. Thus, a student who achieves at, say, the 5.5 grade level may be in a different learning environment if he is in a class in which the average achievement is at the 6.5 grade level than if he is in a class where the average achievement is at the 4.5 grade level.

However, the multilevel view of learning should not be limited to examining the effects of higher level processes on individuals, since the characteristics of students may also affect the structuring of classroom activities, the kinds of teachers and principals who are hired, and the content of the curriculum. Teachers' behavior may be partially affected by the mean, variance, and skewness of the ability distribution of students, while a school district's budgetary policy may be influenced by the characteristics of students. For example, if a large portion of the student body in a specific attendance area do not aspire to go to college, there may be pressures on the district to establish a vocational program; curricular specialization at the secondary school level has extremely important budgetary implications, since vocational schools are, by and large, more expensive to operate than academic high schools.

Burstein (Chapter 3) carefully sorts out the various types of effect and points out the dangers inherent in misspecifying the nature of cross-level influence on learning. We believe that this kind of analysis will be essential reading for researchers who wish to expand knowledge about school effects. Equally important, this methodological discussion provides insights into the nature of a hierarchically structured organization where events occurring at one level affect those occurring at others.

REFERENCE

Wiley, D.E. 1976. "Another Hour, Another Day: Quantity of Schooling, a Potent Path for Policy." In *Schooling and Achievement in American Society*, ed. W.H. Sewell, R.M. Hauser, and D.L. Featherman, pp. 225-65. New York: Academic Press.

Coleman, J.S.; E.Q. Campbell; C.J. Hobson; J. McPartland; A.M. Mood; F. Weinfeld; and R.L. York. 1966. *Equality of Educational Opportunity*. Washington, D.C.: Government Printing Office.

 *Chapter 1*

Models and Measurement for the Study of Cognitive Growth*

Barbara Heyns
University of California, Berkeley

INTRODUCTION

The purpose of this study is threefold. First, I will document the pitfalls and empirical anomalies uncovered in making inferences about cognitive growth from longitudinal test score data. Second, I will endeavor to account for the empirical patterns in a plausible manner, using assumptions and models different from those current in the psychometric literature. Finally, I hope to link issues of measurement and measurement error to substantive concerns in sociology and to suggest ways in which one might assess learning. The study is intended to be both a relatively nontechnical assessment of the theory and measurement models associated with standardized testing and a cautionary tale for the analyst inexperienced with longitudinal data.

The issues to be addressed arose during the course of work on an extensive body of longitudinal data on achievement test scores. Like many other educational researchers, I had become convinced that cross-sectional data were inadequate for testing propositions about learning in schools; to my mind, much of the research in education could and should be criticized on these grounds. One

*Prepared for the University of Chicago Educational Finance and Productivity Center and funded by the National Institute of Education, Grant No. G-74-0037. The computer simulation was completed by Richard Juster; Douglas Jones provided invaluable assistance with the statistical derivations found in the Appendix. Comments and suggestions from Educational Finance and Productivity Conference participants, Chicago, June 6-8, 1978, were enormously helpful.

needed longitudinal data, collected with great care, in order to study learning processes in schools or to make any general statement about the effects of education. This intuition still seems basically correct, although I now think that it seriously underestimates the problem. Even the best longitudinal data do not yield unequivocal results.

The critique of test theory and measurement models that follows is primarily substantive, not statistical. There is an enormous literature describing the hazards involved in inferring change from standardized test scores. Psychometricians have warned of the potential fallacies involved in using change scores or making covariance adjustments in order to compare nonrandom groups. Numerous articles have suggested alternative methods for evaluating growth, many of which provide sound statistical advice and procedures for obtaining estimates. Yet there is a remarkable paucity of conclusive or even credible research on cognitive growth. To be sure, social scientists can frequently be faulted for collecting inadequate data or for paying too little heed to the advice of statisticians. Yet the overriding tendency among analysts is to assume that statistical models and measurement are neutral with respect to theoretical concerns. This is patently false. Classical test theory, like any other theory, involves assumptions that should be subjected to test; the results of such tests should be the basis for an appraisal of the theory. This chapter hopes to raise issues conducive to a critical and constructive reappraisal.

At the outset it is important to clarify what will not be at issue. Perhaps the most frequent criticism of standardized testing concerns the validity of measures. It is commonly asserted that neither cognitive achievement nor intelligence is unidimensional and that no single score, however reliable, captures the diversity of skills and talents in a population. While this seems self-evident, it does not negate the importance of measuring specific skills or of measuring them accurately. I will assume, first, that the test scores constructed to measure vocabulary skills or the ability to reason mathematically do so; second, that the observed test scores reflect adequately the relative degree of skill possessed by children; and, finally, that the fact that children can correctly identify synonyms for a larger proportion of words on nominally parallel forms of a vocabulary test suggests that their vocabulary skills have improved. I will also assume that these skills are consequential and that it is better to have more of them than less. In short, I accept the propositions that the achievement tests measure important skills and that they do so with an acceptable degree of accuracy.

The tests that will be used for illustration were administered biannually by classroom teachers to over 1,000 fifth and sixth grade children in a large urban school district. Four parallel forms, which taken together constitute the complete intermediate battery of the Metropolitan Achievement Test series published by Harcourt, Brace, and World in 1959, were retrieved from the centralized data bank of the school system; test results were matched with questionnaires from a parental survey conducted concurrently with the final period of testing. The sample to be analyzed is restricted to the 745 children for whom test scores were available at all four times, on the most reliable subtest—word knowledge (Heyns, 1978). Each form of this subtest consists of fifty-five multiple-choice items. The observed scores are normally distributed; plotting adjacent time periods reveals substantial linearity between pretests and posttest. The reliability calculated for sample children on the final form (KR-20 = .943) compares favorably with the published reliability of .94. Although it was not possible to do an extensive item analysis on each form, I am convinced that the data are of high quality and probably superior to most data available for educational research and evaluation.[1]

The primary question is, To what extent can the results from these tests be used to infer the amount and pattern of cognitive growth during the two year interval examined? Table 1-1 presents the means for the national norming sample reported by the test publisher for the three most common metrics and the observed means calculated for a portion of the sample. Three observations are readily apparent. First, the means for both the sample and the nation routinely increased irrespective of metric. Statistical tests would reveal that the differences were significant during both school years between October and May and were not significant during the intervening summer. Second, Table 1-1 reveals that the gains are not linear with respect to time; neither the sample children nor the norming population appear to have improved their vocabulary skills as rapidly during the sixth grade as they did during the fifth.[2] The third observation is most troubling of all: the pattern of gains is not consistent across metrics but shows different rates of growth for given increments of raw score points.

Based on these patterns, what can be said about the rate of learning among the sample children? One answer, which is not entirely satisfactory, is that gains or rates of growth differ dramatically according to the scaling or metrics applied. Which metric is best? The answer to this question is a major objective of the discussion to follow. One might imagine a not wholly fabricated conversation between a naive educational researcher and an experienced analyst.

Table 1-1. Comparison of Mean Scores and Gains in Word Knowledge Based on the Intermediate Battery of the Metropolitan Achievement Test—National Averages and Sample Results, by Grade and Metric.

	Test Scores				Gains		
	Fifth Grade		Sixth Grade		School Year	Summer	School Year
Test Scores on Word Knowledge	Fall	Spring	Fall	Spring	(5.1–5.8)	(5.1–6.1)	(6.1–6.8)
National norming sample, published values							
Raw score	25.0	31.5	33.8	37.7	6.5	2.3	3.9
Standard score	44.0	48.0	49.5	52.7	4.0	1.5	3.2
Grade equivalent	5.1	5.8	6.1	6.8	.7	.3	.7
Sample students, white ($N = 513$)							
Raw score	23.9	30.3	32.2	35.8	6.4	1.9	3.6
Standard score	43.2	47.2	48.1	50.6	4.0	.9	2.5
Grade equivalent	4.91	5.99	6.16	6.90	1.08	.17	.74

Source: Heyns, 1978. Used by permission.

"Why don't the sample children increase their standard scores at the same rate as the norming sample? Can I conclude that the schools in this district are failing their pupils?" asks the naive young researcher.

"Longitudinal test scores typically exhibit fan-spread," responds the experienced analyst. "As the means increase, so do the variances of most test scores. Your sample began the fifth grade at a disadvantage; the children appear to fall progressively further behind because the total variability of achievement was increasing steadily. Although it is possible that the schools are in part responsible for these trends, it would be wrong to conclude that they must be . Rates of cognitive growth differ among children; test scores tend to become more variable over time."

The young researcher observes that, indeed, for each metric the sample variances tend to be proportional to the means; cognitive inequality appears to increase both between sample children and the nation and among children within the sample at each point of time. The researcher is now convinced that it does not make sense to hold the schools in this district accountable for the fact that children in the sample progressed less rapidly than the national average. In order to infer differential growth, one must have a comparison group matched by initial scores and perhaps by other characteristics as well. Without such a comparison, it is meaningless to ask whether a given group of children gained more or less than expected during a particular interval, since one cannot assume that a single learning curve characterizes all children.

"Why don't sixth grade children learn as much as fifth graders?" asks the young researcher.

"The vocabulary test may have a ceiling," responds the experienced analyst.

"But it's not just the vocabulary test," says the young researcher. "There appears to be a deceleration of learning over time for every skill tested. Does this mean that the scores for high-scoring children are less reliable than those for low-scoring children?"

"Not at all," responds the psychometric expert. "The item analysis reveals that this test discriminates at least as well among high-scoring as among low-scoring children."

"Then why do high-scoring children learn less on the average than low-scoring children? The data consistently demonstrate that gains are inversely related to initial scores."

"Regression effects," answers the senior analyst. "It is a common observation that the scores of both high- and low-scoring children regress to the mean."

"Then the gains and losses should be equal," says the young researcher. "And the means should be an unbiased estimate of cognitive growth. Could it be that learning rates actually decelerate over time?"

"I suspect they do," responds the experienced analyst. "I have long held to the theory that the innate capacity for learning declines with age. Younger children simply develop skills more quickly than children somewhat older, and your tests reflect this fact."

Somewhat mollified, the young researcher returns to her computer printout. Cognitive growth decreases with time but not at a constant rate for all children since fan-spread occurs. Empirically, one should conceptualize learning as a decelerating function of time but with increasing variability among children. It all makes sense.

Being particularly compulsive, the young researcher proceeds to analyze her data in terms of several different metrics; being sociologically predisposed, she also examines learning rates for children from different backgrounds. It soon becomes apparent that the several metrics yield different distributions of scores and very different conclusions about learning. Raw scores tend to show the largest gains for children from disadvantaged backgrounds, while grade equivalents imply that poor children learned the least during any particular period of time.

"Which metric is right?" she asks.

"They measure different things," answers the experienced analyst.

"They seem to measure different things by national standards than they do in the sample," the researcher complains bitterly, brandishing a table not unlike Table 1-1. "A mean standard score of 52.7 points is equal to a grade equivalent score of 6.8 years in the nation; in the sample, a standard score of 50.6 is equated to 6.9 years."

"The reason," responds the analyst, "for these apparently baffling results is that the metrics you are comparing have unequal intervals. Grade equivalent scores are not linear transformations of either raw scores or standard scores. A given gain in raw scores is worth progressively more in grade equivalent units as one ascends the scale. Had you transformed your raw score values to grade equivalents after averaging, you would not have obtained the same figures."

"But which metric is right?" reiterates the researcher. "I want to determine whether students with college-educated mothers learned more or less than did students with less educated mothers. This table gives me three different answers."

The young researcher displays the puzzling configuration of gains found in Table 1-2 to the veteran and asks once again, "Which metric gives the best estimate of change?"

Table 2-1. Comparison of Mean Gain Scores by Metric and Maternal Education, Metropolitan Achievement Test, Word Knowledge ($N = 745$).

Mother's Education	*Raw Score*	*Standard Score*[a]	*Grade Equivalent Score*[a]
Total	5.5	4.0	.91
Less than high school	6.6	4.0	.53
High school graduate	6.3	4.0	1.02
Some college	5.0	4.1	1.19

[a]Standard scores and grade equivalents were equated to the individual's observed raw score, based on the published norms, and then averaged.

Source: Heyns, 1976. Used by permission.

"You really should not be using difference scores, you know." says the analyst. "Change scores are notoriously unreliable."

"You mean I can't measure learning?" asks the young researcher.

"Of course you can measure learning," says the expert reassuringly. "It's merely change which is problematic."

Puzzled, the young analyst then asks her colleague to explain the results of Table 1-2.

"This table reveals precisely the pattern of effects we have been discussing. Your measure of maternal education covaries with both the pretest and the posttest. The inverse relationship between raw score gains and the covariate is an obvious example of the regression fallacy. Both the pretest and the posttest are measured with error, and since change scores embody both sources of error, they are less reliable than either single score. Errors of measurement frequently result in a negative correlation between gains and pretest scores or with any correlate of pretest—in this case, mother's education."

"But I thought you said that the errors were random?"

"But with fallible measures, the correlation between a pretest and a change score is frequently negative. You have merely demonstrated a variant of the familiar regression fallacy."

"And why do the grade equivalent scores yield a positive association between cognitive growth and maternal education?" asks the neophyte.

"Grade equivalent scores are not very reliable," responds the senior analyst. "I have recommended that they be abolished. What is happening is that the high-scoring students are benefiting from being further up the scale; their gains in raw scores are lower, yet they're credited with a larger increment of gain. The most appropriate metric is the standard score, which tells you that the observed gains for the various levels of maternal education are the same. That is, students learn at a rate that is not affected by the mother's education. That is what you wanted to know."

"That is *not* what I wanted to know," wails the young researcher. "The standard scores were constructed to have equal variances at each date. Why should I expect to see any change in relative position? What I want to know is why, if fan-spread exists, shouldn't one find an increasing educational gap between high and low status children over time? Alternatively, if learning is a decelerating function of time, perhaps it is decelerating more rapidly for the advantaged groups, as the raw scores suggest. I want to know which metric best describes cognitive growth for children from diverse backgrounds."

"My dear, you have much to learn," says the senior analyst. With these words, he gives the young researcher several weighty volumes, a few thin articles replete with mathematical equations, and a bottle of aspirin.

In time, the young researcher learns to accept the psychometric rationale offered and to limit her research to the most reliable measures of achievement available. She discovers that the questions she had been asking were incorrectly framed. As numerous authors demonstrate, a correlational analysis permits one to make inferences about the effects of background on cognitive growth that are consistent and meaningful. She even found herself solemnly passing on the advice she had received: one should not study change directly; rather, one should study the causes of change. And her research tended to support and eventually became the conventional wisdom about educational processes: there is little differential cognitive growth that can be attributed to either family background or schooling.

The moral of this tale is straightforward. Educational tests and measurement rest on a powerful and elegant paradigm that both prescribes procedures for collecting and analyzing data and shapes the kind of questions it is appropriate to ask. If one wishes to explore questions that are somewhat tangential to the orthodox model or that place a somewhat heavier burden on the basic assumptions, one proceeds at one's own risk. When one encounters empirical anomalies in the process of analyzing data, test theory has sophisticated explanations that are internally consistent and convincing.

Classical test theory has contributed immensely to our understanding of individual differences in achievement or ability. The measures derived from this model have justifiably been described as "the most important technical contribution psychology has made to the practical guidance of human affairs" (Cronbach, 1970:197). In recent years, the use of standardized achievement tests for research and evaluation has mushroomed. Almost without exception, such research has sought to discover whether or not educational programs significantly influence the cognitive growth of students. The findings associated with such research, have, with startling regularity, been negative, educational programs of all types have been found to contribute little to the cognitive growth of children. Such results have in turn generated enormous criticism of the schools, as well as a tendency, more or less fully articulated, to regard ability or achievement as an immutable trait, determined to a large degree by genetic factors.

If one accepts the premise that the central questions for educational research and evaluation revolve around learning and cognitive growth, one must ask whether the tests that enjoy such widespread use are capable of measuring change. Although creative explanations for null findings abound, the logically prior question is whether one can use tests to assess growth. Yet this fundamental question is infrequently posed. One must ask whether or not measures and models purporting to assess learning can actually do so. If they cannot, we are wasting an enormous amount of time and money using tests for this objective. If they can, but only under certain assumptions, the implications of these assumptions should be the focus of attention. Begging these questions, or reformulating the problem out of existence, will not lead to a greater understanding of cognitive growth. The dilemmas raised by the measurement and analysis of change scores are a case in point. Analysts are advised not to study learning or change directly, but to utilize correlational techniques for uncovering relationships of interest (Cronbach and Furby, 1970). While such a recommendation is sound statistically, it amounts to suggesting that the causes of change are amenable to study, while the process is not.

In order to infer learning based on achievement tests, one must have a basis for comparing test scores located at different positions on a scale. Hence, the procedures developed for norming and calibrating test scores are crucial for the study of change. One widely accepted method for imputing intervals is based on the assumption that a normally distributed construct underlies the measurement of achievement (Jones, 1971). Invoking this assumption, achievement tests are often scaled to reflect and reproduce such a distribution. If some other distribution was thought to hold, the observed test score metrics would appear very different. The question of metrics and intervals is basic to the study of change. The assumptions imposed by accepting a particular distribution are not neutral with respect to questions of change; they determine in a fundamental way the conclusions reached.

The argument that I will support at some length is, first, that there are both logical and empirical reasons for believing that the underlying skills and aptitudes measured by test scores are not normally distributed but positively skewed; and, second, that the errors of measurement involved in testing are not random with respect to true scores. In the context of longitudinal data, neither assumption seems tenable. Furthermore, these assumptions are consequential; they substantially affect research results and conclusions. Although correlational analyses have many virtues, including consistent results irrespective of the metric assumed, the presence of correlated errors can vitiate many findings. Finally, I will argue that there are alternative models of both learning and test taking that find greater empirical support. The ultimate goal, which exceeds the scope of this chapter by a wide margin, is to arrive at a basis for verifying and validating measurement and measurement models for learning.

MEASUREMENT MODELS AND CLASSICAL TEST THEORY

There are three essential ingredients for measurement: (1) there must be an operationally defined procedure for collecting systematic observations; (2) the measurements should be objective and reproducible; (3) the resulting measures should yield valid indicators of the object or process being studied. In the physical sciences, measurement can typically be repeated in a controlled environment; in the behavioral sciences, in contrast, one cannot assume that the object of research is unaffected by the measurement. Repeated measurements may yield different responses because the context changed, because the individual's response to the context changed, or because the two interact in a more complex manner. Since one is typically interested in behavioral phenomena that are of enduring or general significance, and since one can observe only a finite portion of the relevant behavior obtained under conditions that vary to some extent, measures are inevitably fallible.

Classical test theory derives from an explicit rationale for measurement and from a set of mathematical propositions regarding errors of measurement that links observations to the construct being measured. The basic relationship posited, which is generally regarded as axiomatic, is that an observed test score consists of two independent additive components, a true score and an error. A critical test for any theory, whether expressed mathematically or verbally, is not only how well phenomena are explained but how well the theory accounts for what cannot be explained. Classical test theory, much like the theoretical formulations of less rigorous areas of inquiry, assumes that extraneous factors or errors are random with respect to the observations or processes studied.

The most parsimonious version of test theory can be reduced to four basic propositions regarding errors of measurement:

$$X = T + e; \tag{1.1}$$

$$E(e) = 0; \tag{1.2}$$

$$\rho Te = 0; \tag{1.3}$$

$$\rho e_1 e_2 = 0, \tag{1.4}$$

where X is the observed score, T is the true score, e is an error term, and e_1 and e_2 are independent observations. This formulation does not depend on assumptions about the distribution of unobserved values such as the true score or the error. For this reason, it is argued that distributional assumptions are not integral to the theory (Lord and Novick, 1968). It is assumed that two parallel measurements of a true score are taken and that each contains error. Errors of measurement are of two kinds—systematic and random. If there are systematic errors, the two measurements are by definition not parallel; if the tests yield parallel measurements, it is assumed that only random errors influence the observed scores. If errors are random, their expected value is equal to zero and they are assumed to be independent of true scores. Two parallel tests must, therefore, have equal means and variances; errors of measurement must by definition, have equal variances on parallel tests and must be uncorrelated with each other.

Classical test theory can be derived from these four specifications regarding errors, provided that one accepts the notion of parallel measurement. As Lord and Novick (1968) demonstrate, it is unnecessary to make any assumption about the distributions of either true scores or errors if one can replicate measurement. If two successive measurements have the same true scores and identically distributed errors of measurement, then they are equivalent. Under the assumptions of classical test theory, repeated measurements are parallel if their first and second order moments are equivalent. Hence, by definition, parallel measurements will have equal means and variances.

Parallel measurements, however, cannot be used for studying growth for either individuals or a sample. If the means or the variances of two test forms are shown to differ, as they must if one intends to infer change for all or part of a sample, the measurements are not equivalent. Without equivalent measures, interval assumptions and scaling are crucial. In order to compare results for individuals or for the total sample, one must make additional assumptions about test score distributions. Although it is possible to deduce a considerable portion of classical test theory assuming only ordinal measurement and without stipulating a specific distribution for test scores, interval measurement is essential for studying change.

Distributional assumptions are not troubling if the major interest is the measurement of a static attribute or propensity. However, they are enormously important for an assessment of growth or change. If two measurements differ with respect to either their means or their variances, one cannot assume replicate or equivalent measurement. One cannot distinguish whether the observed differences in the two distributions are due to patterns of individual growth or to changes in the test instrument (Bereiter, 1963). Unless one assumes equal intervals, one cannot compare changes in test scores at different points on a scale.

When pressed, the stance taken by most psychometricians toward measurement and interval assumptions is profoundly agnostic. We cannot observe the true distribution of either ability or achievement; hence, we do not know what intervals are correct. Since ordinal measurement permits any transformation of scale that preserves the relative position of observed scores, a single "proper" metric for measuring achievement cannot be theoretically determined. The criteria for norms and scales are therefore the usefulness and the validity of the measures produced. If test scores are assigned numeric values that prove to be of general utility and that are not a gross violation of the empirical world, one need not question the assumptions imposed (Lord and Novick, 1968: 20-22).

If one applies this line of reasoning to test scores, one concludes that all norming and calibrating procedures are arbitrary; any scale is but a more or less convenient tool without a valid empirical referent. Since means, variances, and intervals are determined by the scales imposed, it makes little sense to ask whether any change has occurred in the underlying construct. One can profitably study the stability of test scores by assessing the similarity between the rank ordering of students at particular junctures, but not the amount of change or the degree to which change is uniform at different points along a scale. In short, if one is unwilling to make distributional , assumptions, one cannot study change or learning directly.

The importance of metric assumptions for the study of change has not gone unnoticed in the literature; however, it does not occupy the position of importance it merits. As Bereiter (1963:10) obs- serves, to "confront the issue fully is to see psychometric theory totter." Both the validity and the reliability of individual achieve- ment tests have been the subject of debate, deliberation, and much research. The point to be made in this context is that the most reliable tests in existence will not yield valid measures of growth unless one posits assumptions about metrics. Measures of learning depend fundamentally on changes observed in the means and var- iances and only secondarily on higher order moments.

As an illustration, suppose that two students are given a particu- lar test and their scores are found to differ. The question of whether the achievement of one student exceeds that of the other is entirely determined by the reliability and validity of the test. If one knows or can estimate its reliability, the probability that the higher-scoring student is more knowledgeable in the skill tested can be determined very accurately. Assume that a second test, an equally valid measure of the skill, is administered at a later time; assume further that one student is observed to have gained more than the other. One can infer which student performed better the second time with some certainty; however, without assuming a specific interval scale, it is not possible to determine which student learned more. Since the two students differed initially, their gains will not encompass comparable portions of the test scale. It is always possible to devise an admissible monotonic transformation that inflates the distance traversed by one student differentially, while not altering their relative positions on either test. A transformation sufficient to reverse the intuitive con- clusion regarding which student gained more would be nonlinear in form, and it might be difficult to justify. However, a transformation of scale capable of such a substantive reversal would not violate the measurement properties of standardized tests in any way.

In sum, distributional assumptions establish the metrics essential for evaluating change and cognitive growth; without such assump- tions, inferences are not possible. Conceived of necessity, metrics assumptions are often regarded as innocent inventions, fathered by convenience. I would argue that they should properly be regarded as the legitimate heirs of classical test theory. Without systematic pro- cedures for interpreting measurement intervals, test theory loses a great deal of practical utility; accepting the need to scrutinize and validate distributional assumptions and patterns of cognitive change adds a new dimension to the concerns of psychometric theory and raises the issue of the adequacy of classical test theory.

DISTRIBUTIONS AND METRICS

One common technique for attributing interval measurement to standardized achievement tests is to normalize raw scores and scale the resulting values in terms of the interval values implied by a normal distribution (Jones, 1971; Angoff, 1971). These procedures are justified in terms of the central limit theorem and by the fact that observed test scores typically approximate a normal distribution reasonably closely when based on a fairly large sample size. The assumption that the underlying distribution of ability or achievement is normal has nearly attained the stature of a scientific truth in the psychometric literature. Since Galton published *Hereditary Genius* in 1869, which claimed to show that all physical traits and natural abilities were distributed according to the Gaussian law of error, the assumption that one would expect intelligence to be normally distributed has not been seriously challenged. Moreover, normal distributions provide statistical advantages that are not found in other metrics.

The justifications for assuming that the unmeasured construct underlying tests of achievement is normally distributed are cogent if not compelling. In order to argue that the metrics imposed by this distribution are invalid, one must be able to show that the interval scales calibrated lack substantive validity and that alternative assumptions would yield more realistic measures. The argument depends on being able to assume that learning is an observable process, that the differences between two distributions reflect this process, and that substantively meaningful interval scales could be validated by comparing gains with actual learning behavior. The objective would be to link scores to a scale that is independent of the distribution of examinees, or to validate gains empirically by examining their relationship to student growth.

The logic of developing such scales is similar to that proposed by Abelson and Tukey (1959), who argue that scales should be based on the additivity of effects. One can imagine calibrating scores to reflect the progressive learning of some finite universe of skills and knowledge or, alternatively, linking scales to temporal norms. Criterion-referenced tests and mastery learning are based on similar objectives (Block, 1971; Bloom, 1976). Recent work with latent trait models devised to yield "person-free test calibration" based on the item-characteristic curves also shows promise (Goulet, Linn, and Tatsouka, 1975).

I suspect that measures of achievement that embody empirically derived metrics for measuring cognitive growth will have substantially more skewed distributions than conventional standardized scores. This assertion is based on two observations drawn from longitudinal test score data. If one assumes that individual test items can be scaled according to the median age or grade level of children capable of successfully answering the item and that a single learning curve characterizes all children, the resulting values would closely resemble grade equivalent scores. Scores based on grade equivalent norms have distributions with substantially different interval properties than do the raw or standard scores; this distribution is invariably more skewed. Although the correlations between raw scores and grade equivalents tend to be close to unity, they portray very different patterns of learning. Increments of gain in raw scores points are weighted progressively more heavily as one ascends the measurement scale; each successive correct answer added to a child's score translates into a progressively greater amount of achievement in temporal units. Thus one finds, as in Tables 1-1 and 1-2, that larger grade equivalent gains accrue to children farther up the scale despite smaller relative increments of raw score or standard score points.

Grade equivalent scores are at best a primitive approximation to a temporal metric; they assume a single learning curve based on the test scores of the child, and they typically contain an unknown amount of interpolating and "smoothing" of values. The balance of opinion discourages their use for educational research. Many of the reasons given are technical rather than substantive: grade equivalent scores are not normally distributed, error terms are quite heteroscedastic, and the measures are less "well behaved" in statistical analysis. Nonetheless, grade equivalent scores are the only commonly available metric that embodies units of growth based on a scale independent of the distribution of children.[3] Further refinements of existing scales are doubtless possible and desirable; however, the distribution of scores scaled relative to time would be more skewed than that observed for raw scores.

The rates of learning by metric depicted in Table 1-2 are instructive. If one assumes that an appropriate metric for scaling achievement items is a child's grade level, one finds that difference scores are predictably related to socioeconomic differentials. By changing the distributional assumptions underlying the metric and imposing an age-graded scale, one achieves intervals that, I would argue, are substantially more realistic sociologically. If achievement is assumed to be normally distributed, one observes "regression toward the mean." If intervals are based on temporal scales, gain scores are sufficiently robust to yield measures of learning. A similar pattern pertains when one compares gain scores by IQ level or by other measures of parental status. I would argue that many of the findings in the literature attributed to "regression effects" are actually artifacts of the intervals or distributions assumed. Studies have consistently documented very low and not infrequently negative correlations between ability levels and the rate of learning among children (Anderson, 1939; Bloom, 1964; Fleishman, 1965; Zeaman and House, 1967). If one were to accept this finding at fact value, it would belie the experience and observation of anyone who has taught children. If one assumes that measurement error is solely responsible, it is difficult to justify using the tests to study learning. The rather modest transformation implied by grade equivalent scores yields more credible metrics, without any assumptions about measurement error. I suspect that a good many of the null findings regarding change that are interpreted as regression effects should be traced to inappropriate interval assumptions. With appropriate metrics, one would discover that both low and high ability students progressed. The observed "regression toward the mean" is the result of learning among low ability children and a systematic devaluation of gains to high ability children.[4]

There are also logical reasons why one might expect that the conventional intervals do not reflect the true distribution of achievement. Ordinarily, raw scores are summed, without weighting; a correct response is assumed to reflect a similar amount of achievement, however difficult or easy any particular item is. The forty-second correct answer adds as much to one's total score as the thirteenth. The items included on achievement tests typically vary considerably in their level of difficulty. It seems plausible to assume that the correct response to a difficult item or to an esoteric question reflects a larger amount of the skill measured by the test than does a correct response to a relatively easy item. Since observed raw scores tend to approximate a normal distribution, weighting items by their relative difficulty would increase the degree of skew; such a procedure would tend to increase the distance between observed scores as a function of scale position. Weighting items would yield intervals, and consequently gains, more similar to grade equivalent scores than to raw scores.

Finally, there are theoretical reasons for expecting that the distribution of "true" achievement is skewed. There is a necessary connection between the form of a distribution and the processes that generate observed outcomes. Numerous experimental studies of learning imply that the rate of skill acquisition is not linear with respect to time. Although learning theorists have concentrated on narrowly defined skills that are probably not directly comparable with the skills tapped by achievement tests, consistent findings about the process have been reported. Stevens and Savin (1962) argue that skill acquisition in a wide range of areas is a power function of the time elapsed or the amount of practice. The actual rates of growth differ, depending on whether one studies nonsense syllables, for example, or psychomotor abilities; yet these studies find that individual growth is proportional to the prior level of skill. If the behavioral processes governing learning are generalizable, perhaps because of behavioral reinforcement, one would expect a skewed skilled distribution that would become more skewed over time (Hamblin, et al., 1971).

In sum, there are sociological, logical, and theoretical reasons for assuming that achievement scores should be skewed, not normal. If one makes modest alterations in the shape of the distribution, such as those suggested by grade equivalent scores, the relative difficulty of items, or a power function, the resulting intervals and metrics describe quite different patterns of learning. While it is not now possible to infer the shape of the underlying true score distribution, it seems reasonable to conclude that it would not be bell-shaped. It is possible to calibrate metrics temporally and to validate intervals or substantively, although this has not been done. Such scales would surely yield a metric more appropriate for studying change.

Assuming that the underlying distribution is skewed rather than normal produces patterns of learning or gain that differ markedly from raw scores. High ability students, as well as students from relatively advantaged backgrounds, achieve consistently more during specific time intervals than is the case when one assumes a normally distributed variable. Furthermore, ability and social class are shown to interact with the effects observed for educational programs (Heyns, 1978). While it is intuitively plausible that educational programs are not equally effective for all students, statistical controls for individual differences in background or ability tend to obscure the patterning of gains and to mask interactions. Unless one is able to randomize groups experimentally, and thereby equate initial scores and other correlates of achievement, mean differences cannot be compared without knowledge or assumptions about intervals. I would contend that a large number of nonexperimental studies of education have erred by introducing statistical controls for individual differences that overwhelmed group effects, under the assumption that an appropriate model was additive rather than interactive. Without valid intervals, interaction effects are meaningless (Wilson, 1971).

When confronted with ordinal measurement, sociologists have typically relied on the reassuring observation that correlations are remarkably stable when subject to monotonic transformations (Labovitz, 1970; Vargo, 1971). Yet many educational problems logically imply an interactive model rather than an additive one. Sociologists have traditionally conceived of social class, for example, as a causal agent, interacting with other environmental influences. If one assumes that social class interacts with other attributes and experiences of individuals, additive models would not yield credible results. Indeed, as the next section details, the conventional assumptions about random measurement error are not warranted when assessing achievement in a longitudinal frame. If errors of measurement are not independent of true scores, interactive effects will tend to be underestimated and inconsistent. The sanguine presumption that correlational techniques yield valid estimates of the effects of other variables would be justified only if one could assume that errors are uncorrelated.

CORRELATED ERRORS OF MEASUREMENT

Longitudinal test score data reveal several other troubling patterns. For example, the correlations between successive forms are observed to increase during successive time intervals (Heyns, 1978). Not only does the effect of the pretest increase, but so does the correlation between achievement and every correlate of achievement when based on nominally equivalent forms. If one were to assume that errors of measurement were uncorrelated with true scores, one would have to conclude either that the true relationship between achievement and every presumed cause of achievement increased with time or that the error variance declined relative to the total observed variance.

Taken alone, the increasing correlations would not disturb many analysts. There are several possible explanations for the pattern. First, it seems plausible to assume that the reliability of the tests increases with an increased observed score variance. Although test score reliability is assumed to be a function of the measurement instrument, it is easily shown that estimates of reliability increase as a function of sample heterogeneity (Lord and Novick, 1968). Second, the tests are constructed to be parallel though not identical forms;

perhaps a sequence of similar tests provides an opportunity for students to practice and consequently decreases the likelihood of random errors. Perhaps repeated testing serves to standardize the procedures for administering and scoring tests accurately, with the same result. Finally, it is possible that the relationship between test scores and the determinants of achievement becomes more predictable over time. Tests tend to become more stable and to exhibit greater reliability as children mature. Perhaps, as Bloom (1964) and others have argued, ability becomes more fixed with age. One would expect to find increasing correlations if the amount of learning declined or if the fluctuation in achievement level became less extreme.

Sociologists have endeavored to separate analytically the effects of test score stability and unreliability. Models designed to disentangle random measurement error from exogenous disturbances using panel data have been proposed and estimated. Following the lead of Coleman (1968), Heise (1969) presents an explicit causal model for separating the effects of temporal instability from measurement error using three waves of observations. His model, which assumes a constant test-retest reliability, is explicated in terms of standardized coefficients. Wiley and Wiley (1970) present an alternative model, which assumes constant error variance over time and thus permits observed test score reliability to increase as a function of sample heterogeneity. Werts, Jöreskog, and Linn (1971) present data from four waves of achievement scores and attempt to test the plausibility of the two alternative models. Their conclusion is somewhat equivocal; the assumption of a constant reliability yields superior statistical fit but unreasonable parameter estimates, while the assumption of equal error variances gives a poorer fit but estimates that are more consistent with theoretical expectations.

Each of these models depends on the critical assumption that errors of measurement are uncorrelated with true scores and are serially uncorrelated. Wiley and Wiley (1974) extend these models to include serially correlated errors and demonstrate that if one assumes equal error variances and constant regression coefficients for both true scores and errors of measurement during fixed time intervals of equal length, it is possible to estimate error directly.

In general, each model suggests that the stability of true scores is substantial and likely to be underestimated by conventional corrections for attenuation. If one assumes serially correlated errors having the structure suggested by Wiley and Wiley (1974), estimates of reliability are consistently lower than they are under the assumption of either constant error variance (Wiley and Wiley, 1970) or constant reliability (Heise, 1969). Wiley and Wiley (1974) note, however, that an adequate model of correlated errors should link the components of measurement error directly to the conditions of measurement.

Psychometricians have extensively examined errors of measurement on tests. Analysis suggests that empirically derived errors of measurement for test scores are not independent of true scores, nor do they appear to be normally distributed. In an interesting empirical paper, Lord (1960) concludes that errors of measurement tend to be a function of true score and to be significantly skewed. In the high ability group, the error variance decreased as true scores increased and errors were negatively skewed; in the low ability group, the error variance increased with true scores and the distribution of errors was positively skewed. Lord began by proposing to test the assumption of uncorrelated, normally distributed errors adopted by classical test theory; although he found substantial reason to view these assumptions as unwarranted, he does not conclude by questioning the theory. Later, Lord and Novick assert that these empirical results "seem reasonable, or can be plausibly rationalized, as a consequence of a floor effect and a ceiling effect" (1968:233), rather than as a challenge to the theory.

It is possible to derive a model of measurement error for test scores that fits empirical data far more plausibly than the classical model does. Psychometricians have long known that multiple-choice exams invite guessing by subjects and that this is a major source of error. A considerable literature exists on formula scoring procedures designed to correct for guessing by subjects. The random guessing model is one of the most elementary. It is assumed that the subject's total score, X, consists of K correct responses to items that are known and G correct guesses. If there are n items on an examination, each with A possible answers, and the student guessed randomly on every item, omitting none, the expected score would be equal to

$$E(X) = \frac{n}{A} \cdot \qquad (1.5)$$

The simple knowledge or random guessing model is deficient in numerous respects. It assumes that the student has either complete knowledge of the information sought by the item or that he or she has no knowledge and therefore must guess. A more plausible model of test taking would assume that a student could successfully eliminate certain incorrect distractors and then judiciously choose among the remainder; although the student would be guessing, the probability of a correct score on an item partially known would be larger than $1/A$.

Despite such drawbacks, a model of random guessing does provide a means of conceptualizing and quantifying measurement error. Such a model does not, however, justify the assumption that errors are uncorrelated with true score.

One might posit a model of observed scores such that

$$X_i = K_i + G_i + e_i, \tag{1.6}$$

where X_i is the observed score, K_i the number of items known, G_i the correct guesses, and e_i a random error term. If one assumes random guessing,

$$E(G) = p\,(n - K), \tag{1.7}$$

where $p = 1/A$. If G is a binomially distributed variable, and $q = 1 - p$, it can be shown that

$$\text{Var}\,(G/K) = pq\,(n - K) \text{ and} \tag{1.8}$$

$$\text{Var}\,(G) = pq\,[n - E(K)] + p^2\,\text{Var}\,(K). \tag{1.9}$$

The random guessing model implies that G is a function of $(n - K)$; the larger the number of items known, the smaller the contribution of random guessing to the observed score is likely to be. If the knowledge level of a group increased, one would expect to find a corresponding decrease in guessing. The covariance between K and G would be negative.

In order to generate estimates of the expected variances and co-variances, the model was simulated by computer. A normal deviate, K_1, was generated with a mean and variance set equal to those observed in the longitudinal data analyzed. The number of test items, n, was set at 55, and p was assumed to be .2; these are the values of n and p for the Metropolitan Achievement Test, word knowledge.

Four sequential simulations were run, each with a case base of 500 students. A learning curve that approximated the observed scores was adopted in which

$$K_t = 2 + (K_{t-1})^{1.05} + e_i. \tag{1.10}$$

This equation produced values of K with increasing means and variances as a function of time. A random error term with a mean of zero and a standard deviation equal to .3 was added to K_2, K_3, and K_4 after the initial simulation. In this model, K_{it} is known,

Table 1-3. Correlation Matrix of Test Scores Generated from Simulation of Guessing Model, where $X_{it} = K_{it} + G_{it} + e_{it}$ and $K_t = 2 + (K_{t-1})^{1.05} + e_i$ (N for simulation set equal to 500).

	K_1	K_2	K_3	K_4	G_1	G_2	G_3	G_4	O_1	O_2	O_3	O_4
Knowledge 1	1.000											
Knowledge 2	.999	1.000										
Knowledge 3	.998	.999	1.000									
Knowledge 4	.995	.995	.997	1.000								
Guess 1	−.547	−.525	−.523	−.520	1.000							
Guess 2	−.651	−.651	−.628	−.628	.387	1.000						
Guess 3	−.732	−.733	−.735	−.735	.389	.409	1.000					
Guess 4	−.793	−.794	−.796	−.796	.375	.476	.550	1.000				
Observed 1	.913	.920	.920	.920	−.229	−.569	−.678	−.750	1.000			
Observed 2	.935	.935	.943	.943	−.484	−.390	−.712	−.758	.869	1.000		
Observed 3	.960	.961	.961	.961	−.500	−.615	−.565	−.770	.887	.904	1.000	
Observed 4	.967	.968	.968	.968	−.516	−.620	−.717	−.666	.884	.906	.929	1.000
Mean	9.40	12.80	16.79	21.40	9.12	8.46	7.49	6.60	18.41	21.34	24.48	28.14
S.D.	9.20	10.84	12.94	15.21	3.18	3.37	3.41	3.72	8.22	9.24	10.86	12.69

while guessing is not. Random guessing is assumed to be a stochastic process generating a binomially distributed random variable with a mean equal to .2 $(55 - K)$. The observed scores, X_{it}, were computed as the sum of K_{it}, G_{it}, and e_{it}. Observed scores that exceeded 55 were arbitrarily set equal to 55; there were only a handful of such cases.

The matrix of correlations generated by the simulation is presented in Table 1-3, with the observed means and standard deviations. As expected, the correlations between successive scores on knowledge, K_t, are close to unity. The variance of knowledge exceeds the observed score variance at each specified time, as it must if the random guessing model holds. The covariances between K_t and G_t are substantial and increasingly negative as the mean value of K increases; these correlations range from $-.547$ to $-.796$. As the expected score of K_t increases, the expected score of G_t declines; since the variance of G_t is a function of the variance of K_t, which is increasing, this value also tends to increase. The adjacent correlations between K_t and the observed score, X_t, increase regularly, from .869 to .929; the negative relationship between guessing and the observed score also increases. Despite the fact that knowledge is almost perfectly predicted from prior knowledge, the observed score correlations suggest far less temporal stability. The model unrealistically assumes K_{it} to be substantially determined by $K_{i(t-1)}$; hence observed scores are more highly correlated than one would expect empirically.

The results from the simulation suggest a perfectly plausible explanation for the increasing correlations between pretest and posttest observed in longitudinal data. Observed scores are attenuated not only by random errors but also by guessing. The dynamics of cognitive growth increase the variance of knowledge among subjects, while a test of fixed length has only a limited number of opportunities for guessing. Since guessing is inversely related to knowledge, the expected covariances between guessing and both knowledge and the observed scores are negative. The total variance in observed scores is a function of both guessing and knowledge; the model implies that the variance explained in a posttest by a pretest will increase as a function of the expected values. This result, as we have seen, is the empirical pattern observed on parallel forms over time.

Conventional reliability theory assumes that it is possible to decompose the observed variance into a component due to true score and a component due to random error that are independent. Errors of measurement under such a model can only deflate the observed relationships. The simulation of guessing raises certain questions about reliability estimates that are not easily resolved. First, if the level of knowledge constrains errors due to guessing, one would expect to find that estimates of test score reliability increase with knowledge even though the instrument is unaffected. Moreover, one would observe high levels of reliability for groups with larger mean scores. The measured determinants of achievement would increase in magnitude at successive times because of the increasing relationship between knowledge and observed scores. The guessing model implies that the observed correlation between how much a student knows and any presumed cause of this knowledge might increase over time, even though the actual relation was constant. If one assumes that measurement error is uncorrelated to true score, one might fallaciously conclude that the relationship between achievement level and either prior achievement or any other cause of achievement increases with time.

The four waves of test score data illustrate this possibility. Table 1-4 gives the correlations, means, and standard deviations observed for the sample; Table 1-5 gives the regressions of posttest on pretest, parental education, family income, race, and IQ for these data for three successive time periods. Perusing Table 1-4, one notices immediately that the zero-order correlations between test scores and the background variables rise over time. The regressions in Table 1-5 indicate that the explanatory power of all variables included (R^2) increases over time; the coefficients tend to do so as well, although the patterns are complex. As Tables 1-4 and 1-5 show clearly, the zero-order correlations between achievement and every other variable increase with time, as does the total explained variance.

If one is willing to assume that guessing is a random process and operates in the rather mechanistic fashion outlines, it is possible to deduce sample estimates for the model described in Figure 1-1. Knowledge, K, is taken to be the underlying variable of interest and to be causally related to both guessing, G, and the observed score, X. Knowledge is a function of previous knowledge and a disturbance term, θ. Estimates of the variances and covariances are derived from the formulas given in the appendix to this chapter.

The model specifies four structural equations for the determination of K_t,

$$K_1 = \theta_1, \tag{1.11}$$

$$K_2 = \alpha_{21}\theta_1 + \theta_2, \tag{1.12}$$

Table 1–4. Correlation Matrix for Sample Children with Test Scores at Four Given Times ($N = 745$).

	(1)	(2)	(3)	(4)	(5)	(6)	(7)	(8)
(1) Test score, fall 1970	1.0							
(2) Test score, spring 1971	.8113	1.0						
(3) Test score, fall 1971	.8263	.8453	1.0					
(4) Test score, spring 1972	.8054	.8487	.8900	1.0				
(5) Family income	.4696	.4540	.5397	.5432	1.0			
(6) Parental education	.4256	.4129	.4661	.4551	.5491	1.0		
(7) Race	.4668	.4898	.5188	.5137	.4380	.2386	1.0	
(8) IQ	.7447	.7659	.7919	.7976	.5277	.4485	.4541	1.0
Mean	17.29	21.91	22.82	26.44	$13,256	11.43	.371	94.11
S.D.	11.26	12.49	12.81	13.52	$5,522	2.73	.483	17.44

Source: Heyns, 1978. Used by permission.

Table 1-5.   Regression Coefficients of Posttest on Pretest Achievement, Family Income, Mean Parental Education, Race, and IQ (N = 745).

Dependent Variable		Prior Test	Family Income ('000)	Parental Education	Race	IQ	R^2
Sixth grade	Spring 1972						
	b	.6822*	.0884	.0777	1.146	.1932*	
	(δ)	(.0336)	(.0526)	(.1108)	(.617)	(.0246)	
	b*	.6462	.0406	.0157	.0410	.2492	.8201
Summer	Fall 1971						
	b	.5356*	.1768*	.2702*	2.013*	.2160*	
	(δ)	(.0330)	(.0542)	(.1143)	(.636)	(.0253)	
	b*	.5224	.0858	.0575	.0760	.2941	.7839
Fifth grade	Spring 1971						
	b	.5486*	.0552	.1773	2.341*	.2636*	
	(δ)	(.0400)	(.0614)	(.1298)	(.715)	(.0278)	
	b*	.4946	.0274	.0387	.0906	.3681	.7270

*Coefficient at least twice as large as its standard error.

Source: Heyns, 1978. Used by permission.

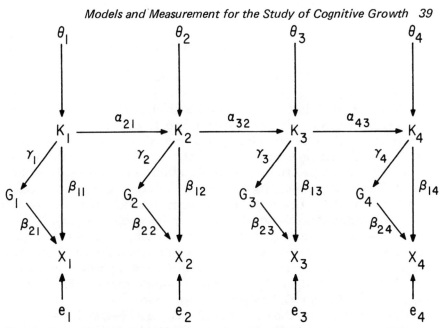

Figure 1-1. Hypothetical Model of Cognitive Growth Based on Observed Scores and Random Guessing as a Function of Knowledge.

$$K_3 = \alpha_{32} \left[\alpha_{21} \theta_1 + \theta_2 \right] + \theta_3, \tag{1.13}$$

$$K_4 = \alpha_{42} \left[\alpha_{32} \alpha_{21} \theta_1 + \alpha_{32} \theta_2 + \theta_3 \right] + \theta_4, \tag{1.14}$$

and four sets of two equations linking knowledge and guessing to observed scores,

$$X_t = \beta_{1t} K_t + \beta_{2t} G_t, \tag{1.15}$$

$$G_t = \gamma_t K_t. \tag{1.16}$$

The variance of observed scores, given the assumptions, is equal to

$$\text{Var}(X) = \text{Var}(K) + \text{Var}(G) + 2\,\text{Cov}(K,G). \tag{1.17}$$

The expected value for the conditional variance of guessing, G_i, can be expressed in terms of the variance in knowledge and the probability of a correct response, p, given random guessing (see equation [1.8]). The variance of guessing is given by

$$\text{Var}(G) = pq\left[n - E(K)\right] + p^2 \,\text{Var}(K), \tag{1.18}$$

and the covariance of guessing and knowledge is equal to

$$\text{Cov } (G,K) = -p \text{ Var } (K) \tag{1.19}.$$

The proof of these last two formulas is given in the appendix to this chapter. For any specific distribution of observed scores, the variance in X is assumed to be completely determined by the variability in K and G, which can be estimated from the equations provided above. Knowledge is assumed to be a linear function of prior knowledge and a disturbance, θ_i; the coefficient, α_{ij}, is set equal to the correlation between K_i and K_j. Given the model, this would be the value necessary to reproduce the observed correlation between x_i and x_j.

The coefficients linking knowledge to guessing, γ_t, and to the observed score, β_{lt}, are estimated assuming no measurement error. The understandardized coefficients are therefore straightforward: $\gamma_t = -.2$, assuming $p = .2$ and β_{1t} and β_{2t} are equal to unity. The correlations between K_i and X_i, however, are less than 1.

Table 1-6 presents the expected means, variances, and covariances based on raw scores in the longitudinal data. Figure 1-2 summarizes the model of learning implied if knowledge operated as a simple

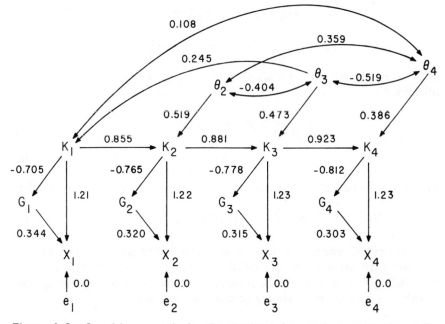

Figure 1-2. Cognitive growth for longitudinal data at four given times. Observed score, X, assumed a function of knowledge, K, and guessing, G.

Table 1-6. Expected and Observed Moments, Covariances, and Correlations between Observed Test Scores, X_i, Knowledge, K_i, and Guessing, G_i, for Longitudinal Data (N = 745).

Date	$E(X_i)$	$E(K_i)$	$E(G_i)$	$Var(X_i)$	$Var(K_i)$	$Var(G_i)$	$Cov(X,K)$	$Cov(K,G)$	$Cov(X,G)$	$\hat{r}_{XK}$	$\hat{r}_{KG}$	$\hat{r}_{XG}$
Fall 1970	17.3	7.9	9.4	126.8	186.3	15.0	149.1	−37.3	−22.3	.969	−.705	−.511
Spring 1971	21.9	13.6	8.3	156.0	233.4	16.0	186.7	−46.7	−30.7	.979	−.765	−.616
Fall 1971	22.8	14.8	8.0	164.1	246.3	16.3	197.1	−49.3	−33.0	.980	−.778	−.638
Spring 1972	26.4	19.3	7.1	182.8	276.7	16.8	221.3	−55.3	−38.6	.984	−.812	−.696

Calculated from observed scores and longitudinal data in Heyns, 1978.

causal chain and the coefficients took on the values specified. The model is overidentified, since it was not necessary to use three of the estimated correlations; in order to reproduce the matrix of estimated correlations, the disturbance terms, θ_t, are permitted to be correlated. These values suggest that a simple causal chain is not adequate to describe the growth of knowledge at successive times.

One objective of the model was to account for the increasing correlations between pretest and posttest over time. Although the correlations between K_{t-1} and K_t are much closer in magnitude than are the correlations between observed scores, the estimated effects still increase during successive intervals. The model of random guessing tends to reduce the disparity between effects on successive measurements but not to eliminate it.

The model implies that any cause or correlate of knowledge that is related to X would be attenuated by errors of measurement introduced by random guessing. Furthermore, it implies that these observed correlations would be likely to increase over time, irrespective of the true effect. Using the techniques of path analysis, it is possible to generate estimates of the relationship between knowledge and any variable presumed to cause it. This correlation would be equal to:

$$\hat{r}_{QK_t} = \frac{\hat{r}_{QX_f}}{\hat{r}_{K_tX_t}} \tag{1.20}$$

When this formula is applied to the observed sample correlations between IQ and achievement and between family income and achievement, the correlations in Table 1-7 can be calculated. As can be seen clearly from these results, the correction for correlated errors due to random guessing yields estimates that are more similar than the original correlations were, but they are not identical to each other. The correlations are still seen to increase with the increasing variance of knowledge over time.

The original intent of the guessing model was to account for the observed increases in the correlations between observed scores and other variables over time. If one inverts a matrix of correlations corrected for errors of measurement due to guessing, one can obtain estimates of the coefficients and the unexplained residual variance for equations similar to those presented in Table 1-5. The R^2 from these regressions are also summarized in Table 1-7. Again, although the correction for random guessing narrow the differential explanatory power of the other variables in the model, the pattern of increasing correlations persists. Corrections for guessing of the order

Table 1-7.   Observed Correlations between Achievement and IQ and Family Income and Predicted Correlations between Knowledge and IQ and Family Income and R^2 for Complete Model at Each Given Time ($N = 739$).

Date	Observed		Predicted		$R^2_{x_t} \cdot x_{t-1}IERQ$	$R^2_{K_t} \cdot K_{t-1}IERQ$
	$r_{x_t Q}$	$r_{x_t}I$	$\hat{r}_{k_t Q}$	$\hat{r}_{k_t}I$		
Fall 1970	.7447	.4696	.7679	.4842		
Spring 1971	.7659	.4540	.7827	.4639	.7270	.7806
Fall 1971	.7919	.5397	.8079	.5506	.7839	.8345
Spring 1972	.7976	.5432	.8104	.5519	.8201	.8684

Calculated from correlations reported in Heyns, 1978.

implied by the model are not sufficient to account for the increments in true score variance observed.

I suspect that one reason the model fails to account for the increasing correlations in their entirety is not that the notion of correlated error due to guessing is wrong but that the model underestimates the extent of the problem. The corrections deduced from the model are not large, since only errors due to random guessing were included; these corrections do not involve substantial modifications of the original correlations. The model imposes a crude dichotomy on the process of test taking; it is assumed that every student either knows or does not know the correct response. If one assumed instead that an even larger portion of the variance attributed to knowledge was due to informed guessing, based on partial knowledge, the model might account to a much greater extent for the increasing explanatory power of other variables. The logic of this argument assumes that, unlike the model elaborated, the behavioral phenomenon of guessing is not an entirely random process; knowledge increases over time, but then so does partial knowledge. The student who can successfully eliminate a larger proportion of wrong answers at time t than at time $t-1$ would be likely to increase his or her score disproportionately during the interval.

Further refinements of this model of test taking that included errors of measurement due to guessing are possible; however, they would involve either more substantive information or more sophisticated assumptions about the process. The model of random guessing assumes that the level of knowledge is the only determinant of the amount of guessing; correct guesses are assumed to be a function of chance and of the number of items for which the answer is not known. This assumption is probably too simplistic. If guessing reflects partial knowledge as well as random choices, one might expect high ability students to guess better than low ability ones and students with more knowledge to guess better than students with less. Such assumptions would further complicate estimation procedures.

In sum, this section has argued that the assumption of errors of measurement uncorrelated with true scores cannot be supported empirically. Although such an assumption is convenient statistically, it does not accord with either the data available or an intuitive understanding of how children take tests. Errors of measurement can be plausibly assumed to result from guessing; models that include guessing tend to yield both a more realistic conception of the process and a better fit to empirical data. Although such models pose methodological difficulties not encountered by classical test theory, they do not appear to be intractable statistically.

Explicating all the ramifications implied by the model of guessing exceeds the scope of this chapter. In passing, however, a few of the more salient issues should be mentioned. First, if one assumes that the relevant attribute to be measured is individual knowledge and that it is related to the observed score in the manner described, much of the literature on test score reliability and corrections for attenuation should be modified. Correlated errors of measurement imply that one cannot decompose observed scores into a component due to true score and an independent error. Moreover, the variance of knowledge must be larger than the variance of observed scores.

Second, if correct responses due to guessing are inversely related to the number of items known, one would expect heteroscedastic errors. Students higher on the scale have both more knowledge and fewer occasions to guess; knowledge would contribute an increasing share of the variance of observed scores as one moves up the scale, while the proportion of the variance due to guessing would decline. I suspect that an empirical puzzle posed by studies of reliability could be explained by such correlated errors. Students who have higher scores tend to exhibit more predictable outcomes than do low-scoring students. Thus one finds that test scores are more "reliable" for whites than for blacks, despite the fact that measures scale equally well for both groups and that observed test scores are often equally variable among both groups. If the level of knowledge is consistently related not only to observed scores but also to errors of measurement due to guessing, this is the pattern one might expect.

Third, correlated error implies that test forms of varying difficulty cannot be equally valid or reliable measures of true knowledge. Procedures for vertically equating tests typically assume that a simple linear transformation of items should suffice. This would not be true unless errors were uncorrelated; I suspect that this is one reason such procedures have not proved very satisfactory (Goulet, Linn, and Tatsouka, 1975).

Finally, the presence of correlated measurement error due to random guessing implies that the level of knowledge is not independent of the causes of knowledge. If the observed increase in correlations over time is the result of a process similar to that hypothesized, one would not expect stable effects irrespective of scale location. As aggregate means increase, so does the proportion of the variance due to "true" knowledge. Thus, the issues of metrics and distributions return through the back door. Analysts have traditionally been satisfied, at least partially, by the consistency and stability of measured effects and have argued that ordinal measurement presented no great problem for this reason. However, this would be true only if errors of measurement were uncorrelated with true scores.

CONCLUSIONS

Cognitive growth, it has been argued, must be assessed in the context of longitudinal data. While it is clear that there is no substitute for accurate and reliable longitudinal data, achievement scores over time raise as many questions as they answer.

Viewed in a longitudinal framework, test scores do not lend much support to the basic assumptions of classical test theory. I have argued that it is impossible to measure growth or change without imposing specific interval assumptions or assumptions about the distribution of true scores; the assumption that the appropriate distribution is normal or that the intervals observed are indentical on true and observed scores seems very weak. If one assumes that metrics for learning must meet minimal criteria of logical and substantive validity, it is clear that a skewed distribution with unequal intervals provides a more credible picture of growth. Furthermore, the four basic assumptions of test theory regarding errors of measurement do not seem tenable. If guessing contributes to measurement error in the manner specified, one would not expect errors to be uncorrelated to true scores or to each other; if effors due to random guessing were a function of "true" knowledge, as posited, their expected values would not be zero, and their standard deviations could not be equal. The model of guessing is deficient in several ways; yet, I would argue, it provides a more plausible explanation of the patterns found in longitudinal data than alternative theories do.

Among educational researchers, there is a tendency to apologize for one's data but never for one's model. If the evidence presented here is convincing, it suggests that basic revisions in test theory are in order. The single most important item on the educational agenda is constructing and validating tests that can measure learning reliably; there are substantial reasons to doubt that those available can do so. Without such measures, educational research is problematic and educational evaluation a charade. The assumption necessary for studying cognitive growth are enormously consequential, as I have tried to show, and fundamentally affect the results obtained. They must be examined both theoretically and empirically. If this study inspires concern about these issues, at least one objective will have been met.

APPENDIX

The model for guessing is given by

$$X_i = K_i + G_i,$$

where X_i is the observed score,

K_i is the student's true knowledge,

G_i is conditionally binomially distributed given K_i,

$$\text{with } E(G_i|K_i) = p(n - K_i),$$

$$\text{and Var }(G|K) = pq(n - K_i).$$

$$
\begin{aligned}
\text{Var}(G) &= E(G^2) - [E(G)]^2, \\
&= E[E(G^2|K)] - [E(G)]^2, \\
&= E[\text{Var}(G|K) + E(G|K)^2] - [E(G)]^2, \\
&= E[pq(n - K) + p(n - K)^2] - [p(n - \overline{K})]^2, \\
&= pq(n - \overline{K}) + p^2 E(n - K)^2 - [p(n - \overline{K})]^2, \\
&= pq(n - \overline{K}) + p^2[n^2 - 2n\overline{K} + E(K^2)] - [p(n - \overline{K})]^2, \\
&= pq(n - \overline{K}) + p^2\{n^2 - 2n\overline{K} + [\text{Var}(K) + \overline{K}^2]\} - p^2(n - \overline{K})^2, \\
&= pq(n - \overline{K}) + p^2[(n - \overline{K})^2 + \text{Var}(K)] - p^2(n - \overline{K})^2, \\
&= p^2 \text{Var}(K) + pq(n - \overline{K}).
\end{aligned}
$$

The solution for the covariance between knowledge, K, and guessing G, is given by:

$$
\begin{aligned}
\text{Cov}(G,K) &= E(GK) - (EG)(EK), \\
&= E\{K[E(G|K)]\} - (EG)(EK), \\
&= p[n\overline{K} - E(K^2)] - p(n - \overline{K})\overline{K}, \\
&= p[n\overline{K} - \overline{K}^2 - \text{Var}(K)] - p(n - \overline{K})K, \\
&= p(n - \overline{K})\overline{K} - p\text{Var}(K) - p(n - \overline{K})\overline{K}, \\
&= -p\text{Var}(K).
\end{aligned}
$$

NOTES

1. For more details regarding the tests and sample, see Chapter 2 and Appendix A of Heyns (1978). The substantive problem for which these data were gathered involved estimating the effects of schooling by contrasting the level and the determinants of achievement during the school year and the summer. Exposure to education was viewed as the "treatment"; cognitive growth in the absence of schooling was taken to reflect the effects of family and peers, while the pattern of learning during the school year was assumed to be the result of family, peers, and schooling.

2. Grade equivalent and standard scores for the norming population represent the published values corresponding to the means for a given raw score; they are not the mean scores calculated for individuals in the population. The grade equivalents are, therefore, arbitrary scale points yielding, by definition, equivalent gains for fixed intervals of time during either school year.

3. Psychometricians have also warned against the indiscriminate use of grade equivalent scores to compare children across several grade levels. It is certainly true that a fifth grade child who tests at the tenth grade level is not equivalent in any meaningful way to an average tenth grader; however, the objection that a posttest is not an equally valid indicator of the skills measured on a pretest applies whatever the time interval or the age of the child. My concern is to show the patterning of achievement between nominally parallel forms taken over intervals of a year or less. I would not recommend the extrapolation of scores beyond these limits. Moreover, the construction of grade equivalent scores involves assumptions and procedures that can be criticized on several grounds; as with any measure adopted for research purposes, the analyst must scrutinize the resulting measure in light of the objectives.

4. Simple gain scores are generally considered suspect by experienced analysts, although one can still find articles recommending their use (Richards, 1975). Regression effects are, under conventional assumptions, ubiquitous. One commonly finds that the correlation between a pretest, X_1, and the gain, $X_2 - X_1$, is negative. It is easy to show that this correlation must be negative whenever the unstandardized regression coefficient, $b_{x_2 x_1}$, is less than unity. While it would not be unreasonable to argue that a regression slope greater than 1 is a defensible criterion for learning, unstandardized coefficients tend to be smaller when estimated by conventional techniques. Alternative estimation procedures, such as weighted least squares, seen preferable for such variables (Heyns, 1978).

REFERENCES

Abelson, R. P., and J. W. Tukey. 1959. "Efficient Conversion of Non-Metric Information into Metric Information." In *American Statistical Association Proceedings of the Social Statistics Section*, pp. 226-30. Washington, D. C.: American Statistical Association.

Anderson, J. E. 1939. "The Limitations of Infant and Preschool Tests in the Measurement of Intelligence." *Journal of Psychology* 8:351-79.

Angoff, W. H. 1971. "Scales, Norms, and Equivalent Scores." In *Educational Measurement,* 2d ed., ed. R. L. Thorndike, pp. 508-600. Washington, D. C.: American Council on Education.

Atkinson, R. C., and J. A. Paulson. 1972. "An Approach to the Psychology of Instruction." *Psychological Bulletin* 78 (1): 49-61.

Bereiter, C. 1963. "Some Persisting Dilemmas in the Measurement of Change," In *Problems in Measuring Change,* ed. C. W. Harris, pp. 3-20. Madison: University of Wisconsin Press.

Blalock, H. M. 1974. "Beyond Ordinal Measurement: Weak Tests of Stronger Theories." In *Measurement in the Social Sciences,* ed. H. M. Blalock, pp. 424-55. Chicago: Aldine.

Block, L. H., ed. 1971. *Mastery Learning: Theory and Practice.* New York: Holt, Rinehart & Winston.

Bloom, Benjamin S. 1964. *Stability and Change in Human Characteristics.* New York: John Wiley and Sons.

––––––. 1976. *Human Characteristics and School Learning.* New York: McGraw-Hill.

Bohrnstedt, G. 1971. "Observations on the Measurement of Change." In *Sociological Methodology 1969,* ed. E. F. Borgatta, pp. 113-33. San Francisco: Jossey-Bass.

Campbell, D. T., and A. Erlebacher. 1970. "How Regression Artifacts in Quasi-Experimental Evaluations Can Mistakenly Make Compensatory Education Look Harmful." In *Compensatory Education: A National Debate,* vol. 3: *The Disadvantaged Child,* ed J. Hellmuth, pp. 185-210. New York: Brunner/Mazel.

Campbell, D. T., and J. C. Stanley. 1963. "Experimental and Quasi-Experimental Designs for Research on Teaching." In *Handbook of Research on Teaching,* ed. N. L. Gage, pp. 171-246. Chicago: Rand McNally.

Carver, Ronald P. 1975. "The Coleman Report: Using Inappropriately Designed Achievement Tests." *American Educational Research Journal* 12 (1): 77-86.

Coleman, J. S. 1968. "The Mathematical Study of Change." In *Methodology in Social Research,* ed. H. M. Blalock and A. B. Blalock, pp. 428-78. New York: McGraw-Hill.

Coleman, J. S.; E. Q. Campbell; C. J. Hobson; J. McPartland; A. M. Mood; F. Weinfeld; and R. L. York. 1966. *Equality of Educational Opportunity.* Washington, D. C.: Government Printing Office.

Coleman, J. S., and N. L. Karweit. 1972. *Information Systems and Performance Measures in Schools.* Englewood Cliffs, N.J.: Educational Technology Publications.

Cronbach, L. J. 1970. *Essentials of Psychological Testing.* 3d ed. New York: Harper and Row.

Cronbach, L. J., and L. Furby. 1970. "How Should We Measure 'Change'—Or Should We?" *Psychological Bulletin* 74 (1): 68-80.

Cronbach, L. J., and R. E. Snow. 1977. *Aptitudes and Instructional Methods.* New York: Irvington.

Fennessey, J. 1973. "Using Achievement Growth to Analyze Educational Programs." Center for Social Organization of Schools, Report no. 151. Baltimore: Johns Hopkins University.

Fennessey, J. 1974. "Understanding 'Fan-Spread' in Achievement Measures." Center for Social Organization of Schools, Report no. 168. Baltimore: Johns Hopkins University.

Fleishman, E. A. 1965. "The Description and Prediction of Perceptual-Motor Skill Learning." In *Training Research and Education*, ed. R. Glaser, pp. 137–75. New York: John Wiley and Sons.

Friedenberg, E. Z. 1969. "Social Consequences of Educational Measurement." In *Proceedings of the 1969 Invitational Conference on Testing Problems*, pp. 23–30. Princeton, N. J.: Educational Testing Service.

Galton, Sir Francis. 1869. *Hereditary Genius: An Inquiry into Its Laws and Consequences.* London: Macmillan.

Glass, G. V.; P. D. Peckham; and J. R. Sanders. 1972. "Consequences of Failure to Meet Assumptions Underlying the Analysis of Variance and Covariance." *Review of Educational Research* 42: 237–88.

Goulet, L.; R. Linn; and M. Tatsouka. 1975. *Investigation of Methodological Problems in Educational Research: Longitudinal Methodology.* Final Report, PN 4-1114. Champaign-Urbana: University of Illinois.

Guildford, J. P. 1956. *Fundamental Statistics in Psychology and Education.* 4th ed. New York: McGraw-Hill.

Gulliksen, H. 1950. *Theory of Mental Tests.* New York: John Wiley and Sons.

Hamblin, R. L.; D. Buckholdt; D. Ferritor; M. Kozloff; and L. Blackwell. 1971. *The Humanization Processes.* New York: John Wiley and Sons.

Heise, D. R. 1969. "Separating Reliability and Stability in Test-Retest Correlation." *American Sociological Review* 34:93–101.

Heyns, B. 1976. "Education, Evaluation, and the Metrics of Learning." *Journal of Teaching and Learning* 2 (April): 2–16.

———. 1978. *Summer Learning and the Effects of Schooling.* New York: Academic Press.

Hoffman, B. 1964. *The Tyranny of Testing.* New York: Collier Books.

Jones, L. V. 1971. "The Nature of Measurement." In *Educational Measurement*, 2d ed., ed. R. L. Thorndike, pp. 335–55. Washington, D. C.: American Council on Education.

Keats, J. A. 1964. "Some Generalizations of a Theoretical Distribution of Mental Test Scores." *Psychometrika* 29:215–31.

Keats, J. A., and F. M. Lord. 1962. "A Theoretical Distribution for Mental Test Scores." *Psychometrika* 27:59–72.

Kerlinger, F. N. 1964. *Foundations of Behavioral Research.* New York: Holt, Rinehart & Winston.

Labovitz, S. 1967. "Some Observations on Measurement and Statistics." *Social Forces* 46 (December): 151–60.

———. 1970. "The Assignment of Numbers to Rank Order Categories." *American Sociological Review* 35 (June): 515–25.

Levine, D. M., and M. J. Bane. 1975. *The "Inequality" Controversy: Schooling and Distributive Justice.* New York: Basic Books.

Levine, M. 1976. "The Academic Achievement Test: Its Historical Context and Social Functions." *American Psychologist* 31 (March): 228–38.

Lord, F. M. 1953. "On the Statistical Treatment of Football Numbers." *American Psychologist* 8:750–51.

————. 1958. "Further Problems in the Measurement of Growth." *Educational and Psychological Measurement* 18:437–54.

————. 1960. "An Empirical Study of the Normality and Independence of Errors of Measurement in Test Scores." *Psychometrika* 25 (March): 91–104.

————. 1967. "A Paradox in the Interpretation of Group Comparisons." *Psychological Bulletin* 68:304–5.

————. 1969. "Statistical Adjustments When Comparing Pre-Existing Groups." *Psychological Bulletin* 72:336–37.

————. 1977. "Practical Applications of Item Characteristic Curve Theory." *Journal of Educational Measurement* 14 (2): 117–38.

Lord, F. M., and M. R. Novick. 1968. *Statistical Theories of Mental Test Scores.* New York: Addison-Wesley.

Marley, A. A. J. 1967. "Abstract One-Parameter Families of Commutative Learning Operators." *Journal of Mathematical Psychology* 4:414–29.

Mayer, L. S. 1970. "Comment on 'The Assignment of Numbers to Rank Order Categories.'" *American Sociological Review* 35 (August): 916–17.

————. 1971. "A Note on Treating Ordinal Data as Interval Data." *American Sociological Review* 36 (June): 519–20.

Richards, J. M. 1975. "A Simulation Study of the Use of Change Measures to Compare Educational Programs." *American Educational Research Journal* 12(3): 299–311.

Rubin, D. B. "Assignment to Treatment Group on the Basis of a Covariate." *Journal of Educational Statistics* 2 (Spring): 1–26.

Spearman, C. 1927. *The Abilities of Man.* London: Macmillan.

Stanley, J. C. 1966. "Analysis of Variance of Gain Scores When Initial Assignment Is Random." *Journal of Educational Measurement* 3:179–82.

————. 1967. "General and Special Formulas for Reliability of Differences." *Journal of Educational Measurement* 4:249–52.

————. 1971. "Reliability." In *Educational Measurement,* 2d ed., ed. R. L. Thorndike, pp. 356–442. Washington, D. C.: American Council on Education.

Stanley, J. C., and M. D. Wang. 1970. "Weighting Test Items and Test-Item Options: An Overview of the Analytical and Empirical Literature." *Educational and Psychological Measurement* 30: 21–35.

Stevens, J. C., and H. B. Savin. 1962. "On the Form of Learning Curves." *Journal of the Experimental Analysis of Behavior* 5 (January: 15–18.

Thorndike, R. L. 1942. "Regression Fallacies in the Matched Groups Experiment." *Psychometrika* 7:85–102.

————. 1951. "Reliability." In *Educational Measurement,* ed. E. F. Lindquist, pp. 560–620. Washington, D. C.: American Council on Education.

Torgerson, W. S. 1958. *Theory and Methods of Scaling.* New York: John Wiley and Sons.

Vargo, L. G. 1971. "Comment on 'The Assignment of Numbers to Rank Order Categories.'" *American Sociological Review* 36 (June): 517–18.

Wang, M. D., and J. C. Stanley. 1970. "Differential Weighting: A Survey of Methods and Empirical Studies." *Review of Educational Research* 40:663–705.

Werts, C. E.; K. G. Jöreskog; and R. L. Linn. 1971. "Comment on 'The Estimation of Measurement Error in Panel Data.'" *American Sociological Review* 36 (February): 110–13.

Werts, C. E., and R. L. Linn. 1971. "Considerations When Making Inferences within the Analysis of Covariance Model." *Educational and Psychological Measurement* 31:407-16.

Wiley, D. E., and J. A. Wiley. 1970. "The Estimation of Measurement Error in Panel Data." *American Sociological Review* 35:112-17.

Wiley, J. A., and M. G. Wiley. 1974. "A Note on Correlated Errors in Repeated Measurements." *Sociological Methods and Research* 3 (November): 172-88.

Wilson, T. P. 1971. "Critique of Ordinal Variables." *Social Forces* 49:432-44.

Zeaman, D., and B. J. House. 1967. "The Relation of IQ and Learning." In *Learning and Individual Differences*, ed. R. M. Gagné, pp. 192-212. Columbus, Ohio: Charles E. Merrill.

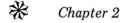

Chapter 2

Production Technologies and Resource Allocations within Classrooms and Schools: Theory and Measurement*

Byron W. Brown and Daniel H. Saks
Michigan State University

There are many ways to look at schools, but the model that has received the most attention recently is that of the school as a utility-maximizing firm using labor (teachers) and capital (equipment and buildings) to process (educate) raw materials (students). Unfortunately, in most previous work such a model has been more a useful analogy than a powerful analytical device. And it has been a positively misleading analogy when insignificant regression coefficients for purchased school inputs in an "input-output" equation were taken to be indicators of zero marginal products for those inputs (cf. Averch et al., 1972).

In this Chapter we hope to clarify just how the simple economic production model needs to be modified to handle the essential elements of educating students in schools. It is our belief that such an effort allows a deeper analysis of allocative choice and that this will help in evaluating alternative technologies, testing management rules

*Commissioned by the Educational Finance and Productivity Center, Department of Education, University of Chicago, under contract from the National Institute of Education. The work reported on here was partially supported by the Institute for Research on Teaching at Michigan State University. The activity that is the subject of this report was supported in whole or in part by the National Institute of Education, Department of Health, Education, and Welfare. However, the opinions expressed herein do not necessarily reflect the position or policy of the NIE, and no official endorsement by the NIE should be inferred.

This study has also benefited from comments received at the Education Finance and Productivity Center conference held in Chicago on June 6-8, 1978. We also wish to thank our many colleagues at the IRT who have contributed more to this work than they may have realized. We especially mention Lee Shulman and Gerald Duffy. Our current work in this area is being supported by a grant from the Spencer Foundation.

of thumb, and generally improving the productivity and operations of schools.

We will cover three levels of analytic complexity: (1) the technology of a single output and multiple inputs; (2) the problem of introducing tastes in the multiple output, multiple input case with no joint products and correctly measured inputs; and (3) the problems of classroom organization in the case of multiple inputs and outputs with joint production and/or improper measurement of inputs. For each of these categories, there are two levels of observation—the individual student and groups or classes of students. We assume at the outset that our model is deterministic, although we will have a bit to say about stochastic elements of the problem including uncertainty, disequilibrium, and person-specific "inefficiency" of production. At the appropriate points we will cite the relevant literature, though we make no attempt to survey the literature for its own sake since others have recently done that.[1]

Consider first the case of the simple textbook production function, or what Keeney and Raiffa (1976) call the "simple value problem," where there is only one output and many inputs. Most of the previous literature has concentrated on this case. Researchers have worried about the measurement of outputs, determination of the array of inputs, and specification of the functional form and stochastic structure of such functions. Unfortunately, this case is most clearly relevant to the education of a single child in a single subject by a tutor. Its relevance to modern schooling in America frankly escapes us.

The next case introduces the notion of groups or classes of students. This results in what Keeney and Raiffa (1976) call the "complex value problem," and it consists of multiple outputs and multiple inputs. Analysis of such a regime requires the introduction of some weighting scheme for the alternative outputs. When there is a market for those outputs, then prices can be used for weighting. But when outputs are not sold, we need a utility function for the decision-makers, whether they be parents, teachers, or administrators.

While the second case introduces multiple outputs, it still assumes that the production relations that determine an individual student's learning are separable from each other. We will demonstrate the nature of such production when students are grouped in classes or tracks. It turns out that individual student production functions or learning curves are identifiable in this case, provided that the inputs to the individual student can be measured correctly (a not inconsequential matter when one talks about students being taught in classes). We will analyze several recent studies that use individual student output data in terms of this model. The analysis shows that these studies may suffer from serious measurement error problems. These problems are not solved by using data on individual students. If the model, particularly the separability assumptions about student learning curves, is accepted, we can suggest how to do a time allocation study that might yield useful results.

The trouble with the assumption of separable individual production functions is that it assumes away all the interesting class organization and mangement problems, since it makes no difference how students are grouped or tracked. There is still, of course, an interesting resource allocation problem in such a model. It comes down to a problem of how to schedule the application of alternate inputs to the particular students. In thinking about this, we have found it instructive to consider the case of the job shop model of production. This model is the polar case from an assembly line. In an assembly line, each item produced goes through the same sequence of processes (e.g., automobile production). In a job shop, each item produced may, depending upon the requirements, go through different processes in different sequences (e.g., an automobile repair shop). These models are too complex for analytical solutions, but they do lend themselves to numerical solutions and could provide the basis for simulation models and testing places for various rules of thumb about teaching strategies. With some simplification, models that contain many of the same attractive features can be handled as dynamic programming problems.

The interesting problems of classroom organization do not arise until we turn to case three—multiple outputs with joint production. We will present a theoretical discussion of the meaning and significance of productive jointness in the multiproduct case. Jointness, roughly speaking, is an interdependence in the learning curves of individual students, a sharing of the same inputs. We cannot assign inputs to outputs in such cases, and this is why it is often indistinguishable from the case where we have difficulty measuring the input applied to a particular output. In one case the measurement is theoretically impossible, and in the other it is impractically difficult. Each student's learning curve may vary with, among other things, how the student is grouped with others having particular characteristics. We illustrate the inherent difficult of specifying and measuring inputs to individual students when jointness obtains.

Once jointness and multiple outputs are admitted, it is the intra-classroom allocation problems that become most important. An important and neglected issue is how such allocations can be achieved when students are not passive about their assignments. We develop these notions in terms of a discussion of the student's supply of effort. We conclude with a brief discussion of the implications of these notions for the design of our current research.

SIMPLE PRODUCTION

The economist's concept of the production function forms the basis of the economic theory of the firm. The function is a summary description of the physical realities of production processes where inputs or resources are turned into outputs or final products. The textbook version of production theory usually begins with the case of a single output being manufactured from a single input. As a pedagogical device, this enables the student to become familiar with some elementary jargon that will be useful in talking about more complicated cases.[2] Suppose $y = f(x)$, in which x is a quantity of some input and y the quantity of output. Economists always assume that the function yields the largest value of y obtainable from some x, given the state of the art in production. Of course, there are many reasons why there may be inefficiency in production or a failure to get the most output from a given input, so we may never observe the values of x and y in the function. This is a problem that has been neglected for the most part in both the educational and economic literature. But see Levin (1974), and Schmidt, Aigner, and Lovell (1977) for examples of work that takes the problem seriously.

What does $y = f(x)$ look like? The function, called the total product curve, is usually assumed to be continuous, differentiable at least twice, nondecreasing, and to satisfy $f(0) = 0$. The first derivative of $f(x)$, dy/dx or the slope of the total product curve, is the marginal product of x, MP_x. The marginal product itself is assumed to be an eventually decreasing function of the input, x, a proposition known to economists as the law of diminishing (marginal) returns.[3]

In Figure 2-1 we show a typical production function and its marginal product curve. An important assumption to keep in mind when using these notions is that both input and output are each homogeneous. Each unit of input is like every other in every relevant respect so that they are perfect substitutes for each other. Empirical work by economists on production functions is often cavalier in making this assumption where it clearly does not apply. A long history of production function estimation in economics that has overlooked the effects of heterogeneity of both inputs and outputs has led to especially serious problems in the education literature. We discuss these problems in detail below. What must be kept in

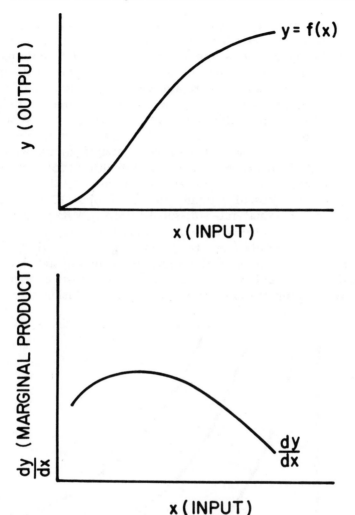

Figure 2-1. Total and marginal product curves.

mind at this point is that the basic theoretical notion rquires both input and output homogeneity.

We could use total product curves like those in Figure 2–1 to describe the process of learning through time. If the input is the amount of time a student spends in a particular activity and the output is the amount learned, the relation between them can be described using the production function notion. In fact, the relation probably looks very much like Figure 2–1, including the idea of diminishing returns. But time alone does not produce learning output.

Other inputs are always present in the production process. Some of these inputs may be variable for the problem we consider and some not. Introducing additional inputs presents no serious complication, but it does increase the amount of jargon we need to discuss the issues. Suppose we assume there are two inputs and a single output: $y = f(x_1, x_2)$, where x_1 and x_2 are inputs measured, as before, in their natural units. By holding x_2 constant, we can vary x_1 and find the marginal product of input 1, MP_1. The law of diminishing returns is again assumed to hold. But with two variable inputs, we can ask about the extent to which they can be substituted for each other in production. More precisely, how much of input 2 does it take to make up for the loss of a small amount of input 1? The answer is dubbed the "marginal rate of substitution" (MRS) between the inputs and can be readily shown to equal the ratio of the marginal products of the inputs (e.g., Ferguson and Gould, 1975). A set of points relating quantities of the inputs for which output is constant is called an isoquant. Several isoquants are shown in Figure 2-2. As we move along an isoquant in the direction of using more x_2, the

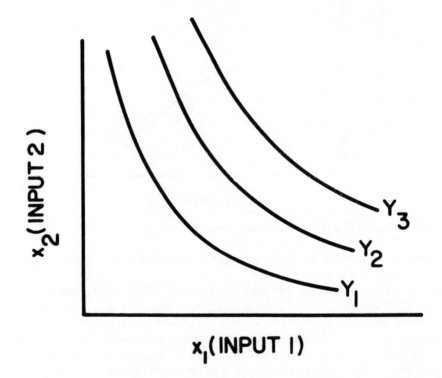

Figure 2-2.   Isoquants for a process that produces one output from two inputs.

marginal rate of substitution or the absolute value of the slope of the isoquant increases. That is, the isoquants are convex when viewed from the origin. Convexity means that as you use less and less of an input it becomes more and more difficult to substitute for it. Put another way, it is easier to produce with mixture of productive inputs.

While they need not do so, isoquants are usually assumed to fill up the positive quadrant of Figure 2-2. The more northeasterly an isoquant, the larger the quantity of output associated with it.

To illustrate the kind of education problems for which this may be useful, suppose that our inputs are the daily amounts of time spent being tutored by a teacher and time spent doing seatwork.[4] Output is the amount of some skill acquired. The isoquants of Figure 2-2 are probably a pretty good representation of the way substitution takes place. Substitution is possible, but the activities are not perfect substitutes. More of either tutoring or studying increases learning, however.

A straightforward question to ask here is: If a fixed amount of time, T, is available, how should it be allocated between tutoring and seatwork if we want to maximize learning? If we denote by T_s and T_t the time spent on seatwork and tutoring, respectively, then any allocation that does not waste time must satisfy $T = T_s + T_t$ or $T_t = T - T_s$. For a given T, this is a linear relation between T_t and T_s and appears as the straight line in Figure 2-3. If we superimpose on Figure 2-3 our isoquants from Figure 2-2, we can see that the optimal allocation is at point A, where the isoquant $y*$ is tangent to our time constraint line. That is the highest isoquant that could be reached without exceeding the constraint. Since the slope of the constraint is -1 at that tangency, the marginal rate of substitution (minus the slope of the isoquant) must equal $+1$. And since the MRS is the same as MP_t/MP_s, our optimizing condition is simply that the marginal products of the two activities should be equal and that the time allocation should be adjusted to accomplish this.

If we knew the parameters of the production function, we would be in a position to judge whether a particular time allocation was optimal or not. We could also put any widely used rules of thumb to the test and see how closely they approximate the optimal allocation. These are interesting questions but are not ones that a person studying teaching is likely to ask or to be much interested in answering. That is because the technology of production suggested by this model stands in such stark contrast to the real world of teaching, in which students are taught many subjects, sometimes at once, and in which pupils of very different backgrounds and abilities are taught together in classrooms, not in one-on-one tutorials.

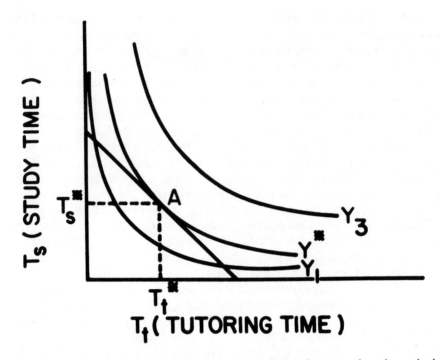

Figure 2-3. A learning maximizing time allocation for a student in a single subject.

It is worth noting, however, that this single output, multiple input model has been widely applied to data generated from actual class-room activities. These studies, many of which are discussed by Hanushek (1978) and Lau (1978), are remarkable for their use of various kinds of aggregation techniques to get rid of the problems posed by the inherent diversity of subject matters and students. Subject matters are aggregated into general math or reading achievement scores for measures of individual student outputs (something we do not find particularly objectionable). Students are aggregated so that class average scores are sometimes used to measure output, a serious difficulty that we examine later. Furthermore, the input measures used may often have only a vague relationship to the actual inputs applied to the students whose scores are being predicted.

PRODUCTION WITH MULTIPLE OUTPUTS

To see why these problems are important and why all studies (including our own) have failed in some important way to isolate and measure accurately the input productivities, we must develop the production model in such a way as to approximate more closely the world in which instruction takes place—namely, in classes in schools.

Schools are places where groups of students are brought together for the purpose of accomplishing some activities. Characteristically, students are placed in subgroups within schools (usually called classes) and may be subdivided further and remixed for different activities in an almost infinite variety. We shall assume that in a school, or in a subgroup within it, the activities and accomplishments of each student count for the school decisionmakers. They are educating all of the students, though not necessarily equally. This is a remarkable assumption, for it forces us to rethink the simple one output, many input production model presented above. If thinking of a school as a firm with a production function is a useful analogy, we must concede that a school is certainly a multiproduct firm, because it has many students.

It turns out that describing the production technology for a multiproduct firm is not nearly so simple as it is for the single output, multiple input case. The most difficult cases, both for theory and for measurement, arise when the several outputs of a firm are not independently produced but are technically related to each other in some fashion. This is too bad, because these cases are also the ones we think most relevant and interesting for understanding how schools work.

Our discussion of the multiproduct (many student) case has two parts. The first is production of a single attribute in students when there is independence among students. The second part deals with joint production.

Having more than one product or student need not present any serious theoretical problems. In the case of two students, we might have

$$y_1 = f(t_1), \text{ and}$$

$$y_2 = g(t_2), \tag{2.1}$$

where y_1 is the first student's learning of some skill and t_1 the amount of input, t, applied to student 1. We define y_2 and t_2 similarly, and the forms of the functions may be different for the two students, perhaps because they have different abilities. In addition, we must have

$$T = t_1 + t_2, \tag{2.2}$$

where T is the total amount of some input available to both students. It may be the total teacher time available for instruction or the amount of some other factor that can be divided between the students. Equation (2.2) says that the total amount of the input is the sum of the amounts applied to the students. Put another way, increasing the input applied to student 1 by one unit, given the total input available, implies decreasing the amount applied to student 2 by one unit. It is this condition that gives us separability in production. If our t's are really teacher's time, we have described a classroom technology, albeit one with only two students, where instruction takes place by the tutorial method. The students need not be physically together in a school; they could just as well be in their own homes, with the teacher coming to them. The students do not interact in any way.

We are in a position to ask a question for this case that we could not ask before—indeed, one which the earlier production model precluded us from asking. How should the teacher's time (or any other resource) be allocated between the two students? Before, even when there were different activities, we had only the problem of maximizing one student's learning. This problem is an order of magnitude more difficult. Economists have devised two ways of solving it, which we might call the market solution and the utility function solution. Both involve techniques for comparing the worth of additional units of achievement for student 1 with that of additional units for student 2. The techniques differ only in where they find the source of the values. The market solution has been applied to firms that sell their products. The prices they can get serve as aggregation weights for valuing the different outputs. In our example, with a fixed amount of some input, the objective of a firm might be to maximize its total sales receipts, R. The problem is to:

$$\text{maximize:} \quad R = P_1 y_1 + P_2 y_2,$$

$$\text{subject to:} \quad y_1 = f(t_1),$$

$$y_2 = g(t_2),$$

$$\overline{T} = t_1 + t_2$$

If the prices of the outputs, P_1 and P_2, are known and fixed, this is a straightforward problem. In fact y_1 and y_2 should be chosen, so that $P_1/P_2 = (\partial g/\partial t_2)/(\partial f/\partial t_1)$, where $\partial g/\partial t_2$ and $\partial f/\partial t_1$ are the marginal products of time in y_2 and y_1, respectively.

While the revenue maximization problem can be solved directly by using standard techniques (for a multitude of examples, see Henderson and Quandt, 1971), a somewhat different way of looking at it will be especially helpful. Pretend the problem has two parts. The first part consists of finding all the output combinations (y_1, y_2) obtainable for a given total input level, $\overline{T}$. We are particularly interested in the combinations for which we have the maximum output of y_1 given any level of the output y_2. That is, we want the combinations that

$$\text{maximize:} \quad y_1 = f(t_1),$$

$$\text{subject to:} \quad y_2 = g(t_2),$$

$$\overline{T} = t_1 + t_2.$$

Since there are only two outputs here and one input that is allocated to the two goods, the problem is trivial. Once a level of y_2 is chosen, there are no extra degrees of freedom in the system; the only solution is the optimal solution. This solution consists of an equation of the type $y_1 = h(y_2, \overline{T})$, which in economists' jargon is called a product transformation curve or a production possibilities curve. Typical examples of such curves are shown in Figure 2-4. CC' contains all the output combinations for a given level of resources, while DD' is the same curve with a greater resource endowment.

If $y_1 = h(y, \overline{T})$ represents the possible combinations we can get along DD', we can once again ask the earlier question, Which (y_1, y_2) combination will maximize total revenue $(R = P_1 y_1 + P_2 y_2)$? The (y_1, y_2) combinations for a given level of revenue are straight lines in output space, $y_2 = R/P_2 - (P_1 P_2) y_1$. The trick is to find the "isorevenue line" that maximizes R (i.e., has the greatest intercept) consistent with the production possibilities curve. As Figure 2-4 shows, this is accomplished for the isorevenue line EE' which is just tangent to the production possibilities curve. For maximum revenue, the slope of the isorevenue line, $-P_1/P_2$ must equal the slope of the production possibilities curve, dy_2/dy_1. But from the solution to the problem we examined earlier, we can see that dy_2/dy_1 must equal $-MP_1/MP_2$, the ratio of the marginal products of time in the two outputs. The numerical value of the slope of the production possibilities curve is usually called the (marginal) rate of product transformation (RPT) and is the amount of one output gained by giving up one unit of another. The RPT is like a production rate of exchange

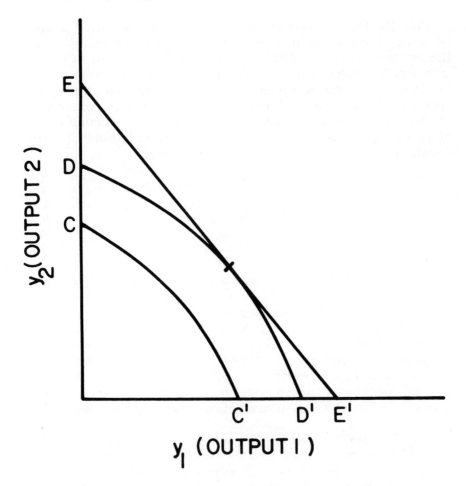

Figure 2-4. Production possibilities curves for two outputs and different levels of input use. *EE'* is an isorevenue curve.

and plays a crucial role in the theoretical development that follows.

The whole point of this analysis was to show that the original maximization problem could be broken up into two subproblems. Solving each subproblem in order would yield the same solution as the original. The division of the problem allows us to construct the production possibilities curve that reveals the alternative outputs we could have. Revenue maximization gave one answer to the question of what we ought to have but relied on the presence of market prices.

The problem of which output combination to choose for classes of students is devoid of market prices. However, the alternative ways to allocate time or resources are still present. This brings us to a step in the analysis of production often overlooked by other researchers—the necessary introduction of nonmarket values. It is less important to us whose values are brought to bear to choose a point on the production possibilities curve than it is to realize that we cannot escape a value judgment in this case. It is this above all else that separates the single output from the multiple output case—the need to make a nontrivial value judgement to find an optimal mix of outputs.

THE UTILITY FUNCTION

Economists solve the problem of subjective value, as opposed to market value, by postulating a utility function. This is simply a rule that assigns a unique level of satisfaction or utility to every combination of goods or services a person might consume. Each individual is assumed to have a utility function that may or may not be similar to other people's. Such functions are maps embodying information about people's preferences.

Consider the utility function for some person trying to decide how to allocate resources to the children whose possible learning outcomes are shown in Figure 2-4. More learning for each might reasonably be a good thing. But our decisionmaker might be willing to trade some learning by one of the students in exchange for a large enough increase in learning by the other.

These basic notions about tastes or the shape of the utility function are often described by economists using the device of the indifference curve. If our decisionmaker's utility function is $U = U(y_1, y_2)$, an indifference curve is a locus of combinations of y_1 and y_2 for which the level of satisfaction, U, is constant. Several indifference curves are shown in Figure 2-5. Higher indifference curves, those denoting higher levels of satisfaction, lie above and to the right of other curves. The curves are negatively sloped and convex when viewed from the origin in order to denote the increasingly difficult substitution possibilities as people have a great deal of one commodity and little of another. The convexity of indifference curves is a way of bringing in the idea that people value variety (see Fair, 1978).

In our simple example of two outcomes, it is easy to see which alternative is best if we want to maximize total utility. Simply choose the outcome mix for which the production possibilities curve is tangent to an indifference curve. If the production possibilities curve and the indifference curves have the slopes illustrated here, there will be a unique optimal outcome.

Economists, unlike psychologists, have not devoted much effort

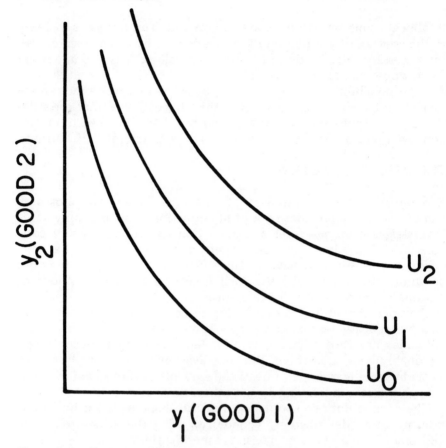

Figure 2-5. Typical indifference curves for a decisionmaker with two goods.

to explicit estimation of utility functions. Since the only safe assumption is that everyone's function is different, some sort of laboratory experiments have been thought to be necessary to reveal preferences. Maybe there is the prospect of some progress in this work along the lines suggested by Keeney and Raiffa (1976). To our knowledge, the only serious attempt to apply their notions to schools (although mostly at the school or district level) is Roche's (1971).

But if tastes are not readily measurable (see Klitgaard [1975] for a particularly pessimistic view), why do we raise the notion here? Because it makes clear that choices among alternatives cannot be escaped in the multiple output case and that not all alternatives are likely to be equally desirable. It is introduced also to show that optimizing behavior is a useful framework for analyzing outcomes.

If some outcomes are better than others, does a best outcome exist, and what is it? This is standard material for economists, and we beg their forbearance if any of them plodded through the preceding pages. It was a mild surprise that in the course of our research, as we spoke with more and more teachers, psychologists, and educators, we found the economic model of optimization under constraints greeted with either tenacious skepticism or unbridled admiration. One of our important tasks is to try to convince those in other disciplines of the virtues of the economic methodology while at the same time learning from them the limitations of the approach for education problems. But if the methodology is to be used, the assumptions must be clearly understood.[5]

EMPIRICAL IMPLICATIONS

Before advancing to the case of joint production in a multiproduct case, we explore the implications for measurement of the cases we have covered so far. It seems that the questions that are always at the center of empirical research are whether there are any inputs that make a difference in determining outputs, and if there are, how "important" are they. Recent summaries of the literature of these questions do not point to conclusions any different from those of a few years ago. In short, the only inputs that consistently seem to make any difference to learning outcomes are students' socioeconomic and racial background measures. Hanushek writes:

> First, almost uniformly, educational production models show no consistent or significant relationship between achievement and expenditures per pupil (either instructional expenditure or total expenditures). Second, analyses of specific purchased inputs (teacher experience, teacher education levels, class size, and administrative/supervisory expenditures) show a similar lack of relationship. (1978:47)

Lau (1978:11-13) stated that there was no consistent relationship between cognitive achievement and such variables as class size, teacher quality, and teacher attitudes. He does allude to several studies that found a relationship between scores and time inputs. But the studies cited use time measures that are grossly different from the microeconomic time-on-task notions that we think are more appropriate. Instead, the time variables usually measure days present, length of school day, or length of school year. (See our discussion of one of these below.) Lau concludes:

None of these rather general conclusions constitutes a startling reversal of any findings of earlier surveys. In fact the conclusion of no consistent observed relationship between cognitive achievement and school resources appears to hold quite well. The only relatively new addition is perhaps the observed importance of student time inputs in education and production for which a substantial amount of evidence has been accumulated over the past few years. (1978:13)

Why might purchased inputs seem to have no effect on learning? After all, if such were really the case, schools would be entirely irrational institutions from an economic perspective. The best explanations of these empirical regularities show them to be the result of using the wrong theoretical model of production—one output produced by many inputs. The correct production model to use in empirical estimation is not the single output version but a multiple output system. The absence of observed productivity effects comes from omitting learning outcomes other than cognitive skills. In one version of the critique, the additional outputs are other student traits such as affective qualities (Gintis, 1971; Bowles and Gintis, 1976; Brown, 1972; or Leekley, 1974). In another version, the neglected outputs are the many students in a class, each of whose learning outcomes is assumed to matter. This implies that it is incorrect to aggregate students in classrooms by taking the mean score or learning level as the measure of output (Klitgaard, 1975; Brown and Saks, 1975a). Indeed, we (1975a) have shown that using a single output model provides the opposite conclusions about the productivity of purchased teacher inputs than does using the multiple output model on exactly the same data. The multiple output model does show that purchased inputs are productive.

The production possibilities curve makes it clear why neglecting the presence of multiple outputs leads to problems. Figure 2-6 shows two product transformation curves for two different levels of input use. We know inputs are productive—that is, have positive marginal products—because DD', the curve representing outputs with the higher input level, lies above and to the right of CC'. The two outputs measured along the axes may be either the scores of different students or the scores of a single student on two different learning outcomes. Assume for a moment the former case and that each student's score matters so that it is efficient to be on the curve CC' or DD' rather than "inside" it.[6] Suppose the resource allocator in the case of fewer resources chooses to be at point Q, while with increased inputs, R is chosen. If we take the mean score of the two students as our measure of output, we find that the average score is lower at R than at Q, and we might be tempted to conclude that the marginal

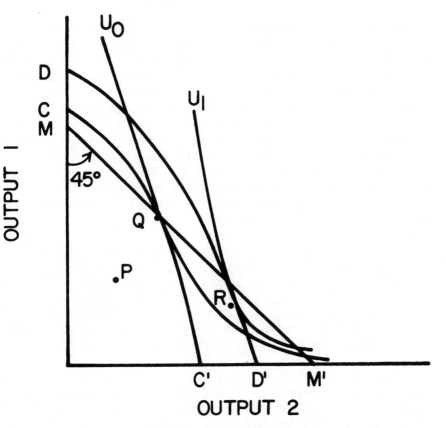

Figure 2-6. Choices between two outputs when the quantity of an input changes.

product of the input is negative. The 45 degree line *MM'* through *Q* is a locus of points for which the mean score is constant. Since *R* lies below *MM'*, we must have a lower mean score. Thus, as we move to a higher production possibility curve because we have used more productive inputs, the mean output falls! The usual simple regression model would conclude that the inputs were not productive. By assumption, that was not the case here.

If the variables in the figure represent different learning outcomes for a particular pupil, say cognitive and affective traits or mathematics and foreign language scores, we confront a similar problem. As resource increase, the production of output 1 decreases, not because of unproductive inputs but because of the structure of tastes. A statistical model that regresses output 1 on inputs would find a negative marginal product. Keeping in mind our objective of identifying input productivities, what is to be done? First, we must try to include all the outputs we can in our model. This is extremely difficult because on the one hand many are in principle not easily measurable (e.g., personality traits) and because on the other hand the number of output measures may be unmanageably large. We as economists do not really have much guidance to offer on this issue. Certainly the problem occurs in all studies outside educational production and is handled after a fashion or assumed away. The test for success or failure seems to be whether other researchers in the field believe the results and the model. Second, many researchers have suggested that both model and data be analyzed at the level of the individual student. Hanushek (1978) seems to take this for granted throughout his paper, and the models he presents are all in terms of the individual student. Lau writes:

> This lack of *identification* of the true relationship of educational production is a problem which plagues a substantial proportion of empirical studies of education production. In principle, this problem is not insurmountable. It does require, however, the collection of detailed student-specific data on the quantities of variable inputs including possibly detailed time budgets of the actors, and a concomitant analysis of the behavioral patterns of the actors in the educational process. (1978:21)

Murnane, in his conclusions about earlier research, lists first among the "lessons that have been learned" that "the unit of observation should be the individual child since intraschool variance in achievement is much larger than interschool variances" (1975:25).

Finally, Summers and Wolfe note that "Past attempts at estimating [production functions] have represented many inputs by school- or district-wide averages, rather than by the more appropriate pupils-specific data . . . . We conclude that the empirical investigations have failed to find potent school effects because the aggregative nature of the data used disguised the school's true impact" (1977: 39–40). They feel that "the use of pupil-specific data, and statistical methods appropriate to such data, account for the cheerier results of [their] study."

In the paragraphs that follow, we will explore the data requirements of the multiple output (i.e., many student) model for analysis at the individual student level. Then we will analyze some of the studies that purported to satisfy the disaggregation requirements of the model. We do this because we believe it is important to realize that individual data will not in general solve these problems.

The multiple output model, when there was no jointness in production, was written in a simple form:

$$y_1 = f(t_1),$$

$$y_2 = g(t_2),$$

$$\overline{T} = t_1 + t_2.$$

The assumption of two inputs and two outputs will not restrict us. The relevant group here is the two students together who "share" a single input quantity, $\overline{T}$. Increasing the amount of t given to one of them is something that is, first of all, presumed to be measurable and that, second, decreases the amount available to the other by the same amount. The data requirements for such a model are for input amounts received by each student, as well as for their output performance (or value added, see Summers and Wolfe [1977]). We show that it is not sufficient to have only input data $(\overline{T})$ for the group, even if we have observations on y_1 and y_2.

All studies using individual student output use classroom level inputs as the lowest level of aggregation.[7] That is, $\overline{T}$ is used in the production equations for y_1 and y_2 instead of t_1 and t_2. Figure 2–7 shows two production possibilities curves for the learning outcomes

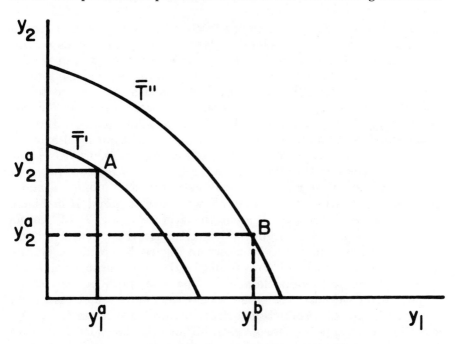

Figure 2-7. Two production possibilities curves for scores of two students.

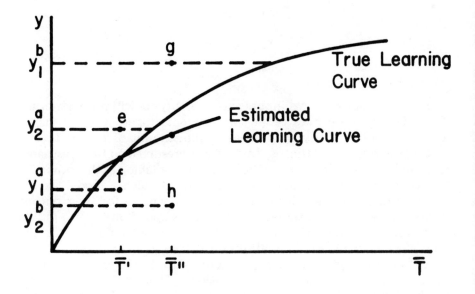

Figure 2-8. The effects of using average input instead of pupil-specific data.

of two students for two different levels of $\overline{T}$. In the best of worlds the students would have identical learning curves, so let us assume that they do. The learning curve appears in Figure 2-8. Can we discover the shape of the learning curve by looking at the relationship between the individual student outcomes and average input to the two students? The answer, in general, is no, because unless $\overline{T}$ is perfectly correlated with both t_1 and t_2, there will be a bias in the estimates of the production parameters. When the input level is at $\overline{T}'$, production takes place at A and the learning outcomes are y_1^a and y_2^a. If we assumed the students each receive the average input $\overline{T}'/2$ instead of the true value, we will have the data points e and f in Figure 2-8. When $\overline{T}$ rises to $\overline{T}''$ we move to point B in Figure 2-7. Again assigning each student the average input, $T''/2$, we get data points g and h. A hypothetical estimate of the learning curve based on these four points is shown in Figure 2-8. While it is positively sloped, it does not correspond to the true learning curve and indeed seems to underestimate the marginal productivity of the input. Again we have the entangling of technology and tastes. We cannot isolate the production effects of a change in an input. We have not been able to disaggregate sufficiently. Lau (1978) at least understands that in this model the problem is solvable, in principle; but no study to date has been able to secure appropriate data.

A CRITIQUE OF THREE NOTEWORTHY
RECENT STUDIES

We would now like to look in detail at a few recent studies that have attracted some attention and that presumably define the state of the art. Summers and Wolfe (1977) is among the very best of these. They use a single equation, single output, many input model to try to discover which inputs matter for student achievement over a three year period from third to sixth grade. Four kinds of explanatory variables (measured for grade 6) are employed: (1) genetic and socioeconomic characteristics of the student, (2) teacher quality variables, (3) other nonteacher school quality variables, and (4) some peer group characteristics. All these variables are stated to be pupil-specific for their 627 students from 103 Philadelphia elementary schools. The statistical analyses in their paper make liberal use of interaction terms involving the right-hand side variables to search for interesting non-linearities in the results.

The results of Summers and Wolfe are claimed to contrast clearly with most earlier work. First, they find inputs that do seem to matter for achievement. A related result of interest, suggested by our earlier model (Brown and Saks 1975a), is that different inputs have different effects with different pupils. They attribute their "cheerier" results to the pupil-specific data set they collected.

What is the Summers and Wolfe model? It is the one output (achievement) production function model that has been used in most studies. They say that the interpretation of their input-output equation should not be as a production function, citing the presence of inputs that cannot be altered by decisionmakers and the assumption that in theory such a function relates maximum attainable output to inputs. However, including fixed inputs in the production equation in no way undermines the notion of a production function or "blurs the distinction between the variables which the educational policymaker can control . . . and those which he cannot . . . " (1977: 639). Indeed, the standard textbook analysis of the short run in production makes just such a distinction.

Summers and Wolfe make an important point in noting that schools are not perfectly efficient so that the points we observe do not lie on the frontier. The implication of this is that the empirical estimates really describe a kind of average rather than peak efficiency. But that seems to us to be as much a problem with the estimation techniques that have been used as with how we ought to interpret the results. They conclude: "It seems preferable, therefore, to view (1) [their achievement equation] as a simple input-output relationship." But if a "single input output relationship" is not a production function, estimated with biases perhaps, we do not know how to interpret it.

Since allocated time is one of the key elements of school production, it was useful for them to try to include such a concept. Unfortunately, their model does not include the time students spend on learning in an important way. It is true that they measure the effects of attendance (latenesses and unexcused absences) and examine the impact of "disruptive incidents." But these are only approximate and, incidentally, very aggregative measures of the time pupils spend trying to learn. Presumably these data, if available, did not show any consistent impact on learning or they would have been included in the final results. This leads us to suspect that unexcused absences and possibly latenesses are not really picking up the effect of time lost but are a proxy for some socioeconomic characteristic. Summers and Wolfe do in fact identify these variables as proxies for "motivation of students" rather than as a production effect of changing time on task (1977:642).

What can we say about their other pupil-specific input measures? These consist of a teacher's college quality rating, teacher experience, class size, and the teacher's score on a national teachers' exam. All these variables seemed to have a significant effect on learning, but after all, that is why they ended up in the final results.

The difficulty we have with these results is that the input data are not pupil-specific but are instead classroom-specific. The variables on teacher quality and class size are measures of classroom resources, not the specific amounts of inputs made available to specific students. The production model with many students requires that output data for each student be matched with the inputs to that student. The inputs in a classroom may be a better measure of resources received by a student than those in the student's school or school district. But the disaggregation in the Summers and Wolfe model is not complete on the input side. So we still have the problem of the interaction between technology and tastes. For example, "Teachers who received B.A.'s from higher rated colleges were associated with students whose learning rate was greater—and it was students from lower income families who benefited most" (1977:644). Were the teachers from the higher-rated colleges more productive than other teachers? Or did they allocate their and their students' time and other classroom resources differently. It may, after all, be that the teachers from the higher rated colleges have different values with respect to the distribution of learning outcomes and as a result use different classroom management strategies. But because we do not observe the amount of input each pupil gets, but only what the class gets, we are unable to disentangle the technology from the values applied in classroom organization.

Teacher experience clearly affects different students differently in Summers and Wolfe's results. Higher achieving students seem to benefit more from experience and low achieving students seemed adversely affected. But again, it is unclear whether we are experiencing the effects of tastes or technology. It is possible, but not determinable in this study, that experience makes teachers more effective with low achieving kids, but that more experienced teachers systematically see to it that more time and resources get allocated to high achievers. We simply do not have the evidence about teachers' or other administrators' values about these things.

Summers and Wolfe's results on the effects of class size also reveal different effects for different kinds of students. Low achieving students seem to do worse in very large classes while high achieving students do better. Class size, as it relates to how classes are organized and time allocated, is an interesting variable. As more children are under the supervision of one teacher, the control problems multiply. Some teachers may see larger classes as an imperative for more sameness in student activities—large group lecturing, study hall, and so forth. Others may see it as raising the value of individual attention to students, particularly in a class where peers are a very heterogeneous group. But without explicit attention to the organizational factors and the resulting time allocations, we must withhold judgment on the effects of changing the class size variable.

Peer group effects seem to be important to achievement. All students seem to benefit most from having 40 to 60 percent black students in the school. An increasing the percentage of high achieving students seems to benefit low achieving students particularly. We can tell stories about why these results might appear. These stories would probably have to do with how the students are mixed together in subgroups within a class and how they interact. If the groups are cleverly chosen, the bright students might teach the not so bright. If the groups were chosen differently, but no less cleverly, the bright students might help themselves, and the teacher would concentrate on the not so bright. Summers and Wolfe do not tell stories like this because their model and data are not designed to discriminate between them. Even though they have data on achievement for individual students, their input data are still aggregated, less so than in other studies perhaps, but still not student-specific.

Perhaps the most interesting results come from their interaction analysis of inputs. As we suggested in 1975 (Brown and Saks, 1975a, 1975b), there has been a near total neglect of the rather obvious fact that schools have very different effects on different students. This means that how a given amount of resources is organized and spread out over the students can have a rather dramatic effect on the standard measures of output, aggregative or not. While Summers and Wolfe may not have had any more success than we did is isolating the productivity from the allocative effects, they point to an important pathway for research. We must try to determine the differences in the productivities across students of different kinds of inputs and the effects of peer group interactions on those productivities. The measurement and analysis of time allocations would seem to be a promising way to proceed, particularly in terms of the theoretical models that we have developed so far. But life is more complicated than we have been willing to admit, since we have assumed independence of the student learning curves as a function of time. After we discuss some other recent studies of achievement, we will develop a model of joint production to study the implications of that realistic extension of the learning model.

Ritzen and Winkler (1977) try to uncover the differences in the productivity of school inputs over time and for "advantaged" and "disadvantaged" children. Because productivities are likely to vary both over students and over time, allocating resources is not likely to be a trivial matter if one wants to optimize the total amount of human capital obtainable from given resources. Ritzen and Winkler most certainly equate learning as measured by achievement tests with human capital—that personal quality associated with higher productivity in labor markets. They state that "new learning by students in a given period of time is a function of their current existing human capital stocks and the current flow of inputs" (1977:428). Then, "Human capital is measured in this paper by percentile scores on standardized examinations of cognitive learning" (1977:430). Indeed, they use scores on IQ and verbal achievement tests. One reason they might prefer to identify their study as one of human capital rather than simply cognitive learning is a desire to associate themselves with the school of thought that identifies the productivity of education as residing in skills and their assumed direct relation to job performance and income. For a contrasting view, one might see Bowles and Gintis (1976) or Gintis (1971).

The Ritzen and Winkler model is one in which the current learning level is a function of the past period's learning level, current home inputs, and current (purchased) school inputs. Learning can depreciate from one period to another, home inputs are assumed constant from year to year (a restriction imposed by the data), and the productivity of a given amount of school inputs is allowed to vary depending on when a student receives it.

Their sample consists of 669 students from a single school district who completed eighth grade in 1965. They report that 356 of the students are black and 313 white. This is important, since they say that race may serve as a proxy for income in their estimates, noting that the difference between black and white mean family incomes differed by almost $2,500 "in the geographic area included in the school district under study" (1977:429).

Their measure of home inputs is an index of the number of cultural items in the home, a variable indicating homeownership, years of education of mother and father, and finally, the number of siblings in the home.

The treatment of school inputs in the model is best put in their own words.

> The quantity of instructional services provided in the school can be assumed to be a function of the capital and labor in the school. Capital includes physical capital such as books, laboratory equipment, special instructional aids, etc., and human capital of the teachers, administrators, and other personnel. At the micro level, labor in the school refers to the quantity of time a teacher allocates to a given child and the pupil's own work effort. Teacher time may be related to class size.
>
> While it would be desirable to have direct measures of capital and labor in the school, we proxy these purchased inputs by current real expenditures per pupil. (1977:431)

The expenditure variable was constructed from information on class sizes, salaries of school personnel, and student academic records. What is clear from the discussion is that the input variable is at best classroom-specific at the elementary level, and they say it is track-specific for the secondary (presumably junior high) school year(s). Since the significance of tracking in their discussion is never made clear, except to note that there are two tracks in the junion high schools, it is not possible to evaluate the data in more detail.

The results that Ritzen and Winkler present show increasing elasticities of achievement with respect to the purchased inputs as grade level increases. In short, it would appear that the marginal products of school inputs are generally positive and increase the farther pupils advance through the grades.

Ritzen and Winkler rerun their equations for subsamples of the data and find marked differences for blacks and whites. Whites demonstrate the pattern of increasing input productivities over time. Blacks, on the other hand, seem to have elasticities of test scores with respect to inputs that are constant over time. That is, the productivity of school remains about constant for blacks as they proceed from grade 1 to 8. Why should this be? Ritzen and Winkler suggest that the difference may be due to the schools having different objectives for blacks and to blacks' different objectives for themselves: "The blacks in this sample are predominantly low income, and low income pupils may not value scholastic achievement as highly as middle and high income pupils, perhaps because they perceive an unimportant relationship between such achievement and future earnings" (1977:434). Now we see the motivation for their earlier assertion that race is a proxy for income. They believe that they have separated the sample along income lines and that low income means a perception of a low payoff to school achievement. They go on to say that blacks tend to be in the vocational track rather than in the college preparatory track and suggest that the school may be attempting to maximize some variable other than achievement. It may, of course, also be true that the tastes and preferences of the school authorities operate in a more insidious fashion and result in fewer resources being allocated to black pupils in elementary school. The aggregative nature of the input variables carefully insures that this possibility, if indeed it occurs, will not be uncovered.

While Ritzen and Winkler may realize the possibility of a confounding of tastes and technology, as in the paragraph quoted above, they seem convinced in the end that they have estimated production parameters—the technology. A page of caveats does not deter them. They dutifully note the difficulty of generalizing their results "to the world as a whole," the difficulty of identifying human capital with test scores, the difficulty of measuring home and school inputs, and finally, the possibility that education technology may change. Yet they venture their policy recommendations: "In those cases when the statistically significant results obtained in the estimation of the model showed production elasticities which continuously increase with time between grades one and eight, the optimal investment trajectory should be one where the quantity of purchased inputs per pupil also increases with time" (1977:436). Thus, the time pattern of expenditures should be one that tends to equate marginal productivities across years. Since with existing allocations the returns for whites are higher in later years, more resources should be shifted in that direction. But blacks have more or less constant returns over time, so their allocation is about optimal.

Ritzen and Winkler's model and conclusions show a lack of sensitivity to the interactive roles of technology and values in the determination of achievement. High returns in some grades for whites may be due to a failure to observe the true input quantities they receive.

If they in fact got more inputs than the classroom or track average and if the inputs they got were productive, we would overestimate the productivity of the observed inputs. But on the other hand, the high returns may be an accurate measure of marginal returns. The point is that we simply do not know and cannot tell from the evidence presented. The results are inconclusive, and the policy prescriptions unjustified.

Murnane (1975) leads us carefully, step by step, through a maze of data and analyses of how and whether schools affect pupils' achievement. In all, he tests thirty hypotheses, ranging from whether the classroom to which a child is assigned affects the child's achievement (it does) to whether black and white teachers show a different relationship between experience and teaching performance (they do not).

Murnane employs the single output, many input production model in which a child's achievement at the end of the school year depends on achievement at the beginning of the year, background characteristics, number of school days attended, and a vector of school and teacher characteristics. His sample consists of 875 inner-city black children.

In the first stages of analysis, he concludes that principals' evaluations of teachers do predict performance in raising the pupils' achievement. Class size and the peer group variables of mean and standard deviation of achievement in a class seemed to have little relation to achievement. With these preliminaries out of the way, Murnane poses an interesting set of questions that really go to the core of some of the issues we want to raise. Does perceived input productivity vary with student achievement level? Are some teachers more productive with certain kinds of children? Does classroom student turnover adversely affect high or low achieving pupils more? These are questions about both the nature of the technology in a classroom and the tastes or values of teachers. Murnane realizes, perhaps better than any researcher whose work we have read, that his answers involve both tastes and technology, so that the regression coefficients in his model should not be interpreted as marginal productivities. His treatment of the effect of turnover is a good example.

> Why would student turnover especially affect the progress of children with high initial reading achievement? One plausible explanation is that teachers compensate for the time lost in dealing with transient students by spending less time with those children who can "best" afford the loss— namely, those children with high achievement levels. If this conjecture is correct, why does the effect not appear in the three math files? The reason

may lie in differences in the way reading and math are taught in the primary grades. Most teachers divide their children into several reading ability groups and allocate time to each group. Thus, the possibility of spending less time with the best readers exists. Math, however, is more often taught to the whole class at the same time at the primary grade level. Thus, there is less of an opportunity to make an explicit decision to spend less time with "high achievers" in order to have more time for other children, (1975:47)

He also tests the hypothesis that "the relatonship between principals' evalations and teacher performance in improving the cognitive skills of students is different for black teachers than it is for white teachers' (1975:49). This is a test of whether principals' evaluations predict the performance of students in the same way depending on whether they had black or white teachers. Indeed, it seems to make a difference (evaluations of blacks are poorer predictors), and Murnane offers two explanations, neither of which has anything to do with any possible productivity differences between the two groups of teachers.

One explanation suggests that black teachers may be especially highly rated for their accomplishments in raising the noncognitive skills of students. This is consistent with Murnane's earlier statement that education has many goals and schools multiple outputs. An alternative is that the principals, most of whom were white, were less capable of evaluating black teachers because they were less familiar with their teaching techniques and styles.

Murnane believes that he has identified—and he may have—some pure productivity effects. Most interesting is the effect of experience on achievement scores. Experience seems to increase teacher productivity up to three to six years of experience. The gains from experience are apparently exhausted after six years and perhaps after as few as three. But any conclusions about other teacher characteristics that may affect learning must be weighed carefully. Murnane's data are another example of individual data on student achievement being joined with classroom level data or inputs, particularly teacher characteristics. Internal organizational factors that reflect values can confound the analysis and prevent us from finding input marginal productivities. But we feel his research represents at least the best link between the single output model and the more realistic and useful models where intraclassroom allocations are fundamental.

JOINT PRODUCTION

We now need to consider cases of multiple outputs where production of one output affects the production of another in more complex ways than simply through the resource constraint. We think that the applicability of this model to classes where inputs get shared in complex ways is obvious. Economic analysis of joint production usually begins with the case of fixed proportions. Suppose some product, y_1, is made using a single input in its production, x. We may write the production function as $y_1 = f(x)$. Suppose also that there is another output, y_2, that is produced along with y_1 in constant proportions without the use of any further inputs. An often used example of such a process is the production of hides and beef. Sometimes one of the outputs is called a by-product. If both of the outputs and the input have constant market prices or values, P_1, P_2, and P_x, we ask what amount of the input, product, and by-product we should choose if we want to maximize profits—the difference between revenues and costs. That is we want to

$$\text{maximize:} \quad R = P_1 y_1 + P_2 y_2 - P_x x,$$

$$\text{subject to:} \quad y_1 = f(x),$$

$$y_2 = k y_1,$$

where k is the (constant) factor of proportionality between the outputs. The solution to the problem is to choose x, the input quantity, to satisfy

$$P_1 \frac{\partial f}{\partial x_1} + P_2 k \frac{\partial f}{\partial x_1} = P_x.$$

The input should be used up to the point where the extra cost of buying another unit, P_x, is equal to the extra return from buying it. This extra return is the sum of two parts, the extra receipts from the scale of the extra y_1 obtained, P_1 $(\partial f / \partial x)$, and the extra receipts from the scale of the extra y_2, $P_2 k (\partial f / \partial x)$.

While this version of the problem certainly makes clear the idea of jointness, there is another way of stating it that is useful for analytical purposes. Consider the following problem, which has the same solution as the one above:

$$\text{maximize:} \quad R = P_1 y_1 + P_2 y_2 - P_x x,$$

$$\text{subject to:} \quad y_1 = f(x_1),$$

$$y_2 = g(x_2),$$

$$x = x_1 = x_2.$$

The best amount of x to choose must satisfy

$$P_1 \frac{\partial f}{\partial x_1} + P_2 \frac{\partial g}{\partial x_2} = P_x,$$

which has the same interpretation as before. Use the input, x, up to the point where the extra cost associated with the use of another unit is equal to the extra benefits. The benefits have two parts, since extra x produces both y_1 and y_2. Indeed, one way of looking at fixed proportions production is to say that each output gets the benefit of all the input. If the amount of input is increased to one product, the increase goes to all the other products as well. All products "consume" the extra input equally.

Notice that this second formulation of the joint production problem is exactly the same as our multiple output case except for the specification of the last constraint. Where separability in production was the rule, we had $x = x_1 + x_2$, so that an increase of x_1 meant an equivalent reduction in x_2, if total x was constant. Here an increase in x_1 does not reduce x_2. In fact, both x_2 and x must rise.

This suggests that there may be intermediate cases of jointness in production and that the fixed proportions and perfect separability cases are only extremes of a more general model. The last input constraint in the above problems holds the key. We want for that constraint a function that will tell us the amount by which an input increase for one good must reduce input availability for other goods. Elsewhere we have called this the "input exhaustion constraint" (Brown and Saks, 1975a), and it is the key to understanding where the gains from jointness arise, if they exist at all. First jointness does not exist if the input exhaustion constraint for x is simply the sum of the amounts of x used to produce all the goods. A quick test is the following: When I increase the amount of x to one output, does this show up as a decrease to all other outputs together in an equal amount? If the answer is no, jointness is present.

As has been pointed out elsewhere, jointness in production has many formal similarities to the economic analyses of public goods and externalities. A pure public good in consumption is one that is consumed in its entirety by everyone ($Z_{total} = A_j$, $j = 1, \ldots n$, for n consumers of Z). Externalities are characterized by lack of independence between production and/or utility functions. It is a matter of choice in some instances whether a particular case of productive interdependence is analyzed as jointness or as an externality. For example, electricity and smoke are produced in fixed proportions from coal. Or smoke is an external effect of electricity production. It usually matters little for the problem at hand which way we choose to imagine the interdependence in production taking place. We shall make use of the similarities between the cases below.

We saw that in the case of independently produced multiple outputs, it was possible to construct a production possibilities curve showing the locus of output possibilities when all inputs are fixed in quantity. This is, in general, also possible in the case of joint production. In fact, the shapes of the production possibilities curves will be similar to those of the independent output case, except in the case of fixed proportions jointness, where the "curve" is just a point in output space.

There are several important implications of the possible existence of jointness for understanding the economics of classrooms. The first is that we cannot understand the production relationship for an individual student in a particular subject by observing the inputs that pupil receives. In the case of the independent production model, that was a proper course in principle, but measurement was difficult. But with jointness, the individual production variables interact in possibly complicated ways. Measurement of individual input applications is not difficult but is theoretically impossible. The problems become apparent with a simple example. Let there be a classroom of two students, A and B, who are taught by a single teacher. The teacher may tutor the students individually or teach them together as a "class" of two pupils.

When the students are tutored, their learning curves (production functions) are

$$L_A = 10 + T_{AT},$$

$$L_B = 5 + 2T_{BT},$$

$$10 = T_{AT} + T_{BT},$$

where L_A and L_B are the learning levels, and T_{AT} and T_{BT} are the tutoring times for A and B. There are ten hours available. The production possibility curve for this technology is shown in Figure 2–9 as the line segment PP'.

Consider now an alternative technology in which the students are grouped in a class and the teacher lectures both at the same time.

$$L_A = 10 + .8T_{AC},$$

$$L_B = 5 + T_{BC},$$

$$10 = T_{AC} = T_{BC}.$$

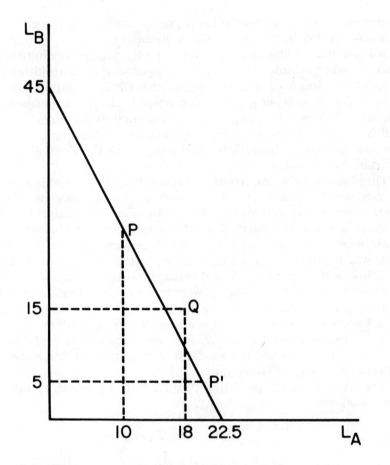

Figure 2-9. Production possibilities for two ways of organizing production.

The last pair of equatios tells us that we have the properties of joint production.

The production possibilities "curve" is the single point ($L_B = 15$, $L_A = 18$) represented as Q in Figure 2-9. Notice that it lies "outside" the production possibilities curve, so the "lecturing" kind of class organization is not dominated by tutoring organizations. Which technique will be picked depends on tastes.

While these cases represent extremes—we might expect a teacher to use some lecturing and some tutoring—we can get a glimpse of the frustration that researchers face if they try to measure input productivities by looking at "time getting instruction" and relating it to outcomes on an individual basis. What we need to know are the times and outcomes, certainly, but we must realize that the results are specific to a particular way of organizing production. If we mix up the data from lecutirng and tutoring classes, say, the results will tell us nothing about the underlying productivities, even if the data are on the level of the individual student. Indeed, in this case (as we have pointed out in Brown and Saks [1975b]), it is essential to aggregate one's data up to the level where all of the jointness is internalized. It is important to realize that in a world of joint production, disaggregated data are not always better.

TOWARD MODELS OF TIME ALLOCATION IN CLASSROOMS

Economists have used two kinds of models to describe the production technologies of firms. The first, and more common, might be called the assembly line. The characteristics of a pure assembly line mode are that (1) each unit of output can be described as having the same set of characteristics as every other unit, (2) each unit of input has the same characteristics as any other unit of that input and (3) in the production of output, every unit passes through the same stages of processing and in exactly the same order as other units. Pure production line technologies are rare, although some subspecies are easy to find—for example, the production of a certain octane gasoline from crude oil of known and consistent chemical composition, or a particular model of automobile with given color, options, and so forth.

The second kind of technology model is the job shop. It is, in most important respects, the exact opposite of the production line. (See Reiter [1966] for a discussion of the features of job shops.) Each unit of output differs from every other; inputs may likewise vary in type or quality, and the process of transforming inputs into outputs differs for each unit of output. While again the pure form is rare, an automobile repair shop or machine tool fabrication and repair facility are suggestive examples.

One of the features of real world job shops is that they may occasionally process orders where many units require the same inputs and transformation procedures. Because the set-up time for a particular process is usually not zero, the units requiring similar treatment may all be done together (the technical term is "streaming"). This results in a kind of mini–production line run in what is basically a job shop technology. It is easy to see that any particular real world technology may have elements of both models.

Basic to our discussion is the idea that the production of a unit of a commodity can be thought of as being broken down into a set of tasks or operations on inputs. Thus the tune-up of an auto engine may entail raising the hood, removing and checking spark plugs, attaching wires for certain measuring devices, and so forth. Each operation requires the time of a person or a machine with special characteristics. Furthermore, some operations may have to be done in a particular order—for example, the hood must be raised before the spark plugs are removed. We shall assume that the tasks to be done in making a unit of output, though not necessarily their order or mode of completion, can be specified independently of whether the task is ultimately carried out in a job shop or on a production line. It then becomes an important economic question whether a good should be produced in an assembly line or a job shop mode of production.

One further difference between the assembly line and the job shop is important. Because units of assembly line inputs and outputs are homogeneous, the measurement of input and output are relatively easy on the plant level. Indeed, this can be accomplished by measuring simple statistics on total or average production, since there are no relevant variations among individual output units. For the job shop, however, describing output can be difficult unless we are willing to settle for a complete list of units produced, along with their characteristics. What is in the assembly line a simple question of more or less becomes a large data-handling or aggregation problem for the job shop, where the issue is often which goods to produce today and which not. A related aspect of job shops is that the complexity makes analytic solutions to the scheduling problem almost impossible. Rules of thumb are commonly used for allocation and management.

We believe that the dichotomy between assembly line and job shop modes can yield useful insights into the functioning and evaluation of schools as production units. We have argued elsewhere (Brown and Saks, 1975a) that the task of schools is to change the characteristics of particular students. In a typical school, or even in a classroom within a school, we find a wide diversity among the students. They may differ in their initial endowments of knowledge or skill or social traits. They may acquire traits at different rates, depending on the characteristics of classmates, teachers, or instructional materials or on how activities within the classroom are organized. The final desired set of characteristics that are the result of schooling may vary from student to student. Because the inputs are unique to students and because students are probably not homogeneous, the classroom would seem to be a good example of job shop production. It is the multiple output, joint production perspective of teaching that makes the analysis of job shops relevant to education.

There is an important distinction between a school and a typical industrial job shop, however. The school could be (and some are) operated like production lines in the sense that all units are treated exactly the same way. While it would probably occur to no one to operate an auto repair shop like an assembly line, such is not the case with schools. In fact, it seems to us that many of the innovations in modern education are really technical changes of the kinds that organize existing inputs differently, as opposed to using new hardware. The use of "tracking" or ability grouping may be a good example of trying to "stream" the processing of nearly homogeneous input units.

In the next section we examine some production technologies for individual students. Following that, we explore the implications of grouping students in classrooms and the effects of allocating classroom resources in different ways.

CHANGES IN STUDENT TRAITS

For purposes of illustration, we shall assume that the change in a student's learning trait (say, the number of words that can be sight-read or spelled or the knowledge of the "sevens" row of the multiplication tables) is a function of three sets of variables: the student's learning traits acquired up to a time t^*, some characteristics of the students with whom our student is grouped, and the productivity of various kinds of inputs. This learning gain function for a student is, at least for now, assumed to be deterministic and monotonic in the independent variables. Ordinarily, though not necessarily, the effects of increasing inputs will be positive. We have no strong prior judgments to make about the signs of the effects of the other variables.

Because we are interested primarily in the effects of reallocating inputs under various conditions, it will be helpful to think of the input productivities themselves as depending on the other factors.

Now suppose we have a group of N students with different but known learning gain curves. There are assumed to be available at least a teacher and some other inputs such as books, chalk, chairs, desks, and maybe even a teaching machine. The problem we wish to investigate, and the one that confronts every teacher, is how to allocate the limited resources among the students. This encompasses the narrower question of the order in which certain resources are used, and whether or not the students are better off in particular subgroups.

This problem is clearly very much like the one faced by the manager of a job shop. Given the utility or profit value of each kind of output, the manager will allocate the scarce inputs so that the objective function is maximized. This is, in general, a nonlinear dynamic programming problem that depending on the particulars, may not be easy to solve. Such problems are, in principle at least, capable of solution by complete enumeration to any desired degree of accuracy.

Because such problems are not readily solved in real world situations, we are not concerned with the problem of finding optimal solutions or with the characteristics of such ideal outcomes. Rather, because such problems are tackled instead of applying rules of thumb, we shall concentrate on comparing the implications of different kinds of management strategies. This is the approach taken by Radner and Rothschild (1975) and would seem to be a particularly fruitful one for classroom management, since optimal control there seems to be a particularly distant prospect. Indeed, much of the history of classroom structure and organization can be described in terms of rules of thumb—the Lancasterian memorization lockstep methods of the nineteenth century, the somewhat less rigorous age-sex groupings of the early twentieth century and the age groupings of the present day, ability grouping or tracking, self-posed instruction, and even busing to correct racial imbalance.

Our approach, then, is to take the underlying microstructure of learning curves for individual students and to apply rules of thumb for classroom organization and management. Very simple models using few students and uncomplicated learning curves will be explored as an example.

HYPOTHETICAL CASE

Suppose there are two students with learning curves

$$G_{ij} = t_{ij}{}^{\alpha_{ij}-\beta_{ij}\delta_j} \qquad (i, j = 1, 2),$$

where G_{ij} is the score gain in a subject for student i when he used mode j for learning. The "time on task" is t_{ij} and equal $\bar{t}_{ij} - \bar{T}$, where $\bar{T}$ is the set-up time necessary to begin operation in a mode. The Kronecker delta, δ_j, will assume values of 0 or 1 depending on the mode used to organize instruction, while α_{ij} and β_{ij} are measures of the responsiveness of the gain score to additional time spent. We require $\alpha_{ij} - \beta_{ij} > 0$ for either value of δ.

In our example, two modes will be used for illustrative purposes—grouping ($\delta_j = 1$) and tracking ($\delta_j = 0$). Grouping means the students always work on the same task and in the same mode. Tracking means, in this case, that the two students are always using different modes. To assist our thinking about the problem, we might imagine one mode to be "receiving instruction directly from the teacher" and the other to be "studying and doing problems in a workbook."

We can illustrate how this sort of analysis might work by choosing some hypothetical values for the parameters of the learning curves. For example, we arbitrarily set:

$$G_{11} = t_{11}^{.85 - .10\delta_1}$$
$$G_{12} = t_{12}^{.4 - .10\delta_2} \qquad \text{for student 1;}$$

$$G_{21} = t_{21}^{.5 - .10\delta_1}$$
$$G_{22} = t_{22}^{.25 - .10\delta_2} \qquad \text{for student 2.}$$

Thus, for the first student the elasticity of gain score with respect to time receiving instruction is .85 (= .85 − .10[0]) if the teacher works with the student alone, .75 (= .85 − .10) if the students are taught together. Instructional time, in this example, is more productive for both students than workbook or seatwork time. And when the students are grouped to do tasks, time is less effective.

First consider the score outcomes for the two students. Let the time the teacher has to devote to instruction be 240 minutes. If the tracking mode ($j = 0$) is adopted, each student may receive from 0 to 240 minutes of direct instruction. The student not receiving instruction works alone. The possible scores for the students are shown by the curve labeled "tracked" in Figure 2-10. If, on the other hand, the students are grouped so that they are always engaged in the same activity ($j = 1$), the possible scores are shown as the line labeled "grouped." There is more than one "grouped" outcome because the teacher still has the option of varying his or her time with the students from 0 to 240 minutes.

Note that under what many people would consider reasonable assumptions, most of the points in the "grouped" set are inefficient. But which mode of organization and which time allocation within that mode will be chosen depends on the relative values attached to gains for the two students. We have suggested elsewhere (Brown and Saks, 1975a) that the distribution of scores can be conveniently summarized in terms of its mean and standard deviation. In this simple example, we can use the mean and range. The mean-range combinations for the two modes of organization in this example are shown in Figure 2-11.

While the tracked mode might seem to be a superior method of organization, this is not necessarily the case. For tastes that put a great value on reducing the differences between students (extreme

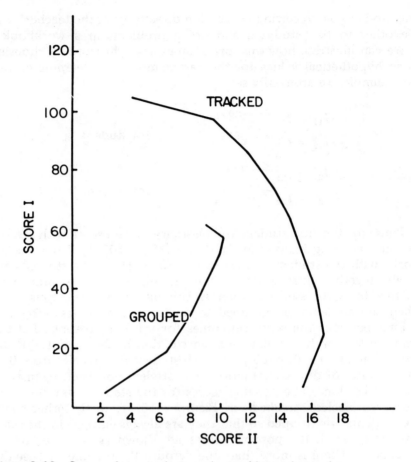

Figure 2-10. Scores of two students under tracking and grouping.

"levelers"), the grouped mode might be chosen because it will give the lowest range of scores. Note also that within the tracking mode, a higher mean is always associated with a higher range, so that maximizing the mean score also means maximizing the range. If increasing the range given the mean is perceived to be bad, some intermediate time allocation may be chosen. One might even choose a lower mean in the tracking mode than would be possible under some time allocations in the grouping mode because of the effect on the range. Thus, tracking need not result in greater variance or range than some grouping allocations.

Let us summarize. The model of many outputs with joint production suggests that the job shop may be a fruitful analogy for understanding classroom organization. Because job shops, and indeed

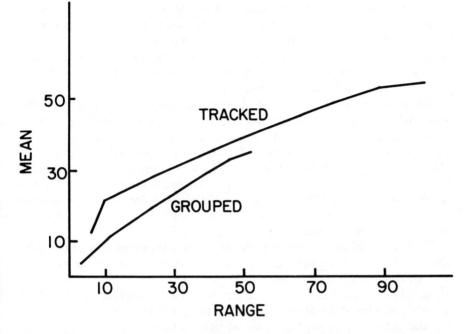

Figure 2-11. Mean and range of scores of two students under tracking and grouping.

classrooms, are so complex, it is useful to examine the results of applying different rules of thumb. It will not generally be possible to decide among rules without applying some value scheme or utility function.

Harnischfeger and Wiley (1976) take up the question of classroom organization as a problem in the allocation of time. They begin with the "abundantly obvious" hypothesis that "the more time an individual spends trying to learn, the more he will learn" (p. 6). With time as the focus of the analysis, they assert that we ought to look at the nature of classroom activities, their content, and their duration. The nature and content of activities is expected to vary from school to school and even from student to student. Duration is just another way of describing the frequency and intensity of the activities a student may undertake.

The task of the classroom teacher is the allocation of resources, the principal one of which is time. Harnischfeger and Wiley contrast their approach, quite rightly, with an analysis of teaching effectiveness that emphasizes subject matter content or teaching style. There is simply more to teaching than setting curricula and letting teachers teach it. Teachers can control, within rather wide bounds, how much time they will devote to particular pupils and how the pupils will be grouped together for certain specific activities. Cooperation and interaction among pupils and teachers play a central role in their analysis, as illustrated by their lengthy example (1976: 23–27), which we reconsider in detail below.

We find Harnischfeger and Wiley's approach very much in the spirit of what we are suggesting. As we do in our model, they look at the individual student and how learning in a subject varies with time spent and with how the student is grouped with others in a class. They consider grouping of students and time spent on learning tasks as the main objects of teacher management strategy. As a model for future empirical studies, their work points up the necessity for finding the individual student learning curves under different assumptions about grouping students.

However, although the Harnischfeger and Wiley model of the production of skills is similar to ours, we find their treatment and evaluation of the grouping strategies inadequate. Their example hypothesizes three classrooms that do not differ from each other in pupils' characteristics. The students in each class are grouped into thirds (upper, middle, and lower) on the basis of prior achievement. Though they do not make it explicit, it is best to think of each third as being homogeneous in every way. The teachers for the three classes have "equivalent skills," an assumption designed to get rid of idiosyncratic characteristics that might make some teachers more or less productive with the same students and to emphasize the effects of different management strategies. The analysis is based on a table of marginal productivities of spending extra hours of instruction on integer addition (the task). The marginal products vary by student achievement group and by whether the hour is spent in total class work, in a subgroup made up of those in the same their of past achievement, or in seatwork. Table 2–1 (their Table 3) shows these data.

Studying the table, we see that the upper third is at least as productive in each instructional setting as any other group. Except for the middle third, seatwork and work as a subgroup are more productive than total classwork.

Harnischfeger and Wiley's production framework includes the characteristics of jointness in production, the interrelations among productive units that we explored earlier. For example, an hour spent with the upper third as a subgroup increases achievement by 2 units. When the other two-thirds of the cass are added, giving us the total class setting, the hour generates only 1 unit for the upper

Table 2-1. Hypothetical Margin Products (in achievement units) of an Hour Spent on Integer Addition.

Achievement Group	*Instructional Setting*		
	Total Class	*Subgroup*	*Seatwork*
Upper third	1.0	2.0	2.0
Middle third	1.0	1.5	1.0
Lower third	.5	1.0	1.0

Source: Harnischfeger and Wiley, 1976. Table 3. Used by permission.

third. Total class instruction is, in fact, a good example of fixed proportions jointness in the sense that in that setting, adding an hour of instruction to one group increases the input to every group by exactly the same amount.

Another interesting feature of the example is that some learning can be produced with no teacher input at all. The upper third, in fact, does best if they are simply ignored by the teacher and left to do seatwork perpetually. Only the middle third shows any gain from subgroup (individualized) instruction over what could be gotten from seatwork. Jointness in production results in an hour of classwork being more productive than an hour spent with any subgroup. Thus, shifting an hour of subgroup instruction from the upper third, with a loss of 2 units, to total class instruction, with a gain of 2.5 units, would increase the total achievement of the class.

Harnischfeger and Wiley then created three teachers, Buehler, Ewald, and Oates, each of whom employs a different time allocation or classroom management strategy. Each teacher and student has 3 hours to spend. These hypothetical allocations are set out in Table 2-2. Buehler has an affinity for total class and subgroup work, and Ewald shuns total class instruction entirely. Oates, like Buehler, spends half the time with the total class and half on subgroup instruction with the lower two-thirds. The effects of these allocations on achievement are given in Table 2-3.

We find these results interesting for several reasons. One thing that Harnischfeger and Wiley do is draw our attention immediately to the average score gain in each classroom. But the strategies treat different students differently, and since student's achievement gain matters to us in the end, we must be wary of evaluating the success of a strategy in terms of its effect on mean achievement. Teacher Ewald,

Table 2-2. The Allocation of Time to Teacher Activities and Pupil Pursuits (in hours).

				Pupil Time		
Achievement Group	*Teacher Time*	*Total Class*	*Sub-group*	*Seatwork (addition)*	*Seatwork (other)*	*Total*
Teacher Buehler's grouping strategy						
Total class	1.5					
Upper third	0.5	1.5	0.5	0.0	1.0	3.0
Middle third	0.5	1.5	0.5	0.5	0.5	3.0
Lower third	0.5	1.5	0.5	1.0	0.0	3.0
Total	3.0					
Teacher Ewald's grouping strategy						
Total class	0.0					
Upper third	0.5	0.0	0.5	1.0	1.5	3.0
Middle third	1.0	0.0	1.0	1.5	0.5	3.0
Lower third	1.5	0.0	1.5	1.5	0.0	3.0
Total	3.0					
Teacher Oates's grouping strategy						
Total class	1.5					
Upper third	0.0	1.5	0.0	0.5	1.0	3.0
Middle third	0.5	1.5	0.5	1.0	0.0	3.0
Lower third	1.0	1.5	1.0	0.5	0.0	3.0
Total	3.0					

Source: Harnischfeger and Wiley, 1976, Table 2. Used by permission.

Table 2-3. The Effects of Grouping on Achievement (in achievement units).

	Achievement Group			
Teacher	*Upper Third*	*Middle Third*	*Lower Third*	*Average Gain*
Buehler	2.5	2.75	2.25	2.5
Ewald	3.0	3.0	3.0	3.0
Oates	2.5	3.25	2.67	2.67

Source: Harnischfeger and Wiley, 1976. Table 4. Used by permission.

with an average gain of 3 increases all the students' scores by exactly the same amount. Oates by contrast favors the middle third over the upper and lower thirds. Is Ewald's strategy superior to Oates's because it results in a higher mean? Certainly not, unless we are prepared to neglect differential treatement of students as irrelevant to the evaluation process. If gains to the middle third are disproportionately valued, then Oates, whose strategy favors the middle, may be more efficient.

It would appear the Buehler's strategy is inferior to those of Ewald and Oates under what many people would consider an acceptable value judgment. That is, a strategy is superior—more efficient—if it can be shown to raise some students' scores without reducing anyone's. Ewald's strategy raises every grup's score by more than Buehler's; Oates's raises the middle and lower thirds and keeps even with Buehler for the upper third. We saw in our own example above how one could identify the set of superior strategies defined in this way. Our discussion showed that the choices among superior strategies can be made only with the aid of a utility function that can judge the relative values of achievement for different students.

Another interesting aspect of the strategies that Harnischfeger and Wiley present is that in terms of any criteria that value only learning arithmetic, all of them are inefficient. Each assigns at least some of the students some of the time to do something called "Seatwork (Other)." This is presumably some kind of activity other than arithmetic that occupies student time but not teacher time. Clearly, if that time were simply transferred to arithmetic seatwork, the mean score of the affected groups would be raised. The teachers must have their reasons for assigning "Seatwork (Other)" activities, but we are not given any information about what the payoff from this work is or how it might be evaluated against further gains in arithmetic.

Finally, we were immediately tempted to ask whether there existed one or more strategies than the ones given that could maximize even the average achievement gain. An allocation of three hours of seatwork to both the upper and lower thirds and of three hours of subgroup work for the middle third will given an average gain of 4.5 units. Thus, maximizing the average has the teacher ignoring two-thirds of the class and putting all her or his resources into the single group where the relative (though not absolute) advantage is greatest. This result illustrates more clearly than any other the bizarre outcomes we can get from trying to maximize the average.

LEARNING CURVES AND THE
FREQUENCY OF LESSONS

If learning curves display diminishing returns to time spent and also require set-up times, we can work out an instructive example of how to analyze the question of optimal frequency and duration of lessons. The example shows how these questions might be analyzed in a way that relates to variables that we could observe in the world.

Consider that there is a measure of student competence by detailed subject matter and call this measure S for test score. Confining ourselves to production in school, consider the following linear production function for schools

$$\Delta S = \sum_{ijk}\sum\sum\sum_{l} \underline{a}_{i,j,k,l} \, T_{i,j,k,l}, \tag{2.3}$$

where the flow of added competency, ΔS, is due to standardized time, T, spent on different tasks related to learning the subject, and $\underline{a}$ is the marginal score produced by another unit of T. Obviously, $\underline{a}$ is very sensitive to the design of the test, but if test design is controlled, $\underline{a}$ is a measure of the marginal product of T. Since we expect productivity to vary with the particular subject being taught, the techniques of instruction, the characteristics of the teachers, and the characteristics of the students, the $\underline{a}$s and Ts are indexed over at least four dimensions.

One can develop some relations between the Ts that will exist in the optimal school, given valuation of scores for different students and subjects and given the a's or technical relations. But here we wish to focus on the issue of standardized time when we know that in designing lesson length there is a trade-off between set-up costs (getting ready for the new lesson) and fatigue associated with spending too much time on one task. We want to partition the lesson length problem from the time allocation to subject matter problem. Time, T, is really a proxy for a unit of learning here.

Perhaps the meaning will be clearer as we proceed with a particular specification. Suppressing the subscripts, the amount of learning (or standardized time, T) will be the product of the frequency of the lesson, F, and the learning L, per lesson, which is itself a function of the duration, d, of the lesson:

$$T = F \cdot L(d).$$

Assuming that there are diminishing learning returns to increasing duration, $L(d)$ will look like the curve in Figure 2–12. Because

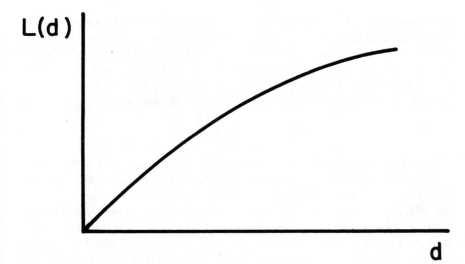

Figure 2-12. Learning as a function of the duration of a lesson.

$\partial L/\partial d > 0$, $\partial L^2/\partial^2 d < 0$, there is a trade-off in producing a given level of T between higher frequency or higher duration (see Figure 2-13). The $MRTS_{F,d}$ (the marginal rate of technical substitution of F for d) is the ratio of the marginal T products of F and d:

$$MRTS_{F,d} = \frac{L(d)}{F \dfrac{\partial L}{\partial d}} = \frac{\partial T/\partial F}{\partial T/\partial d}.$$

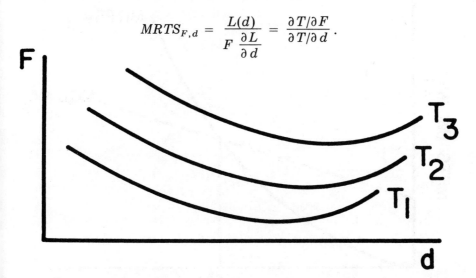

Figure 2-13. The trade-off between frequency and duration of lessons for different levels of learning.

This tells us about the technical psychological trade-off between frequency and duration. To reach an optimal decision, we need to know about costs of making alternative decisions. In the case of schools with inputs fixed in the short run, the relevant costs are time costs, C_T. These fall into two categories—set-up time for each lesson, C_S, and the time devoted to the lesson itself, d. We can write

$$C_T = F \cdot C_S + F \cdot d.$$

The marginal time cost of frequency of lessons is $\partial C_T / \partial F = C_S + d$, and the marginal time cost of duration of lessons is $\partial C_T / \partial d = F$. The ratio of these marginal costs $(C_S + d)/F$ must be set equal to the $MRTS_{F,d}$ at the point where minimum time is spent on the production of standardized learning time. Figure 2–14 shows the selection of optimal lesson lengths, d^*. The ratio of marginal costs is a straight line with slope equal to $1/F$ and intercept equal to C_S/F. Because of the shape of $L(d)$, the $MRTS_{F,d}$ function starts at the origin and is convex from below. Select d^* where

$$\frac{L(d)}{F \dfrac{\partial L}{\partial d}} = \frac{C_s + d}{F}.$$

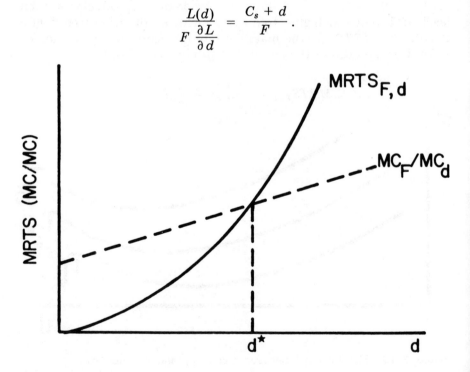

Figure 2-14.   Choice of optimal lesson length.

Notice that the optimal lesson length is independent of the amount of T that is being produced. (This also assumes an interior solution and no other binding restraints.)

This is, of course, a static equilibrium formation of the problem, and we can only suggest some of the dynamics. For example, if set-up time increases because of a decline in discipline in the school, the cost curve will shift up, and $d*$ should increase. But it may not be possible in the short run to readjust the schedule of the school, particularly if times get fixed by lesson plans in textbooks and by school customs. In that case, the analysis may have to incorporate adjustment costs. Similarly, if there is a desire to increase the emphasis (T_1 to T_2) on a particular subject (e.g., toward science because Russia sends up a Sputnik), there may be more problem in adjusting, say, frequency rather than duration, and the school may be in temporary disequilibrium with an adjustment path shown by the arrows in Figure 2-15. Alternatively, we could show the relation as in Figure 2-16. Here, the change in the utility of the composite score can be shown as a function of the frequency of the optimal length lessons in a particular subject. This curve is concave from below,

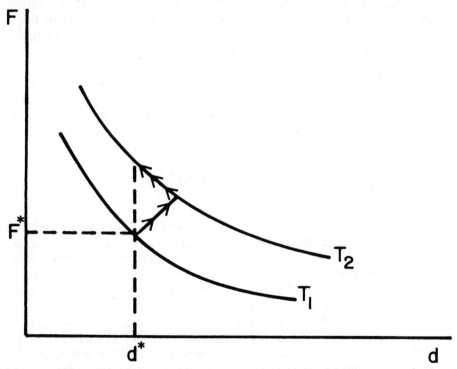

Figure 2-15. Adjustment of frequency and duration of lessons over time.

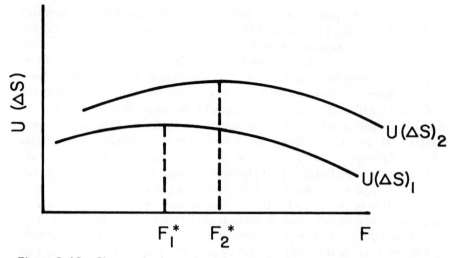

Figure 2-16. Changes in the optimal frequency of lessons because of changes in taste.

reflecting the diminishing marginal utility of more and more emphasis on one subject to the exclusion of others. With a shift in tastes toward the given subject, the utility curve shifts to the northeast, and frequency should increase. But it may not be able to do so immediately.

As a final note, we must realize that we are thinking of learning material in a linear sequential fashion where there is always more to learn and that we are not thinking at all about situations where lessons must have a fixed structure. In production terms, lessons may be lumpy or indivisible. Is this a problem? We do not know.

INCENTIVE STRUCTURES AND STUDENT ALLOCATIONS OF EFFORT

In the typical thinking about production of education in school, students are treated as passive inputs or raw materials that get processed by other factors of production. As we have emphasized, in the multiple output, joint products case, it is the allocation of resources within the unit of production that becomes the important component of the analysis. In the last section, we focused on the allocation of teacher effort and continued to assume that students were passive recipients of assignments—that they do what they are told and that even though learning curves may differ systematically among students, the parameters of those curves are given to the teacher, who has to make decisions accordingly. If students respond in fixed ways to teaching techniques, if teachers know a lot about these responses, and if the classroom is authoritarian, this might be an adequate model of intraclassroom allocation.

What we are saying is that the learning curves embody both "ability" and "motivation" or "effort" and that the teacher can pick the optimal points on the learning curve for each student and subject. Yet in making such assumptions we would be ignoring the potential relevance of several important schools of thought. The recent literature on the optimal lifetime accumulation of human capital (see, for example, Heckman [1976]) concentrates on the choices of individuals who have to allocate their time among consumption, production, and investment in human capital. To the extent that children have freedom, they must make choices about how to allocate their fixed time to alternative activities. Unfortunately, one of the frequent assumptions of this literature is that adults act so as to maximize the present value of lifetime income, and it is hard to think of children being so calculating over such a long planning horizon. But it is clear that children do have to make the decision about how to spend their time within the constraints imposed on them. It is very likely that the field of labor economics, which deals with the behavior of labor inputs in the production process, has many suggestive analogies that should be considered in analyzing student behavior in schools. And it is the range of student choices that those most familiar with the institutional iterature on schools (cf. Thomas, 1977) have emphasized. In this section, we will suggest some of the important issues raised by student choice.

When we discuss student allocation of effort, we need to focus on two dimensions—time spent on particular activities and the intensity of work performed in that time. In the production context, we would be talking about the number of hours working on the assembly line and the speed at which the line operates. In the learning curve context, we are talking about where the student moves along the curve (i.e., how much time is spent on the activity) and also the slope of the curve.[8] While the measure of time spent is relatively straightforward in theory, the measure of pace, intensity, or difficulty may be extremely hard to identify. The problem stems from the meaning of learning curves and ability. A learning curve tells us how much a student learns in any period of time under given conditions of production. That curve reflects both ability and effort. As a practical matter, ability would have to be defined as the component of learning that was fixed from the point of view of the student, and effort would be that component of learning that the student could adjust under the right incentives. It is exactly analogous to the difference between the short and the long run in economic analysis of the firm. The "short run" is the economist's shorthand for optimization when some of the production variables are fixed and some are adjustable, and the "long run" describes optimization when all variables, including fixed plant and equipment, can be adjusted. The shapes of learning curves may appear to be fixed for any technique of teaching, but there may be costly policies that would modify those curves but be quite beyond the ability of policymakers to change in the short run. These might range from nutrition of the fetus to parents' attitudes toward school. On the other hand, there may be costly policies (and remember that when economists use the word "costs" they do not mean money costs only) that could change the slope of the learning curve in the short run.[9]

In standard production theory, it is assumed that the managers have already explored all possibilities and are on the production frontier, given their possible choices about technique. When you are talking about how to manage a plant, you do not want to assume away the plant manager's problem. The teacher's problem is how to organize the classroom and the incentive system that operates there to get the "best" student response to teaching technique. And the student's problem is how to behave in that environment in order to make the "best" of it from his or her point of view. Of course, teachers may also be responding to incentives that students establish, so that classrooms may be thought of as markets where two sides are making exchanges. Students know how to use good and bad behavior, enthusiasm, respect, and performance to "reinforce" desirable teacher behavior. The things being determined in such a market are the pace and time devoted to particular subjects and the techniques of instruction. These get translated through the learning curves into learning by subject or skill. One could envision a supply curve of student time and effort to an activity and a teacher's demand for the student to spend time and effort on such an activity.

The market analogy is hardly fanciful. In some classrooms teachers go so far as to draw up formal contracts on the basis of "negotiatons" with explicit rewards and penalties. Where the student sets the pace of production ("self-paced learning"), the allocations can be manipulated by explicit incentive systems. Whether such formal markets are the best way of organizing production depends on many things. Perhaps the most famous economic analysis of the problem was Ronald Coase's ([1937] 1952) essay, "The Nature of the Firm." Coase emphasizes that there are costs of using the price mechanism and that the most important are the costs of "discovering what the relevant prices are" and the "cost of negotiating and concluding a separate contract for each exchange transaction which takes place in a market . . . " (p. 336). We know of no studies that evaluate such costs, but the fact that classrooms using formal market mechanisms are rare might suggest that the costs are perceived to be considerable. But even where a formal market mechanism is not visible, the teacher-manager still has to deal with the problems that a market makes explicit.

Consider the teacher's problem of manipulating the student. The teacher has two main control variables—the rewards that can be given to students and the pace at which the material to be learned is covered. These are shorthand for a host of things. Rewards would include grades, gold stars, enlisting the parents for home reinforcement of the teacher's incentives,[10] letting the student spend more time on desirable or fun activities, and the like. There is also the lifetime component of rewards for performance in school. Better students get to go farther in school and have both higher income and higher status jobs. Since grades are a good predictor of the amount of schooling that will be taken,[11] we prefer to ignore the question of the relative importance of lifetime and immediate rewards. It may be, however, that student variations in utility assigned to higher grades reflect variations in their valuations of the lifetime consequences of such grades.

Similarly, the pace of work refers to a whole variety of characteristics of the learning situation. In some sense, pace and difficulty of the material covered are almost indistinguishable, since speed must always be relative to the level of difficulty. Thomas (1977) stresses the attractiveness and quality of complementary inputs such as "well-educated parents, competent teachers . . . , well-written textbooks, well-equipped science laboratories, and good libraries . . . " (p. 108). All of these are analogous in the labor economics literature to job characteristics (e.g., safety, boredom, physical discomfort, etc.) for which there will be compensating wage variations.[12]

We are ready now to develop a simple model of student choice of effort or pace. The two major elements of it are (1) the student's preference with respect to rewards and pace, and (2) the incentive system imposed by the teacher or school authorities. The two parts together will determine the level of student effort where the student has choice.[13]

Consider a student who has well-behaved preferences with respect to the pace of instruction and the rewards that he or she is receiving in school. We can, following usual conventions, write a utility function for such a student and draw the contour of the function (an indifference map):

$$U^1 = u^1(R, P), \text{ and}$$

$$MRS_{P,R} = -dR/dP$$
$$U^1 = \text{constant,}$$

where R is rewards, P is pace, U^1 refers to the utility function of the first student, and $MRS_{P,R}$ is the marginal rate of substitution of pace for reward that leaves a student's level of utility unchanged. Figure 2-17 displays some indifference curves (combinations of pace and reward among which the particular student is indifferent) for two different students. Higher curves represent higher levels of satisfaction (i.e., higher reward for a given pace).

The two students we happened to pick had somewhat different attitudes toward pace. For the first student, higher pace is always a "bad" that needs to be offset with some reward. But for student 2,

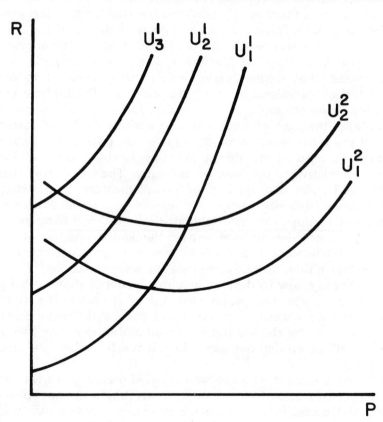

Figure 2-17. Indifference curves for two students.

too slow a pace is also undesirable (perhaps because of boredom or a feeling that valuable time is being wasted) so that the marginal rate of substitution of pace for rewards actually changes sign. It will be important later to realize that a student with higher ability is more likely to have the preferences of student 2 on the grounds that higher ability means that a given pace would not be so arduous and too slow a pace may induce boredom. Let us ignore this for the moment.

Now that we have a map of students' preferences, we need to know about the incentive system that, given their preferences, will determine their pace. We need two relations to generate the reward structure for pace—a relation describing how rewards depend on learning (output) and pace and a relation (production function) describing how learning depends upon pace, ability, and time spent on the activity:

$$R = r(Q, P) \qquad \text{(the general reward structure)},$$

$$Q = q(P, A, t) \qquad \text{(the production function)},$$

where R is reward, P is pace, Q is measured output or learning, A is ability, and t is time spent on the activity. The reward structure for pace will be those values of R and P that are consistent with these two equations.

To proceed, we need to know what these functions look like. There is some "experimental" evidence on the shape of the reward structure.[14] Figure 2–18 shows the apparently typical results of asking adults playing teacher to assign rewards to various students who display varying amounts of effort, ability, and achievement on tests measuring learning. It is clear that rewards are given not only for performance but also independently for higher effort. There is also an ability component to the reward structure, although it takes the form of penalizing "underachievers," and we regard it as an additional correction for inadequate effort. A reasonable question is why effort should be separately rewarded from output, which requires both effort and ability. We can think of several reasons. First, by paying extra rewards for effort, the incentive system is placing a premium on the cause of learning that is, by definition, most under the student's power to control. Second, as Bowles and Gintis (1976) and others have pointed out, schools do more than teach cognitive skills, and hard work is one of the behaviors that they try to inculcate so that students may become productive members of society. Third, the harder a student is working, the easier it is for the teacher to pursue the goals for the class. In terms of the input exhaustion

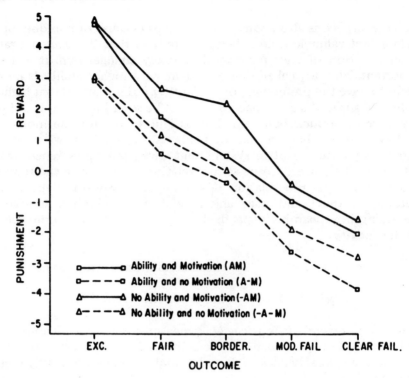

Source: Weiner and Kukla, 1970. Copyright 1970 by the American Psychological Association. Reprinted by permission.

Figure 2-18. Evaluation (reward and punishment) as a function of pupil ability, motivation, and examination outcome.

for joint production, high effort and the order implied by such behavior should make a jointly applied input go further. Let us defer the more difficult question of just what the shape of the reward structure ought to be.

The shape of the production relation (or learning curve) has already been partially discussed. We might assume that the curve displays diminishing returns to increased pace, and indeed it is not hard to imagine cases of negative marginal returns where higher pace begins actually to confuse the learner.

Figure 2-19 puts the two relationships together. All variables are measured in positive units from the origin of the graph. The southeast quadrant shows the production relation for a given lvel of ability and given time spent on the activity. The northwest quadrant is a stylized version of Figure 2-18 where R is approximately linear

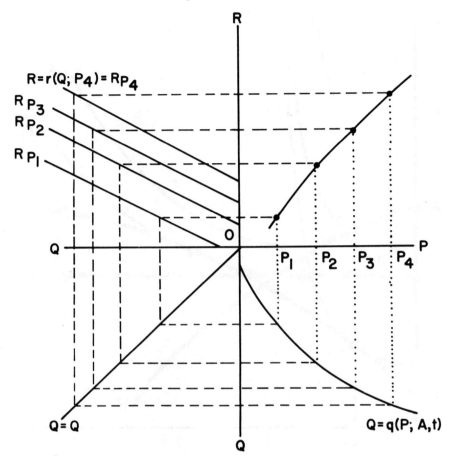

Figure 2-19. Generation of reward structure for higher pace.

(with positive partial derivatives) in Q and P. The northeast quadrant shows the locus of combinations of R and P that are consistent with the given equations. One finds such points by picking a P (e.g., P_1), finding the level of Q that will be produced, and then determining the level of R that corresponds to that P and Q. We can see that a fall in the marginal product of pace will reduce the slope of the reward for pace curve, although that could be offset by changing the slope or intercepts of the general reward structure. By manipulating the curves in the northwest quadrant, we can trace out a variety of different reward for pace curves. Indeed, if we made the partial derivative of reward with respect to pace sufficiently negative (i.e., by punishing students that get too far ahead of the others), we would draw a downward sloping reward for pace curve.

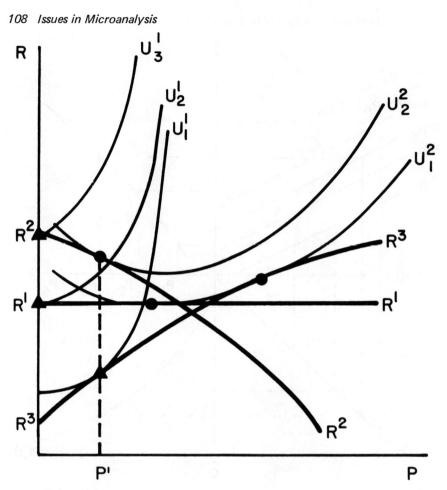

Figure 2-20. Selection of pace.

The two parts of the decision problem are joined together in Figure 2-20. Three different reward structures are displayed there— R^1, R^2, and R^3. Given the reward structure that is attainable, the student tries to get to the highest possible indifference curve. That tangency will determine reward and pace. These points are shown as triangles for student 1 and as small circles for student 2. We can see that by manipulating the reward structures, we can obtain a variety of different distributions of learning in the classroom. Further, if we were to insist on everyone proceeding at the same pace, we can do so with heterogeneous student tastes and homogeneous abilities only if we have reward structures that correspond to each different type of student. Thus, applying R^3 to student 1 and R^2 to student 2 will cause both to proceed at pace P^1.[15] In the example drawn, it should also be noted that each would be much happier with the other's incentive scheme. What are the costs of maintaining such a differentiated reward structure within the same classroom? What are the costs of having everyone proceeding at their own pace? These are the kinds of questions that this sort of analysis suggests.

How should the incentive structure, and the distribution of ensuing efforts, be designed? In the case where the teacher or other school authorities have well-defined preferences over alternative distributions of school outcomes $(Q_1, Q_2, \ldots, Q_n)$, they would pick that feasible incentive scheme that maximized their utility function. The reward structure would be associated with marginal valuation of outputs just as wages are related to marginal value product in the neoclassical economic model of the labor market.

There has been some recent interest shown by economists in questions of the design of incentive systems, and some of these are of potential interest to the problems we have been discussing here. For example, is it better to reward on the basis of measured inputs of time, effort, and ability, or is it better to reward performance? In the labor market context, this is the difference between wage rates for hours worked and piece rate payments for output. The answer depends on the relative costs of measuring the various inputs, the production costs of making a measurement mistake, and the consequences of different systems of compensation for the supply of inputs. For example, there is measurement error in all of the variables in the reward structure equation presented above. We have observed grade inflation[16] in recent years. Is it because in more open and decentralized classrooms, there is an increase in the measurement error for effort, time allocation, and ability variables, and the teacher's loss function is asymmetrical such that making a mistake by giving too low a grade incurs relatively high loses?[17] Or is it because in decentralized open classes the premium for input allocation has had to rise in order to induce students to do voluntarily what they used to do under force, so that the grade associated with any performance ability level is higher? What are the consequences of such phenomena for the structure and stability of the school incentive system and the portions of the economy that rely on such signals? How will changes in the relative weights of performance and input affect morale in the classroom? These are all questions that are of interest to economists as well as to sociologists because production and allocation will be affected.

The issue of measurement error and informational uncertainty is especially important in discussing incentive systems. We have supposed that students were approximately homogeneous in abilities, but this is not very likely in any randomly drawn group of students. This may be symptomatic of a more general uncertainty about the precise shape of the learning curve. The teacher in such a situation has two general strategies that might help. First, the teacher might use some indicator variable[18] that is correlated (the teacher believes) with the variable in question, in this case ability and marginal product of time and pace. Indicator variables might be diagnostic results (cf. Rosenthal and Jacobson, 1968) or social or class status indicators. They may not be very good, but we are assuming that better indicators are not worth the expense of acquisition. Indeed, there is an implicit market for information, and one could work out the appropriate rules for determining whether better diagnostics are worth the extra cost. Under the right conditions, including some restrictions on the teacher's utility function, the teacher would allocate time and other resources to the students with the higher expected abilities (because of their higher marginal products) and make the beliefs self-fulfilling because students who received more inputs would indeed show more learning.

The second teacher strategy would be to let the equations portrayed in, say, Figure 2-20 operate to sort the students by ability. One help to successful sorting would be a correlation between the tastes of high ability students and their preferences. We would expect student 2 to have higher ability than student 1. This means that student 2's learning curve is higher. The consequences of this are shown in Figure 2-21, where R^2 is the reward for pace curve that would be generated for student 2 and R^1 is the reward for pace curve for student 1. Both the differences in generated rewards and the differences in pace would help to sort the students by ability. That differences in pace reflect ability is the notion behind what Dahlloff (1971) emphasizes in the analysis of steering groups or fram frame theory. Some educational researchers believe that teachers often set their pace so that the tenth to twenty-fifth percentile in the class is just keeping up. Why teachers look to this "steering group" in determining pace in unclear. On sampling grounds alone it makes sense to watch just a few children's progress with regularity. But the important point is that the "steering group" is fixed, and it seems as if the teacher has used desired pace as an index of basic ability in the way our model predicts. Why the pace is set too fast for the lowest portion of the class is an interesting question. Akerlof (1976) has a model of the speed of the assembly line that predicts it will be set so everyone is working faster than they would like because rewards are based on the average product of the line and by turning up the speed the slowest workers are weeded out and

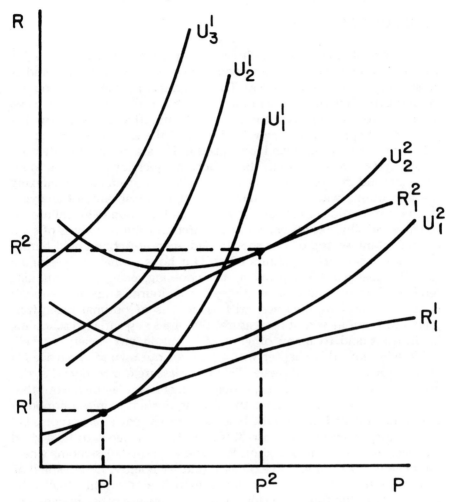

Figure 2-21. Reward for pace when abilities vary.

rewards do not have to be shared with that group. Is this what happens in classrooms where ability groups get tracked in what amounts to a self-selection process? It is an interesting question to which we do not have an answer.

In this section of the chapter, we have sketched just the barest outline of what we would take to be the elements of a serious analysis of the student supply of effort and its role in the production of learning in schools. This has been the domain of psychologists and sociologists, but in thinking about these matters, we have come to believe that perhaps economists also have something to contribute.

CONCLUSIONS

In our critical analysis of the literature on production functions for schools, we have become more convinced than ever that the models most used are also most useless. That is a harsh judgment on a booming industry, but the problem has been that tools always have to be modified to fit the institution studied, and that is only now beginning to happen in the new field we call the economics of schooling. If multiple outputs and joint production are not a minor feature of our system of education, the important questions are going to revolve around determining values for multiple outputs and analyzing the allocations within what have been the typical units of analysis. If the production function literature and its apparent failure to generate sensible results causes this redirection and reanalysis of such an important sector of our society and economy, one could hardly write the work off as unimportant. Our hope is that in developing tools to deal with the problems of schooling, economists will also refresh their own discipline. Indeed, the journals are increasingly filled with articles that deal with questions of optimal incentives, joint production, and other features that are so essential to schooling institutions and to many other institutions in our society as well.

We will close this chapter with a hint of our own research agenda over the next couple of years. This will reassure our readers that our criticism has not bred despair, though foolishness may be a word that comes to some minds. Time is the most important scarce commodity that gets allocated in schools. It is clear to us that as classrooms become more open and decentralized, the teacher needs to be a good manager as well as an expositor. We have witnessed classrooms where the decentralization was so extensive that we could not help standing in awe at teachers who could manage such a situation effectively. This suggests the following steps: (1) collect or use other researchers' data on time allocations in classrooms to test some of our theories and to calibrate models of classroom organization and allocation, (2) use such models to develop and evaluate various rules of thumb about teaching and also perhaps to help in the training of teachers, and (3) use such models as a framework for evaluating new instructional techniques. Our own view (Brown and Saks, 1978) is that such work can be done effectively only in collaboration with experts from other disciplines and with people who understand what goes on in classrooms. Collecting data and working with practitioners are not things that economists have had much experience doing. We are encouraged, however, by the fact that people as diverse and thoughtful as Barr and Dreeben (sociology), Thomas (education), and Walberg (psychology) are all converging with us on similar perspectives and, more important, on agreement about the key questions that need to be answered. As we proceed, however, maybe we should be looking over our shoulders at another dimension that we seem to be leaving behind. Perhaps this is a good point to remember Weber's plea from the closing passages of *The Protest Ethic and the Spirt of Capitalism*:

> ——— the modern economic order . . . is now bound to the technical and economic conditions of machine production which today determine the lives of all the individuals who are born into this mechanism, not only those directly concerned with economic acquisition, with irresistible force . . . .
>
> No one knows who will live in this cage in the future, or whether at the end of this tremendous development entirely new prophets will arise, or there will be a great rebirth of old ideas and ideals, or, if neither, mechanized petrification, embellished with a sort of convulsive self-importance. For of the last stage of this cultural development, it might truly be said: "Specialists without spirit, sensualists without heart; this nullity imagines that it has attained a level of civilization never before achieved." (1958: 181-82)

NOTES

1. See Hanushek (1978) and Lau (1978) for review by economists. The most perceptive review of this literature from the classroom perspective is in Barr and Dreeban (1977).

2. Readers with a better economics background should skim the next few sections. We take the space here to develop those notions because some people seem confused about what the simple model implies and why it has to be modified for particular applications.

3. There are various explanations for the phenomen. The most plausible is that there is some other factor of production that is held fixed, and so, as more and more of x is mixed with that excluded factor, the marginal product must decline.

4. How is the time to be allocated over a day? Is each activity done once or several times? What about time lost in passing from one activity to another (one of Adam Smith's arguments for total specialization)? We shall take up these problems later on. For now, assume each activity is done at most once.

5. Take an example of the application of the above theory to a school resource allocation problem. Thomas (1977:67-69) analyzes the case of two students for whom the production (learning) functions involving time differ. Thomas equates higher total productivity with greater efficiency (1977:2). Thus he says, "Students with higher efficiency (or time value) can produce more learning in a given period of time. . . . " We are on the verge of a confusion here between total (or average) and marginal productivity, for he goes

on to add that "production theory suggests that in their [students with high efficiency] cases, a given amount of students' time will be combined with a greater than average amount of purchased resources" (p. 67). Thomas cites the proverb, "To them who hath shall be given" (p. 68). Frankly, we do not understand the argument, and its conclusions seem inconsistent with the results of economic theory. Efficiency requires that resources be allocated where the additional (i.e., marginal) payoff is greatest, not where total payoff is already highest.

In the context of classical production theory, how should time and other resources be allocated to two students when one of them always achieves at a higher level than the other for any input combination? Suppose the students each have the same amount of their time devoted to a learning process and that the question is, How should purchased inputs be allocated between them. The answer is that the inputs should be allocated so as to get on the production possibilities curve, rather than be stuck inside it. Further, we want to choose the right point on the possibilities curve, based on the values to the teacher of the outcomes of the students. This argument does not favor the high achieving ("efficient") student or, in fact, the low achiever. Indeed, the optimal allocation is determined as much by tastes as by productivity. Thus Thomas's conclusion that "if we make comparisons among school districts or within classrooms, we will expect to find that those students who have already received large investments at home and in school for the development of their cognitive skills will be likely to be the recipients of larger educational expenditures, better quality teachers, and superior books and equipment than those students who have not benefited from substantial home and school investment" (1977:68) is unwarranted. The rich may indeed get richer, but an economic rationale would depend either on their having higher marginal (not total) outputs or on their being favored individuals in the scale of social values. The teachers have to have "elitist" preference functions in our (Brown and Saks, 1975a) sense.

6. Notice that under the usual assumptions about utility functions not every point on the curve is superior to each point inside it. What is generally the case is that for any point inside the curve, say P, there is some point on the curve that is better.

7. The only possible exception appears to be some measure of time, usually student days attended.

8. For some reason, when Thomas (1977) addresses this problem, he worries not about the marginal product of time (the slope of the learning curve) but about the average product of time. He defines "the quality of a student's time as the ratio of learning produced (in a given subject) to time expended . . . " and remarks that it is equivalent to student "efficiency" (1977:58). In terms of classical production theory, it is marginal learning per unit of time spent that is important. Presumably, students allocate their efforts or have them allocated so that marginal value learning per unit of additional allocated time is the same for all activities.

9. Some writers, including even Thomas (1977:58), try to separate nature (genes) from nurture (past human capital investment) in accounting for the

short-run fixity of the learning curve. This may be an interesting question for geneticists, but it has nothing to do with economics. For the economist, the parameters are for whatever reason fixed with respect to some policies and variable with respect to others. After all, genetically caused problems are not necessarily best dealt with by genetic policies. Myopia is efficiently handled by prescribing eyeglasses. Knowing that the deficiency is caused by unusual genes may not be of interest in evaluating a policy of providing appropriate corrective lenses.

10. This is analogous to the effect of unearned income on labor supply in the standard consumer model. If the child gets a high level of reward at home irrespective of school performance, the teacher's incentive structure will have a different impact on effort than if parents reinforce that structure.

11. See Wallach (1976) for a discussion of the relation between test scores and grades and success. He finds a weak relation. For the relation between schooling and success, though, there is ample correlational evidence. For a good review, see Welch (1974).

12. This literature begins with Book 1, Chapter 10 of Adam Smith ([1776] 1937). For more recent references, see Rosen (1974) and Lucas (1977). Thomas (1977) stresses two other variables affecting student supply of labor—instructional differentiation and student ability. We believe these enter the model in a different way (see below).

13. We are not concerned about time allocation here, although it would be straightforward to extend the analysis to student determination of time spent in alternative activities. Here, we assume that the teacher assigns time allocations and the student obeys. In decentralized classroom or where homework is important, this is an important omission.

14. These results are rported in Weiner (1976) and are from a study by Winer and Kukla (1970).

15. Thomas (1977:109) suggests that student preferences can be adjusted by using different instructional methodologies for the different students. His discussion is in terms of student time allocation, but presumably the argument also applies to effort. It is an empirical question whether the benefits of such "technological differentiation" outweight the costs.

16. For some evidence on this, see Bills (1977).

17. Readers who wonder about this might try the following experiment. Next time a student comes to complain about a grade, begin by asking whether the student felt the grade was too high or too low.

18. This is one of Arrow's (1973) models of economic discrimination, and it is related to Allport's (1958) explanation of prejudice as faulty categorization.

REFERENCES

Akerlof, George A. 1976. "The Economics of Caste and of the Rat Race and Other Woeful Tales." *Quarterly Journal of Economics* 90 (November): 599-617.

Allport, Gordon W. 1958. *The Nature of Prejudice.* Garden City, N.Y.: Anchor Press.

Arrow, Kenneth J. 1973. "The Theory of Discrimination." In *Discrimination in Labor Markets*, ed. Orley Ashenfelter and Albert Rees, pp. 3-33, Princeton, N.J.: Princeton University Press.

Averch, Harvey; Stephen Carroll; Theodore S. Donaldson; Herbert J. Kiesling; and John Pincus. 1972. *How Effective Is Schooling? A Critical Review and Synthesis of Research Findings.* Santa Monica, Calif.: Rand Corporation.

Barr, Rebecca, and Robert Dreeban. 1977. "Instruction in Classrooms." *Review of Research in Education* 5:89-162.

Bills, David. 1977. "An Analysis of the Decline in ACT College Admissions Scores." Institute for Research on Poverty Discussion Papers, no. 432-77. University of Wisconsin. Mimeo.

Bowles, Samuel, and Herbert Gintis. 1976. *Schooling in Capitalist America.* New York: Basic Books.

Brown, Byron W. 1972. "Achievement, Costs, and the Demand for Public Education." *Western Economic Journal* 10, no. 2 (June): 198-219.

Brown, Byron W., and Daniel H. Saks. 1975a. "The Production and Distribution of Cognitive Skills Within Schools." *Journal of Political Economy* 83 no. 3 (May-June): 571-93.

———. 1975b. "Proper Data Aggregation for Economic Analysis of School Effectiveness." *Review of Public Data Use* 3 (October): 13-18.

———. 1978. "An Econometric Perspective on Classroom Reading Instruction." Paper presented at the Annual Meetings of the International Reading Association, Houston, May.

Coase, Ronald, [1937] 1952. "The Nature of the Firm." In *Readings in Price Theory*, ed. George J. Stigler and Kenneth Boulding, pp. 331-51. Homewood, Ill.: Richard D. Irwin.

Dahlloff, U. S. 1971. *Ability Grouping, Content Validity, and Curriculum Process Analysis.* New York: Teachers College Press.

Fair, Ray C. 1978. "A Theory of Extramarital Affairs." *Journal of Political Economy* 86, no. 1 (February): 45-61.

Ferguson, C. E., and J. P. Gould. 1975. *Microeconomic Theory.* 4th ed. Homewood, Ill.: Richard D. Irwin.

Gintis, Herbert. 1971. "Educational, Technology, and the Characteristics of Worker Productivity." *American Economic Review* 61, no. 2 (May): 266-79.

Hanushek, Eric A. 1978. "A Reader's Guide to Educational Production Functions." Paper presented at the National Invitational Conference on School Organization and Effects, San Diego, California, January 27-29.

Harnischfeger, Annegret, and David E. Wiley. 1976. "The Teaching-Learning Process in Elementary Schools: A Synoptic View." *Curriculum Inquiry* 6 (1): 5-43.

Heckman, James J. 1976. "A Life-Cycle Model of Earnings, Learning, and Consumption." *Journal of Political Economy* 84, no. 4, pt. 2 (August): 11-44.

Henderson, James M., and Richard E. Quandt. 1971. *Microeconomic Theory: A Mathematical Approach.* 2nd ed. Hightstown, N.J.: McGraw-Hill.

Keeney, Ralph L., and Howard Raiffa. 1976. *Decisions with Multiple Objectives.* New York: John Wiley and Sons.

Klitgaard, R. E. 1975. "Going Beyond the Mean in Educational Evaluation." *Public Policy* 23 (Winter): 59-79.

Lau, Lawrence J. 1978. "Educational Production Functions." Paper presented at the National Invitational Conference on School Organization and Effects, San Diego, California, January 27-29.

Leekley, Robert M. 1974. "A Multiple Output Approach to Public Education." Ph.D. dissertation, Michigan State University.

Levin, Henry M. 1974. "Measuring Efficiency in Educational Production." *Public Finance Quarterly* 2, no. 1 (January): 3-23.

Lucas, Robert E. B. 1977. "Hedonic Wage Equations and Psychic Wages in the Returns to Schooling." *American Economic Review* 67, no. 4 (September): 549-58.

Murnane, Richard J. 1975. *The Impact of School Resources on the Learning of Inner City Children*. Cambridge, Mass.: Ballinger Publishing Company.

Radner, Roy, and Michael Rothschild. 1975. "On the Allocation of Effort." *Journal of Economic Theory* 10:358-76.

Reiter, Stanley. 1966. "A System for Managing Job-Shop Production." *Journal of Business* 39 (July): 371-93.

Ritzen, Jozef, and Donald R. Winkler. 1977. "The Production of Human Capital Over Time." *Review of Economics and Statistics* 59, no. 4 (November): 427-37.

Roche, J. G. 1971. "Preference Tradeoffs Among Instructional Programs: An Investigation of Cost-Benefit and Decision Making." Ph.D. dissertation, Harvard University.

Rosen, Sherwin. 1974. "Hedonic Prices and Implicit Markets: Product Differentiation in Pure Competition." *Journal of Political Economy* 82 (January-February): 34-55.

Rosenthal, Robert, and Lenore Jacobson. 1968. *Pygmalion in the Classroom*. New York: Holt, Rinehart & Winston.

Schmidt, Peter; Dennis Aigner; and C. A. Knox Lovell. 1977. "Formulation and Estimation of Stochastic Frontier Production Function Models." *Journal of Econometrics* 5 (July): 21-38.

Smith, Adam. [1776] 1937. *An Inquiry Into the Nature and Causes of the Wealth of Nations*. New York: Random House.

Summers, Anita A., and Barbara L. Wolfe. 1977. "Do Schools Make a Difference?" *American Economic Review* 67, no. 4 (September): 639-52.

Thomas, J. Alan. 1977. *Resource Allocation in Classrooms*. Educational Finance and Productivity Center. University of Chicago.

Wallach, Michael. 1976. "Tests Tell Us Little About Talent." *American Scientist* 64 (January-February): 57-63.

Weber, Max. 1958. *The Protestant Ethic and the Spirit of Capitalism*. New York: Charles Scribner's Sons.

Weiner, Bernard. 1976. "An Attributional Approach for Educational Psychology." In *Review of Research in Education*, 4 ed. Lee S. Shulman, pp. 179-209. Etasca, Ill.: F. E. Peacock.

Weiner, Bernard, and A. Kukla. 1970. "An Attributional Analysis of Achievement Motivation." *Journal of Personality and Social Psychology* 15: 1-20.

Welch, Finis. 1974. "Relationships Between Income and Schooling." In *Review of Research in Education*, 2 ed. Fred N. Kerlinger, pp. 179-201. Itasca, Ill.: F. E. Peacock.

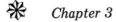 *Chapter 3*

The Role of Levels of Analysis in the Specification of Education Effects*

Leigh Burstein
University of California
Los Angeles

One of the chief functions of educational research is to specify school- and home-based factors that influence educational performance and to ascertain their effects. This question is the focus of much of the sociological literature on school effects (e.g., Alwin, 1976; Coleman et al., 1966; Coleman, 1975, Peaker, 1975; Sorenson and Hallinan, 1977; Mood, 1970), the economics literature on educational production functions (e.g., Averch et al., 1972; Brown and Saks, 1975; Hanushek, 1972; Murnane, 1975), the educational psychology literature on teacher-classroom effectiveness (e.g., Berliner et al., 1976; Brophy, Biddle, and Good, 1975; McDonald and Elias, 1976), and the literature on the evaluation of educational interventions (e.g., Circirelli et al., 1969; Cline et al., 1974; Smith and Bissell, 1970; Stebbins et al., 1977).

Invariably, studies in each of these areas encounter complications caused by the nature of the educational enterprise. A central element of these complications is that educational data are inherently multilevel. That is, education involves students taught by teachers in class-

*This study draws heavily from work I previously conducted as principal investigator for the Consortium on Methodology for Aggregating Data in Educational Research, Vasquez Associates, Ltd., Milwaukee, Wisconsin, and for the Multilevel Analysis Project, Center for the Study of Evaluation, University of California, Los Angeles, under contracts from the National Institute of Education. Frank Capell and David Rogosa provided valuable comments on earlier drafts. Discussions with Robert L. Linn and J. Ward Keesling were also extremely beneficial. M. David Miller generated the empirical analyses of the data from the Six Subjects Survey by the International Association for Evaluation of Educational Achievement. Chris Miller, Linda Powell, and Mary Gannon typed accurate readable drafts from often indecipherable prose.

rooms in scholls in school districts and so on. As a consequence, one would expect that any attempt to identify the factors that affect educational performance would involve analyses of multi-level educational data.

OBJECTIVES AND ORGANIZATION

The purpose of this chapter is to present a comprehensive treatment of the role of levels of analysis in the specification of educational effects. The issues to be considered include:

1. The conditions under which unbiased estimates of microlevel (individual level) processes can be derived from macrolevel (aggregate or group level) data (problems in cross-level inference),
2. The identification and interpretation of the effects of macrolevel variables on microlevel processes (group-structural-contextual-composition effects);
3. The basis for choosing an appropriate unit of analysis in a given context (appropriate unit of analysis); and
4. The specification of an appropriate analytical model in the estimation of relationships from multilevel data (specification of analytical model).

Like multilevel educational data, the four issues are hierarchically nested in many respects. The last issue—specification of an analytical model—subsumes the rest. The results from work on each issue will be discussed in turn, and problems that warrant further attention will be identified.

The emphasis throughout will be on large-scale regression-based analyses of multilevel data from surveys, quasi-experiments, and field studies. I will not attempt to address the large literature on multilevel data in experimental research or research with strictly ordinal or categorical data except as these areas shed light on issues in other types of research.

PROBLEMS IN CROSS-LEVEL INFERENCE

The difficulties involved in making inferences across levels (units) of analysis have been extensively investigated by social scientists (e.g., Hannan, 1971). Work on change in units of analysis (Blalock, 1964), ecological inference (Alker, 1969; Duncan and Davis, 1953; Goodman, 1953, 1959; Menzel, 1950; Robinson, 1950; Scheuch, 1966, 1969), aggregation bias (Burstein, 1974, 1975a, 1975b; Feige and

Watts, 1972; Green, 1964; Grunfield and Griliches, 1960; Theil, 1954), correlations based on grouped data (Gehlke and Biehl, 1934; Pearson, 1896; Thorndike, 1939; Walker, 1928; Yule and Kendall, 1937), and grouping of observations (Burstein, 1978c; Cramer, 1964; Haitovsky, 1966, 1973; Firebaugh, 1978; Hannan and Burstein, 1974; Johnston, 1972; Prais and Aitchison, 1954) all stem from concern about making inferences about relationships at one level from relationships found in data at a different level.

Since research on educational effects involves multilevel data (pupils, teachers, classrooms, schools, etc.), problems of cross-level inference invariably arise. The problem of concern here is how to answer the question, What are the conditions under which unbiased estimates of parameters of microlevel processes can be derived from macrolevel data?

We know a great deal about the consequences of comparisons of analyses at two distinct levels of aggregation. Under contract from the National Institute of Education (NIE), the Consortium on Methodology for Aggregating Data in Educational Research reviewed, classified, interpreted, and expanded the work on change in units of analysis problems previously associated with such sociologists as Blalock (1964) and Robinson (1950) and with such economists as Cramer (1964), Prais and Aitchison (1954), and Feige and Watts (1972). Most of the findings from the work of the Consortium (elgl, Burstein, 1975a, 1975b, 1978c; Burstein and Knapp, 1975; Burstein and Linn, 1976, Hannan, 1976; Hannan, Freeman, and Meyer, 1976; Hannan and Young, 1976a; Hannan, Nielsen, and Young, 1975) are directed specifically to the estimation of parameters from structural regression models. However, the literature on the effects of cross-level inference in experiments (Glendening, 1976) and on categorical data (Goodman, 1959; Shively, 1969; Iversen 1973; Maw, 1976) reflects similar trends.

The main findings about the differences between regression models at two levels can be summarized as follows:

1. *Consistency of Estimation*—Estimates of regression coefficients from different levels of analysis are inconsistent (asymptotically biased) unless groups are formed randomly, on the basis of the values of the regressors (grouping on the independent variable) or on the disturbances (assuming that the disturbances are uncorrelated with the regressors).

2. *Determinants of Consistency*—The magnitude of the differences between coefficients from individual and group level data is a function of the relationship of the grouping variable(s) (rule,

methods) to the regressors, to the dependent variable net of the regressors, and to the ratios of the variances of the regressors at the two levels of analysis. Grouping directly on the outcome variable yields particularly poor results.

3. *Specification Bias and Inconsistency*—Differences in coefficients across levels of inference are a clear indication of specification bias (the deletion of causally relevant regressors correlated with other regressors in the model) except in the special case when groups are formed directly on the basis of values of the dependent variable.

4. *Efficiency of Estimation*—Even when consistent, estimates of coefficients from one level of analysis are inefficient for estimating coefficients from another level unless observations are grouped according to values of the regressors.

5. *Generality of Principles*—The above principles appear to be applicable to both simple and multiple regression models, to nonrecursive models, and to longitudinal models.

6. *Variable Efficiency in Multiple Regression*—In multiple regression models, estimates of coefficients are more efficient for the regressors that determine group membership than for the other regressors in the model.

7. *Effects of Collinearity*—Collinearity among regressor seriously affects the consistency and efficiency of estimation across levels.

8. *Aggregation Gain*—Aggregation gain is possible in at least two special cases: when grouping minimizes grouped variation in confounding variables and when regressors at the lower level of aggregation are measured with error.

9. *Preconditions for Assessing Group Effects*—Knowledge of the process that groups observations and the nature of the substantive problem and research design is crucial to the determination of the consequences of grouping.

Theoretical Results for Different Types of Grouping

The reader who is willing to accept the above summary or who is concerned only with the practical effects of cross-level inference for research on the effects of education is encouraged to skip to the "Empirical Illustrations" section below. For others, I provide further explanation of the summarized findings by considering the effects of misspecification and grouping on a two regressor linear model:

$$Y = \alpha + \beta_1 X_1 + \beta_2 X_2 + u, \tag{3.1}$$

where the disturbance, u, has a mean zero, constant variance σ_u^2, and is asymptotically uncorrelated with the regressors X_1 and X_2. The least-square estimates, b_1 and b_2 from

$$\hat{Y} = a + b_1 X_1 + b_2 X_2 \qquad (3.2)$$

are consistent estimators of β_1 and β_2 in equation (3.1).

If the investigator fails to include X_2 and instead estimates a model

$$Y = \alpha' + \beta_1' X_1 + w, \qquad (3.3)$$

following Theil (1971), the least-squares estimator, b_1', of β_1' converges asymptotically to

$$plim(b_1') = \beta_1 + \beta_2 b_{21}, \qquad (3.4)$$

where b_{21} is the coefficient in the sample from the regression of X_2 on X_1. As long as X_1 and X_2 are correlated, least squares applied to equation (3.3) yields inconsistent estimates of β_1 in equation (3.1). The magnitude of this discrepancy,

$$plim(b_1') - \beta_1 = \beta_2 b_{21}, \qquad (3.5)$$

is called the specification bias of b_1' as an estimator of β_1.

When observations on individuals are grouped into m groups (for simplicity, we assume equal size groups of size n), the group level analogues to equations (3.1) and (3.3) can be written as

$$\overline{Y} = \alpha + \overline{\beta}_1 \overline{X}_1 + \overline{\beta}_2 \overline{X}_2 + \overline{u} \qquad (3.6)$$

and $$\overline{Y} = a' + \overline{\beta}_1' \overline{X}_1 + \overline{w}. \qquad (3.7)$$

Least squares applied to equation (3.7) yields an estimator $\overline{b}_1'$ such that

$$plim(\overline{b}_1) = \overline{\beta}_1' + \overline{\beta}_2 \overline{b}_{21}. \qquad (3.8)$$

As with the individual level models, when $\overline{X}_1$ and $\overline{X}_2$ are correlated, $\overline{b}_1'$ is an inconsistent estimator of $\overline{\beta}_1$ with discrepancy

$$plim(\overline{b}_1') - \overline{\beta}_1 = \beta_2 \overline{b}_{21}. \qquad (3.9)$$

By comparing the least-squares estimators from various combinations of the two individual level models (equations [3.1] and [3.3]) and the two group level models (equations [3.6] and [3.7], we can illustrate all the results on bias (inconsistency) in estimation from grouped observations.[1] Three distinct sets of circumstances warrant discussion: (1) group level regressors and disturbances uncorrelated, (2) group level regressors and disturbances correlated, and (3) grouping with a misspecified model.

Case A: Group Level Regressors and Disturbances Uncorrelated. If the assignment of individual to groups does not create a correlation between the regressor(s) and the disturbance—that is, between $\overline{X_1}\,\overline{X_2}$, and $\overline{u}$ in equation (3.6) or between $\overline{X_1}$ and $\overline{w}$ in equation (3.7)—then the parameters from the group level and individual level models will be the same. The implications of the above for estimation can be stated as follows:

If $\overline{X_1}$ and $\overline{X_2}$ are uncorrelated with $\overline{u}$, and $\overline{X_1}$ and $\overline{w}$ are uncorrelated, then

$$\overline{\beta}_1 = \beta_1, \overline{\beta}_2 = \beta_2, \overline{\beta}'_1 = \beta'_1, \tag{3.10}$$

and correspondingly,

$$\overline{b}_1 = b_1, \overline{b}_2 = b_2, \overline{b}'_1 = b'_1.$$

The kinds of grouping practices that ensure that the group level regressors are uncorrelated with group level disturbances include random grouping, grouping by the regressors (X_1 or X_2 in equation [3.1] or X_1 in equation [3.3] if X_1 and X_2 are uncorrelated) or grouping by the disturbances (u in equation [3.1], w in equation [3.3]. Several investigators have demonstrated the above by a variety of different analytical approaches (Blalock, 1964; Burstein, 1974, 1975b, 1978c; Cramer, 1964; Feige and Watts, 1972; Firebaugh, 1978; Hannan, 1971; Hannan and Burstein, 1974).

Note that under random grouping and grouping by the disturbances, there may be no between group variation in the regressors (Cronbach, 1976). If the latter occurs, the denominators of $\overline{b}_1$, $\overline{b}_2$, and $\overline{b}'_1$ go to zero, and the corresponding estimates cannot be determined. In practice, pure cases of random grouping and especially grouping by the disturbance occur only rarely.

The results on efficiency of least-squares estimators in equations (3.6) and (3.7) are also well known (Burstein, 1975b; Cramer, 1964;

Feige and Watts, 1972; Hannan and Burstein, 1974; Prais and Aitchison, 1954). Random grouping reduces both systematic (associated with X_1 and X_2 in equation [3.1]) and error variation (u in equation [3.1], w in equation [3.3]). Thus, random grouping is considerably more damaging to the efficiency of least squares than is grouping by X. In finite populations (of N observations) with m equal size groups, the efficiency of random grouping is approximately $m-1/N-1c$.

In terms of efficiency, grouping by the disturbances only is worse than random grouping. Since u and X are uncorrelated, variation in X is decreased as in random grouping. But, in addition, variation in u is maximized; $\sigma_{\bar{u}}^2 \cong \sigma_u^2$. Both of these effects reduce efficiency.

Grouping by the regressors maximizes the variation in X and thereby minimizes the information loss through grouping (Cramer, 1964; Prais and Aitchison, 1954). In fact, grouping by the regressors is optimal in the sense that no other grouping method can yield group level estimators with smaller variances.

When data are grouped by a subset of the regressors (e.g., by X_1 in equation [3.1], the discussion of efficiency of grouping by the regressor requires further elaboration. While group level estimators of all parameters remain consistent when grouping is based on a subset of the regressors (Burstein, 1965b; Haitovsky, 1966, 1975; Hannan and Young, 1976a), the estimators for the regressors determining group membership are much more efficient than the remaining estimators. That is, if observations are grouped by X_1 in equation (3.1), then the efficiency of $\bar{b}_1$ as an estimator of β_1 is much superior to the efficiency of $\bar{b}_2$ as an estimator of β_2.

The effect of grouping by a subset of regressors can be seen in the data from the Houthakker and Haldi study presented in Haitovsky (1966, 1973). The data are from the regression of automobile purchases, Y, on income, X_1, and initial automobile inventory, X_2. When data are grouped by X_1, $SE(\bar{b}_2)$ is larger than $SE(\bar{b}_1)$, even though for the ungrouped data $SE(b_2) < SE(b_1)$. Similarly, when the data are grouped by inventory, X_2, only $SE(\bar{b}_1) > SE(b_2)$.

Hannan and Young (1976a) found that when data were grouped by X_1, the efficiency of $\bar{b}_2$ was only slightly better than for random grouping. They attribute the inefficiency of the estimator to the opposing influences of the correlation of X_1 and X_2 (ρ_{12}) on r_{12} and on $var(\bar{X}_2)$. Hannan and Young (1976a) define the relative efficiency of b_2 to be

$$eff(b_2, \bar{b}_2) = \frac{var(b_2)}{var(\bar{b}_2)} \cong \frac{1 - \bar{r}^2_{12}}{1 - r^2_{12}} \quad \frac{var(\bar{X}_2)}{var(X_2)}$$

As ρ_{12} increases, the first ratio on the right-hand side decreases while the second ratio increases. Hannan and Young (1976a) conclude that the two tendencies offset each other, so that the efficiency of $\overline{b}_2$ is no better than random grouping.

Before leaving this case, it is useful to note one instance in which grouping by the regressors actually improves estimation. Under classical assumptions about errors in variables, when regressors are fallibly measured (i.e., the Xs are measured with error), least-squares estimation from the ungrouped fallible observations yields attenuated estimates of the true parameters ($r_{XX'}\beta$ rather than β, where r_{XX}, is the reliability of X). It has been shown (Bartlett, 1949; Madansky, 1959; Wald, 1940) that if groups are formed on the true values of the regressors, the group level estimator, $\overline{b}$, of β has smaller bias than the ungrouped estimator, b, based on fallible measures.

Several investigators (Aigner and Goldfeld, 1974; Blalock, Wells, and Carter, 1970; Hannan, 1976) have provided evidence that grouping on the fallible regressor (rather than on the true regressor) can also yield estimates with smaller bias than the ungrouped estimator. If it is true that grouping on the fallible regressor yields better estimators, it may be practially possible to have an aggregation gain (Grunfield and Griliches, 1960; Hannan, 1976). While it is not feasible to determine the true values of the regressor from fallible observed values, an investigator can systematically plan to group on observed values of the regressor and thereby at least partially disattenuate his fallible ungrouped estimates.

Case B: Correlation Between Group Level Regressors and Disturbances. It is possible that the assignment of individuals to groups may cause the group level regressors and disturbances to be correlated. The example of this case that is most frequently cited is grouping by Y (Blalock, 1964; Burstein, 1975b; Feige and Watts, 1972; Hannan and Burstein, 1974).

When observations are grouped by Y, the corresponding group level and individual level parameters (β_1 and $\overline{\beta}_1$, β_2 and $\overline{\beta}_2'$ $\overline{\beta}_1'$ and β_1') will no longer be the same. As a result, the group level estimators ($\overline{b}_1$ and $\overline{b}_2$ for $\overline{\beta}_1$ and $\overline{\beta}_2$, $\overline{b}_1'$ for $\overline{\beta}_1'$) will yield inconsistent estimates of the ungrouped parameters (β_1, β_2, and β_1'). The above occurs because when Y is positively related to its regressors (i.e., β_1, β_2 positive), grouping by Y tends to place high values of X_1, X_2, and u (X_1 and w for equation [3.3]) in the same group and low values of X_1 and X_2 and u in the same group. Thus, while X_1 and X_2 are uncorrelated with u, X_1 and X_2 will be correlated with $\overline{u}$.

Blalock (1964) described the consequences of grouping by Y on regression coefficients (b_{YX}, b_{XY}) and on correlation coefficients (r_{XY}). He pointed out that although grouping on Y does not bias the estimator of b_{XY} (i.e., $b_{\overline{XY}} = b_{XY}$), assuming b_{YX} and r_{XY} are positive, it does inflate the corresponding correlation coefficient ($r_{\overline{XY}} > r_{XY}$). But since $b_{\overline{XY}} b_{\overline{YX}} = r^2_{\overline{XY}} > r^2_{XY} = b_{XY} b_{YX} = b_{\overline{XY}} b_{YX}$, then $b_{\overline{YX}} > b_{YX}$. Thus, grouping by Y inflates the regression coefficient when Y is the dependent variable.

The mean-squared error for grouping by Y is always greater than the mean-squared error for grouping by X. Although grouping by Y may be as efficient as grouping by X, grouping by Y always introduces a component of bias to the mean-squared error—that is, *MSE ($\overline{b}$) = (bias [$\overline{b}$])^2 + Var ($\overline{b}$)*, where *Var ($\overline{b}$)* is measured relative to the group level parameter $\overline{\beta}$.

When the bias from grouping by Y is small, grouping by Y can yield more efficient estimates than random grouping (Burstein, 1975b). This would occur because grouping by Y is systematically related to X, while random grouping is not. Admittedly, the notion of small bias arising from grouping by Y is hard to imagine. However, it is conceivable that when few groups are formed and there is a strong relationship between Y and X, some impiovement can occur.

Case C: Grouping and Specification Bias. In reality, the groups in educational effects research are rarely formed on the basis of a variable unrelated to X and Y, on the basis of the regressors, or on the basis of outcomes. In general, the exact mechanism controlling grouping cannot be determined.

It can be argued, however, that students are grouped into schools according to some complex combination of their own background characteristics (parental education and occupation; student ability), the characteristics of the communities in which they live (community wealth and demographic properties), and some random influences. Grouping into classrooms within schools may have a different but equally complex set of determinants.

If the above argument is correct and the grouping mechanism is not systematically included in the individual level model, problems in estimating microlevel educational effects from macrolevel data are bound to occur. The complications can be traced to two factors: (1) a misspecified individual level model and (2) exacerbating the misspecification by grouping (Burstein, 1975b; Hannan and Burstein, 1974; Hannan and Young, 1976a; Hannan, Nielsen, and Young, 1975; Hanushek, Jackson, and Kain, 1974). We can demonstrate this case by returning to the individual level (equation [3.1] and

[3.3] and group level models (equation [3.6] and [3.7]) introduced earlier.

For the case of grouping by an omitted regressor (i.e., by factors
selecting students into schools, classes, etc.), the investigator specifies the relationship of interest to be as in equation (3.3):

$$Y = \alpha' + \beta'_1 X_1 + w. \tag{3.3}$$

In so doing, he or she ignores the grouping mechanism, X_2, which
is correlated with both x_1 and w. That is, if the investigator had
achnowledged the potential effects of group membership, the correct
specification would be as in equation (3.1):

$$Y = \alpha + \beta_1 X_1 + \beta_2 X_2 + u. \tag{3.1}$$

As pointed out earlier, under these conditions the least-squares
estimator, b'_1, or β'_1 yields inconsistent estimates of β_1 from the
correctly specified model. This bias—more accurately, specification
bias—occurs from failing to recognize the role of group membership
at the individual level.

In substantive terms, the coefficient from the individual level
(total) regression of outcome, Y, on the regressor, X_1, is the wrong
coefficient when group membership, X_2, is systematically related
to both Y and X_1. Under such conditions, the coefficient of interest
should be β_1, which can be shown to be the coefficient from the
pooled within group regression of Y on X_1 (cf., e.g., Burstein,
1975b, 1978c; Duncan, Cuzzort, and Duncan, 1961; Firebaugh,
1978; Werts and Linn, 1971). This point reappears later on.

Earlier, the bias from using b'_1 to estimate β_1 was said to be

$$plim \ (b'_1) - \beta_1 = \beta_2 b_{21}. \tag{3.5}$$

Note that this expression is zero when x_2 is unrelated either to
x_1 ($b_{21} = 0$) or to Y after controlling for X_1 ($\beta_2 = 0$). Under these
circumstances, the disturbance in equation (3.3),

$$w = \beta_2 X_2 + u,$$

is uncorrelated with X_1, and so no specification bias occurs.

When individuals are grouped by X_2 while it is incorrectly assumed
that equation (3.3) is the underlying model to be estimated, the
effects of misspecification are compounded by the effects of grouping. We would be erroneously using $\bar{b}'_1$, the estimator for β'_1 in equa-

tion (3.7), as an estimator of β_1' in equation (3.1). The resulting bias is

$$plim\ (\bar{b}_1') - \beta_1 = (\beta_1 + \beta_2 \bar{b}_{21}) - \beta_1$$

$$= \beta_2 \bar{b}_{21},$$

since groups are formed on the basis of X_2, $\bar{b}_{21} > b_{21}$ (see the discussion of grouping by Y under Case B). Thus, the bias from estimating β_1 from grouped data (i.e., by $\bar{b}_1'$) when the grouping variable is positively related to both the regressor and the outcome and has been left out of the individual level regression is larger than the specification bias alone. That is,

$$plim\ \bar{b}_1' - \beta_1 > plim\ b_1' - \beta_1$$

$$\beta_2 \bar{b}_{21} > \beta_2 b_{21},$$

as long as β_2 and b_{21} are positive.

Unfortunately, the investigator is likely to be in the case described above when attempting to make inferences about microlevel relations from macrolevel data. It is exceedingly rare to find an investigation of educational effects in which all the necessary variables affecting outcomes have been identified and accurately measured. If these conditions (proper specification and measurement) are met, grouping does not bias estimation. When they are not, the investigator can only take some small comfort in the realization that the differences between macrolevel and microlevel estimates suggest that the model was most likely misspecified (because of the exclusion of correlated regressors representing group differences or because of fallibly measured regressors) in the first place.

Empirical Illustrations

We can illustrate the problems of cross-level inferences described above in a variety of ways. First, data are presented on the differences, in terms of bias and efficiency, among the cases described earlier. These illustrations are followed by examples drawn from actual research on school effects.

Illustrations over Different Types of Grouping. Burstein (1974, 1975a, 1975b, 1978c) and Hannan and Burstein (1974) present data from entering freshmen in a large midwestern university to illustrate the consequences of the various kinds of grouping. A subset of these data are used for our present purposes; the reader is referred to Burstein (1975b) for a more detailed discussion.

The basic results from estimating the simple linear regression of the total score on an entering achievement test battery (ACH) on total score on the Scholastic Aptitude Test (SAT) from grouped data are contained in Table 3-1. The estimate of the individual level regression is

$$\text{ACH} = .839 \text{ SAT}, \, SE \, (b) = .011.$$

(Note that all variables were initially standardized at the individual level.)

The present model corresponds to equation (3.3). The micro-level observations on ACH and SAT were grouped by the variable indicated in Table 3-1, and weighted regressions of the group means on ACH on the group means on SAT were calculated. The grouping variables were classified on the basis of their known relationships to ACH and SAT according to the following types—random grouping, grouping by the included regressor (X_1), grouping by an omitted regressor (X_2) that is uncorrelated with Y after controlling for X_1, grouping by Y, and grouping by an omitted regressor (X_2(that is correlated with both X_1 and $Y \cdot X_1$ (Y controlling for X_1).

For each grouping variable, Table 3-1 presents the number of groups formed; the group level estimates, b_1'; their standard errors; the estimated standard error of $\bar{b}_1'$ as an estimator of β_1'; and the partial regression coefficient $b_{YX_1} \cdot X_2$. The points made earlier about the different cases are illustrated. The "advantage" of grouping on the regressor (SAT2) over virtually all other methods is evident. The efficiency of random grouping (ID2 forms about nine times as many groups as does any other variable) is also apparent. Grouping by Y (ACH2) yields particularly poor estimates; even so, its mean-squared error approximates random grouping with the same number of groups.

If one is fortunate enought to group by some variable that is unrelated to Y after controlling for the included regressors, group level estimates are typically very good. But when grouping is by some characteristic related to both Y, controlling for X_1, and X_1 (a mis-specified microlevel model), group level estimation can be disastrous.

By comparing $\bar{b}_1'$ and b_1' to $b_{YX_1} \cdot X_2$, we gain some idea of the relative impact of specification bias when compounded by grouping. In every reasonable case (excluding random grouping and grouping on X_1), grouping exacerbates the bias due to misspecification, assuming, of course, that the model including both X_1 and X_2 is more correctly specified.

Table 3-1. Estimates from Grouped Data of Regression of ACH on SAT.

Grouping Variable	Number of Groups	$\bar{b}_1'$ [a]	Observed Bias $(\bar{b}_1' - b_1')$	$SE(\bar{b}_1')$ [a]	$\sqrt{MSE}(b_1')$ [b]	$bYX_1 \cdot X_2$
Random Grouping						
ID2	100	.832	-.007	.059	.059	.839
ID1	10	1.053	.214	.217	.304	.839
Grouping by X_1						
SAT2	13	.838	-.001	.019	.019	.884
Grouping by X_2 uncorrelated to $Y \cdot X_1$						
PARINC	10	.817	-.022	.060	.064	.838
POPED	6	.877	.039	.069	.079	.838
PARASP	5	.744	-.095	.090	.131	.839
NOBOOK	5	.718	-.121	.037	.127	.844
Grouping by Y						
ACH2	10	1.168	.329	.054	.334	.082
Grouping by X_2 correlated with $Y \cdot X_1$ and X_1						
SRAA2	5	.899	.060	.054	.081	.811
HSPHYS	5	1.237	.398	.042	.400	.811
HSMATH	5	1.396	.557	.048	.559	.765

Note: The grouping variables are: last two digits of student identification (ID2), last digit of student identification (ID1), highest two digits of SAT (SAT2), highest two digits of achievement (ACH2), student's estimate of parental income (PARINC), student's report of father's education (POPED), highest digit of composite self-rating of academic ability (SRAA2), student's report of semesters of high school mathematics (HSMATH), student's report of semesters of high school physical sciences (HSPHYS), student's report of number of books in the home (NOBOOK), highest level of education parents hope student will complete (PARASP).

[a] Estimates from ungrouped data: $b_1' = .839$; $SE(b_1') = .011$.

[b] $\sqrt{MSE}(b_1') = \sqrt{(OSERVED\ BIAS)^2 + SE(b_1')^2}$

Source: Burstein, 1975b.

Examples from School Effects Research. Studies of educational effects have been conducted at many levels and with data from multiple levels. Averch et al. (1972) provide short descriptions of a wide range of studies. The most frequently cited results from the Coleman Report (Coleman et al., 1966) are based on between school analyses and a mixed model with individual level measures of pupil outcomes and pupil backgrounds and aggregate measures of school and teacher characteristics. The Six Subject Surveys conducted by the International Association for the Evaluation of Educational Achievement (IEA) (Comber and Keeves, 1973; Peaker, 1975) report similar analyses.

Both the Coleman Report and the IEA studies analytical models that decrease the likelihood of identifying important teacher, classroom, and school characteristics (Bidwell and Kasarda, 1977; Burstein, 1976b; Burstein and Miller, 1978; Burstein and Smith, 1977). Data from students were not matched with the characteristics of their own teachers in either study. This practice by itself could limit the possibility of capturing the educational process as it affects individual students—except in the unlikely event that the process is uniform within and across classrooms within a given school. Moreover, when teacher variables such as experience and instructional practices are measured only at the school aggregate level, they are distal school resource characteristics that can be expected to behave like such global school characteristics as books in the library, overall per pupil expenditures, and characteristics of the principal.

In general, between school analyses tend to accentuate the effects of background, because students from similar backgrounds tend to be grouped together. That is, at the school level, aggregate student background measures reflect community characteristics that at least for the United States, determine to a large degree the resources (per pupil expenditures, teacher quality, etc.) available to run school programs. Moreover, communities with high quality school programs attract families from all social class levels who are motivated enough to move to obtain higher quality education. Whatever the mechanism, this aggregation process does not reduce background variation to the extent that it does variation in teacher and classroom characteristics. As a result, background factors typically fare better in between school analyses than they do in between student analyses, as the data in Table 3-2 indicate. The between school coefficients for POPOCC and BOKHOM are much larger than their between student counterparts. Moreover, the between student background effects were already large relative to the effects of school characteristics (EXPLORE, SCISTUDY). In contrast, the between school coefficients for SCISTUDY and EXPLORE increase very little.

Table 3-2. Between School and Between Student Regression Analyses of the Factors Affecting Schience Achievement (RSCI) for U. S. fourteen year olds in the IEA Study.

Variable	Between Students	Between Schools	Differences in Effects	Correlation Ratio
SEX	−4.157 (11.87)[a]	−6.620 (3.90)	−2.463	.09
RWK	.861 (23.22)	.876 (6.47)	.015	.21
POPOCC	.487 (6.39)	.843 (2.87)	.356	.23
BOKHOM	1.661 (7.20)	3.577 (3.37)	.916	.16
GRADE	1.912 (5.24)	1.390 (1.69)	−.522	.41
SCISTUDY	.066 (4.29)	.110 (2.34)	.040	.25
EXPLORE	.130 (2.52)	.240 (1.50)	.110	.21
R^2	.39	.72		
N observations	1,806	107		

Note: The variables included are: raw total science score (RSCI), raw word knowledge score (RWK), sex of student (SEX), student's report of father's occupation (POPOCC), student's report of number of books in the home (BOKHOM), grade in school (GRADE), student's report of exposure to science (SCISTUDY), student's report of degree of use of exporation in science in science instruction (EXPLORE).

[a]The t statistics are in parentheses.

Source: Burstein, Fischer, and Miller, 1978.

It should be noted that the coefficient for RWK, a measure of concurrent verbal ability, remains relatively stable across levels. Apparently, the grouping mechanism that allocates students to schools does not distort the estimate of the relationship of verbal ability to science achievement (though evidence presented below calls this interpretation into question).

Other studies with analyses at multiple levels provide further evidence of the consequences of grouping. Haney (1974) and Hannan, Freeman, and Meyer (1976) report empirical analyses at three levels. As expected from the theoretical results on analyses at different levels, the coefficients at the various levels in the Haney and the Hannan et al. reports differ in magnitude, different variables enter models at different levels, and aggregation generally inflates the estimated effects of background relative to the effects of school factors.

In an analysis at the student level with school aggregate teacher and classroom characteristics and global school characteristics, the aggregate measures begin with a disadvantage relative to the student level background factors. Since the former are measured only at the school level, they can influence only the mean outcomes for the school, which account for about 20–25 percent of the overall variation in student achievement ($\eta^2_{RSCI} = .23$ and $\eta^2_{RWK} = .21$ in Table 3–2). In contrast, the individual level student background measures can be associated with within school variation in outcome as well as with between school variation. This explanation provides an additional technical consideration that can help explain the poor showings of school level measures of the education a student receives. But these explanations are not likely to explain away the typically strong effects of background and the weak effects of schooling. The remainder of the truth lies elsewhere.

Concluding Comments about Cross-Level Inferences

Both the theoretical underpinnings and realistic examples of the consequences of attempting to estimate parameters of microlevel processes from macrolevel data have been presented. If one agrees with Averch et al. (1972) that "the researcher would like to examine the relationships among the school resources an individual student receives, his background, and the influences of his peers on one hand and his educational outcome on the other" (p. 38), then individual level data or at least the assurance that the aggregation process does not distort the relationships among important variables are necessary.

In general, it appears to be impossible to avoid distortion through aggregation in school effects research if microlevel processes are of interest. The grouping mechanism that allocates students to schools and to classrooms within schools is just too complex to specify adequately. Therefore, when the purpose is to identify factors affecting individual student achievement, I would discourage cross-level inference. Thus, the many studies that use either schools (Katzman, 1968; Thomas, 1962), school districts (Bidwell and Kasarda, 1975; Kiesling, 1969), or even states (Walberg and Rasher, 1974) as units of analysis are likely to yield misleading estimates of corresponding effects in student level analyses. One would also expect that school effects studies using the student as the unit of analysis (see, e.g., Hanushek, 1972; Murnane, 1975; Summers and Wolfe, 1975) are more likely to yield accurate estimates of the factors influencing individual student achievement.

We shall later place some conditions on the assertions in the last paragraph. Nevertheless, in order to conduct an adequate investigation of educational effects on individual student performance, it appears that the investigator must measure every variable at its lowest possible level and be able to match each student's data with the data from the teacher, classroom, classmates, and school (Burstein, 1975a, 1975b; Burstein and Smith, 1977). Otherwise, the study of the effects of education on individual students might as well be forgotten.

GROUP-STRUCTURAL-CONTEXTUAL COMPOSITIONAL EFFECTS

In this section, we consider the issues and problems that occur when macrolevel variables are specified to affect microlevel outcomes in an analysis of educational effects. This study of the effects of properties of groups or collectives on individuals is generally called "contextual analysis" (Lazarsfeld and Menzel, 1961).

Since properties of teachers (e.g., instructional practices), classrooms (e.g., availability of aides), and schools (e.g., variety of program offerings) are at a macrolevel with respect to students within classes and schools (the microlevel for present purposes), analyses that mix student level outcomes with group level independent variables are prevalent. The between student analyses in the Coleman Report (Coleman et al., 1966) and in the IEA studies (Comber and Keeves, 1973) were carried out in this manner. Indeed, most educational effects research involves specifications with group level explanatory variables. As the term is used by sociologists and economists, "school effects" research (Alwin, 1976; Alexander and Eckland, 1975; Coleman et al., 1966; Hauser, Sewell, and Alwin, 1976) generally involves this type of analysis. The terms, "teacher effects" and "classroom effects" in the research on teaching literature also typically refer to models involving macrolevel explanatory factors.

Inconsistencies in Terminology
The above notwithstanding, the juxtaposition of the four "visually distinct" modifiers of "effects" in the section title reflects the definitional and theoretical confusion that abounds in the social science literature on models that incorporate variables from multiple levels. There have been numerous attempts to disentangle the semantic morass implied by the four terms (group, structural, contextual, and compositional), beginning with the studies of the American

soldier reported by Stouffer et al. (1949) and winding through the so-called Columbia School tradition (see, e.g., Lazarsfeld and Menzel, 1961), several chapters in the compendium on quantitative ecological analysis in the social sciences edited by Dogan and Rokkan (1969, see especially Valkonen [1969]), and recent papers by Firebaugh (1977) and by Karweit, Fennessey, and Daiger (1978).

Unfortunately, the various clarifying papers also disagree on terminology. For the time being, we shall adopt a compromise set of meanings. "Group effects" and "structural effects" (Blau, 1960) shall be used interchangeably to denote the generic effects of macrolevel properties on individual level behavior. Both global (macrolevel properties not based on aggregation of individual characteristics—e.g., teacher sex for a classroom) and aggregate properties of groups (classrooms, schools, etc.) are subsumed under these terms.

"Contextual effects" and "compositional effects" will denote the effects of aggregate properties of groups only. Initially, contextual effects will be measured by the effect on microlevel outcomes of the group mean of a microlevel explanatory variable net of the microlevel values on the corresponding variable (Alwin, 1976; Farkas, 1974; Firebaugh, 1977; Hauser, 1970, 1971, 1974). That is, a contextual effect for ability is said to occur when group mean ability ($\overline{X}$) is related to individual outcomes (Y) after controlling for individual ability (X). The term compositional will refer to a more general set of operationalizations of aggregate properties (e.g., Davis, Spaeth, and Huson, 1961; Valkonen, 1969).

The methodological discussion of contextual effects considers two additional types of effects—individual and frog-pond. Individual effects refer to the impact of microlevel properties (X) on microlevel outcomes (Y) in models with variables from mixed levels. Individual ability, X_{ij}, (where i = group, j = person within group) is such a variable in models with group mean ability, $\overline{X}_{i.}$, and individual outcome, Y_{ij}.

The frog-pond or comparison effect is based on "the key social psychological principle . . . that success is judged by relative standing in the social group" (Davis, 1966:25). Thus, an individual's performance is a function of one's relative standing in the group (classroom, school) to which one belongs. Davis (1966) suggests that a student's performance may improve by attending a less competitive school, because self-concept is enhanced by ranking relatively higher in ability (thus, the "big frog in a small pond" metaphor).

Variations on the frog-pond concept permeate a variety of substantive work on the social-psychological effects of status within groups. The notion is basic to reference group theory (e.g., Merton and Kitt, 1950), to social evaluation theory (Pettigrew, 1967), and to the relative deprivation hypothesis in the interpretation of school effects (e.g., Alexander and Eckland, 1975; Davis, 1966; Hauser, Sewell, and Alwin, 1976; Meyer, 1970; St. John, 1971).

Operationally, frog-pond effects in educational effects research are typically measured by the impact of the individual's deviation from the mean of his or her group $(X_{ij} - \overline{X}_{i.})$ on individual level outcomes (Y_{ij}). An example would be the effect of a student's ability relative to the class mean ability on the student's performance on an achievement test.

Specification and Identification of Group Effects

We turn now to issues in the specification and identification of group and contextual effects in research on the effects of education. Group effects on individual educational outcomes have been demonstrated repeatedly. Affirmative answers to questions about school-to-school and classroom-to-classroom differences in individual outcomes are evidence of group effects.

Source. What is left unmentioned by the above, however, is the origin of between group differences. On the one hand, between group differences in outcomes may be attributable to properties of the groups themselves or to processes within the groups. On the other hand, such differences may simply be a function of the "selection rules" that govern assignment to groups (see, e.g., Cronbach 1976:1.17c).

In more concrete terms, selection effects in education can occur through systematic processes or "naturally." For example, systematic selection effects result when colleges establish selective admissions procedures, thereby increasing their chances of a high level of student attainment (e.g., higher average performance on the Graduate Record Examinations). Thus, the selection process can give a direct linkage between the average ability of the institution's entering students and the average achievement of its graduates.

The predominance of local control and financing of education in the United States leads to "natural" selection effects. These occur as a consequence of the symbiotic relationship between community characteristics and the quality and motivation of the students available. High wealth areas attract achievement-oriented families. At the same time, communities with highly educated (and wealthy) families can and do expect more from their children and their schools and provide more in personal investments of both time and money. Whatever the mechanism, the result is the same: schools differ in the mean backgrounds (entering ability, socioeconomic character-istics) of their students. And typically, these mean entering differ-ences translate into between school differences in outcomes that may have little to do with the quality of the school's educational program.

If selection factors can account for between school and between classroom differences, other substantive interpretations of school effects are unwarranted. There is one important caveat to this state-ment, however. If the effects of classrooms and schools are cor-related with the effects of selection into groups (e.g., ability determines assignment to classrooms, but the classroom effect is also greater for higher [lower] ability students than for lower [high-er] students, partitioning the group effect into causal (substantive) and spurious (due to assignment into groups) components is virtually impossible. This confounding of group membership with school resource variables (the educational "treatment") is the source of much of the methodological controversy surrounding Coleman et al.'s (1966) interpretation of the relative influence of school and home background on achievement. The IEA studies experienced similar difficulties in interpretation (Peaker, 1975; Schwille, 1975). The problems associated with the relationship between assignment to groups and "treatment" in quasi-experiments with nonequivalent control group designs also fall within this domain (Cronbach, 1976; Cronbach, Rogosa, Floden, and Price, 1977).

The usual way to remove selection or grouping mechanisms as an explanation of group effects is to specify the grouping mechanism within the model. That is, if assignment to schools is on the basis of socioeconomic background, the model used to estimate school ef-fects should also adequately specify socioeconomic background (the "inputs" to the school). While such models do not solve the problem of correlation between the selection and causal effects of group membership, the effects attributed to causal mechanisms in such models are typically conservative. So the existence of significant effects (after controlling for selection) is impressive evidence that some causal mechanism of the group (school, classroom), as yet unspecified, is operating on the student.

Empirical Illustrations. Data from three studies (Tables 3–3 to 3–5) are provided to illustrate the magnitude of school and classroom effects. The estimates of proportions of variation from the Wiley and Bock (1967) data and from the Early Childhood Education Evalua-tion (ECE) data (Baker, 1976) are generated from a hierarchically nested analysis of variance model (pupils within classrooms within schools):

Table 3-3. Proportion of Total Variation in Treatment[a] Mean Attributable to Classrooms and Schools for Fifth Grade Pupils on the Stanford Achievement Test.

| Subtest | Proportion of Variation | |
	Classrooms (N = 19)	*Schools (N = 10)*
Word meaning	.18	.62
Paragraph meaning	.18	.65
Spelling	.13	.52
Language	.50	.31
Arithmetic computation	.68	.14
Arithmetic concepts	.59	.11
Arithmetic application	.38	.32
Social studies	.44	.38
Science	.06	.72

[a]The proportions of variance were actually reconstructed by Wiley and Bock from the variance components under the assumption that each "treatment" is represented by one classroom of thirty pupils in each school. The proportions are variance in "treatment" means.

Source: Wiley and Bock, 1967.

$$Y = \mu + \alpha_s + \beta_{(c):s} + \gamma_{(p):cs}, \qquad (3.11)$$

where α_s, $\beta_{(c):s}$, and $\gamma_{(p):cs}$ represent effects of schools, classrooms within schools, and pupils with classrooms, respectively.

Background factors have not been taken into account in either of these sets of analyses. The studies, however, do reflect variations in sampling frame that should be associated with the likelihood of selection mechanisms. The Wiley-Bock data come from a single suburban community in northern Illinois and probably reflect essentially random mechanisms for allocation to schools. The ECE data are drawn from schools in moderate- to large-sized California school districts. Moreover, schools receiving some compensatory education funding and ECE funding (based on poverty, partly on willingness to "reform") were overrepresented because the purpose of the study was to evaluate the effects of ECE and of compensatory funding plus ECE.

Taken at face value, the data from Tables 3-3 and 3-4 suggest several comments about school and classroom effects.

Wiley-Bock data:
1. School and classroom effects are large.
2. The variation associated with classrooms or schools differs according to content area, with more between school variation in

Table 3-4. Proportion of Variation between Schools and between Classrooms within Schools for Different Criterion-referenced Tests for Grades 2 and 3 Used in the ECE Evaluation.[a]

| Content Area | School | | | | | Classroom within School | | | | |
| | Form 1 | | Form 2 | | | Form 1 | | Form 2 | | |
	Grade 2 (N = 72)	Grade 3 (N = 71)	Grade 2 (N = 71)	Grade 3 (N = 72)	Median	Grade 2 (N = 159)	Grade 3 (N = 154)	Grade 2 (N = 157)	Grade 3 (N = 158)	Median
Reading										
Sight word	.11	.17	.15	.16	.16	.12	.09	.11	.12	.10
Word attack	.13	.19	.19	.13	.16	.11	.08	.11	.14	.11
Literature Composition	.02	.09	.15	.11	.10	.14	.11	.02	.06	.09
Total	.10	.18	.19	.17	.18	.15	.13	.11	.13	.13
Math										
Operations (addition, subtraction, multiplication)	.01	.04	.06	.16	.05	.31	.19	.19	.07	.19
Word problems	.04	.08	.10	.15	.09	.13	.11	.05	.06	.09
Coins	.06	.06	.03	.03	.05	.08	.05	.10	.06	.07
Total	.02	.07	.08	.16	.08	.27	.18	.18	.10	.18

[a]The data reported are taken from the files of the Evaluation of the California Early Childhood Education Program by the Center for the Study of Evaluation (see Baker, 1976). All tests were short, with total testing time of less than an hour. Each class included received both forms. The data for approximately 800 students are the basis of this analysis.

Table 3-5. Proportion of Variation in Student Outcomes (R^2) Associated with Classroom and School After Controlling for Student and School Background Characteristics for Children in the Murnane Study.[a]

| | Cohort 1 | | | | Cohort 2 | | Medians | | |
| | Grade 2 | | Grade 3 | | Grade 3 | | | | |
Source[b]	Reading	Math	Reading	Math	Reading	Math	Reading	Math	Overall
Schools (N = 14 or 15)	.05[c]	.12	.08	.08	.03	.06	.05	.08	.07
Classrooms (N = 38–40)	.11	.22	.15	.20	.13	.16	.13	.20	.16
Classrooms within schools	.06	.10	.07	.12	.10	.10	.07	.10	.10
Background factors only (N = 410–42 students)	.43	.35	.50	.39	.53	.52	.50	.39	.44

[a]The data are from a single school district (New Haven, Connecticut) for grades 2 and 3 black children in Title 1 schools. Outcomes are spring test scores for the specific grade. The background variables included in the model are scores for the previous spring, sex of student, number of days student attended school during the year, whether student lived in publicly subsidized housing, percentage of low cost rental units on block in which the child lived, and percentage of population under eighteen on the child's block living in female-headed families.

[b]The proportions of variation attributed to the school and classroom were determined by including dummy variables for schools or classrooms (separate models) in the model with the background factors. The proportion of variation in classrooms within schools was determined by subtraction (R^2background, classroom dummies − R^2background, school dummies).

[c]All proportions of variation exhibited in the table are significant at the p = .05 level using corresponding mean square residual for students as the denominator for the F-test.

Source: Murnane, 1975.

reading, spelling, and science and more class within school variation in mathematics, social studies, and language.

ECE data:
3. School and classroom effects assessed by criterion-referenced tests
   are moderate at best in both grades 2 and 3.
4. Classroom within school effects are larger than between school
   effects in math, while the reverse is true in reading.

Murnane (1975) attempted to specify properly student and community inputs to schools and classrooms so that any residual effects
could be attributed to classroom or school effects. The contribution
of classroom and school membership to variation in spring achievement test scores was determined after controlling for the pupils'
previous spring test scores, community background, sex, and attendance.

Though the Murnane study involves second and third grade
children, as does the ECE study, his schools were all Title I schools
in New Haven, Connecticut. The sample is much more restricted than
in the ECE study. This homogeneity provides a further control for
the selection mechanism that might be used to explain any group
effects. The results from Murnane's study suggest the following
interpretations.

Murnane data:
5. Moderate school and classroom effects exist even after controlling
   for inputs.
6. The effects are somewhat larger in math than in reading.
7. The effects associated with classrooms within schools are slightly
   though consistently larger than the effects associated with schools.

Interpretations.   The studies cited vary along several dimensions.
In fact, the main similarity among them is the existence of statistically and practically significant effects of classrooms and schools.
Of course, the magnitude of the effects reported vary as a function
of grade, sampling frame, subject matter, and degree of control for
individual background factors and selection effects. However, the
pattern of effects is not unreasonable. They are larger for the more
homogeneous samples at the elementary grades (Murnane and
Wiley-Bock as opposed to ECE).

The differences in effects across subject matter are particularly
informative. Mathematics instruction exhibits stronger effects than
reading does across grades, with most of the impact associated with

classroom-to-classroom differences. This latter finding is as expected. While home influences have a stronger impact on reading, mathematics is a subject matter largely learned in school (with, perhaps, the exception of number recognition and counting). Moreover, while mathematics, like reading, is offered in virtually all elementary school classes, teachers' skills in instruction and their attitudes toward mathematics—which together presumably determine the overall quantity, variety, and quality of mathematics instruction in the elementary grades—vary greatly among classrooms within schools (cf., e.g., Burstein, 1978b, Dishaw, 1977; Filby and Fisher, 1977). These variations in skill and attitude are presumably much smaller between schools. In contrast, the quantity and coverage of reading instruction are presumably more homogeneous across classrooms. These differences in the relative magnitudes of classroom and school effects for mathematics, both by themselves and also when compared with reading, can be explained by the influence of pupil background and by the differences in teacher skills and attitudes within schools.

While the existence of group effects at the classroom and school levels is evident from the above examples, we have not provided any indication about how these effects arise. The two types of analyses presented (nested analysis of variance and regression analyses with classroom and teacher dummy variables) can serve only one limited purpose: they can tell the investigator whether it is important to consider school and classroom influences on pupil outcomes. Assuming no interactions between individual background and classroom-school factors, these analyses provide an upper bound on the amount of variation in individual outcomes that can be attributed to classroom or school level variables.

Specification and Identification of Contextual Effects

As mentioned in the previous section, the use of classroom or school dummy variables to account for individual outcomes can determine the existence of group effects, but it cannot identify their source. Other more proximal measures of school and classroom processes are needed to identify them. Research on contextual effects (Alexander and Eckland, 1975; Alexander, Cook, and McDill, 1978; Alwin, 1976; Campbell and Alexander, 1965; Farkas, 1974; Firebaugh, 1977; Hauser, 1970, 1971, 1974; McDill and Rigsby, 1973; Meyer, 1970; Nelson, 1972; among many others) represents one attempt at more direct assessment of group effects on individual outcomes.

Typically, context has been operationalized by aggregating the observations of group members, X_{ij}, on the variable of interest. Then so-called contextual effects refer to the effect of this aggregate measure of context, $\overline{X}_1$, on individual outcomes, Y_{ij}, net of the individual's effect, X_{ij}, for the same variable. The analytical results for contextual effects, frog-pond effect, and individual effects are developed below. The presentation draws heavily from Firebaugh (1977).

Preliminary Specification. For a single independent variable, the structural equation for the contextual effects model can be written as

$$Y_{ij} = \alpha + \beta_{YX \cdot \overline{X}} X_{ij} + \beta_{Y\overline{X} \cdot X} \overline{X}_{i.} + \epsilon, \tag{3.12}$$

where Y_{ij} and X_{ij} are individual level measures on Y and X for person j in group i, $\overline{X}_{i.}$ is the mean for group i on variable X, and ϵ is a random disturbance term with the usual least-squares properties.

The coefficient $\beta_{Y\overline{X} \cdot X}$ in equation (3.12) is the standard measure of the contextual effect. If $\beta_{Y\overline{X} \cdot X}$ is significantly different from zero, group context is said to have an independent effect on individual outcomes (Alwin, 1976; Farkas, 1974; Firebaugh, 1977, 1978; Hauser, 1971, 1974). That is, in a study of the effects of ability on achievement, a significant $\beta_{Y\overline{X} \cdot X}$ is interpreted to mean that the level of ability of the group (as measured by $\overline{X}$) has an independent effect on individual achievement. An ability context is then given a substantive interpretation (see e.g., Alexander and Eckland, 1975).

The so-called individual effect is measured by the coefficient $\beta_{YX \cdot \overline{X}}$. If $\beta_{YX \cdot \overline{X}}$ is significant, an individual's ability is said to have an independent effect on the individual's achievement after controlling for the effects of group mean ability.

Intuitively, the results from an application of equation (3.12) in the example described would seem to be theoretically sound. That is, all things being equal, we would expect an individual's ability to have a significant impact on performance. Moreover, group mean ability can be expected to influence instructional practices by causing the teacher (school) to adjust instruction to the level of the students in the class (school). As a result of the ability context effect on instructional practices, individual students within the class (school) can be expected to learn more or less than they would in other classes (schools).

The theoretical interpretations of individual and contextual effects presented above emphasize the role of two learning principles—learning ability and opportunity to learn—on the achievement process. That is, on an absolute scale, individuals learn more (less) because (1) they begin with higher (lower) ability and (2) they learn in groups where instructional practices offer more (high ability group) or less (low ability group) content to be learned. To make the point even more concrete, Jane cannot solve fractions problems because either (1) she lacks the ability to solve fractions (an individual effect) or (2) though capable if taught, she was not given the opportunity to learn fractions because the teacher felt that the class was not ready for the topic or needed more instruction in multiplication instead.

Most of the sociological literature on school context effects does not base interpretations of such effects on such psychological grounds as opportunity to learn. Instead, sociological or social-psychological interpretations are offered. According to a standard interpretation, group values on X affect the individual by "setting and enforcing standards for the person" (Kelly, 1952; see also Alwin, 1976; Firebaugh, 1977; Meyer, 1970) and by functioning as "comparison point(s) against which the person can evaluate himself" (Kelly, 1952:413; see also Davis, 1966; Firebaugh, 1977; St. John, 1971). These descriptions refer to contextual and frog-pond effects, respectively. According to the former, the motivation associated with either peer pressure or social sanctions causes Jane to achieve higher (lower) than she would have otherwise. If the fact that Jane is high (low) when compared with the ability of her class (school) causes her to perform lower (higher) or higher (lower) than she would have otherwise, a frog-pond effect, presumably due to the motivational effects of one's relative standing within the group, is said to exist.

A structural model that includes both contextual and frog-pond effects can be written as

$$Y_{ij} = \alpha + \beta_{Y(X - \overline{X}) \cdot \overline{X}} (X_{ij} - \overline{X}_{i.}) + \beta_{Y\overline{X} \cdot (X - \overline{X})} \overline{X}_{i.} + \epsilon, \quad (3.13)$$

where $(X_{ij} - \overline{X}_{i.})$ is the measure of relative standing of a person j in group i, $\beta_{Y(X - \overline{X}) \cdot x}$ is the coefficient associated with the frog-pond effect, and $\beta_{Y\overline{X} \cdot (X - \overline{X})}$ is the coefficient associated with the contextual effect. We could have written the coefficients as $\beta_{Y(X - \overline{X})}$ and $\beta_{Y\overline{X}}$ since $(X - \overline{X})$ and $\overline{X}$ are uncorrelated.

Note that equation (3.13) does not include a measure of the individual effect, X_{ij}. Only relative standing and group mean performance are specified to affect microlevel outcomes. Instead, we might have argued on psychological grounds that only individual pupil ability, X_{ij}, and relative ability within the group, $X_{ij} - \overline{X}_{i.}$, might affect individual outcomes. According to this view, a student's relative standing within the group could determine the amount of instructional resources that the teacher allocates to the student and hence the amount that the student learns over and above level of ability.[2] A structural model incorporating individual and frog-pond effects can be written as

$$Y_{ij} = \alpha + \beta_{YX \cdot (X - \overline{X})} X_{ij} + \beta_{Y(X - \overline{X}) \cdot X} (X_{ij} - \overline{X}_{i.}) + \epsilon, \text{(3.14)}$$

where the coefficient $\beta_{YK \cdot (X - \overline{X})}$ is interpreted to measure the individual effect while $\beta_{Y(X - \overline{X}) \cdot X}$ measures the frog-pond effect.

It should be obvious to the reader that (1) plausible alternative sociological and psychological interpretations of contextual and frog-pond effects have been offered and (2) models involving potentially different estimates of all three effects (individual, contextual, and frog-pond) have been generated. Table 3–6 summarizes both the substantive interpretations and possible estimators of the three effects of ability on achievement, with class defining the group membership in the two effect models. Similar interpretations can be offered for socioeconomic background (SES) and other input characteristics, for other outcomes besides achievement, and for other group membership indexes (e.g., school, school district, etc.).

We can carry this theoretical exercise one step further and argue that all three factors (individual ability, group mean ability, and the individual's ability relative to that of the group) affect individual level outcomes. The specification of this model is given by the structural equation

$$Y = \alpha^* + \beta_1 X_{ij} + \beta_2 \overline{X}_{i.} + \beta_3 (X_{ij} - \overline{X}_{i.}) + \epsilon, \qquad \text{(3.15)}$$

with β_1, β_2, and β_3 representing the coefficients for individual (X_{ij}), contextual ($\overline{X}_{i.}$) and frog-pond ($X_{ij} - \overline{X}_{i.}$) effects, respectively.

Analytical Complications. Unfortunately, the model represented by equation (3.15) is not estimable by any standard means. That is, β_1, β_2, and β_3 cannot be estimated simultaneously, since X_{ij}, $\overline{X}_{i.}$, and $X_{ij} - \overline{X}_{i.}$ are linearly dependent (Burstein and Miller, 1978; Cronbach, 1976; Firebaugh, 1977). As a result, the same data can be generated by a variety of alternative combinations of individual, contextual, and frog-pond effects. Thus, when measured by X_{ij}, $\overline{X}_{i.}$, and $X_{ij} - \overline{X}_{i.}$, respectively, these three effects cannot be estimated simultaneously.

Table 3-6. Substantive Interpretations and Estimators of Individual, Contextual, and Frog-Pond Effects of Ability on Achievement in Classrooms in Two Effect Models.

Type of Effect	*Alternative Interpretations*	*Estimators[a]*
Individual	1. A student's ability affects the student's learning and hence measured achievement	$\beta_{YX \cdot \bar{X}}$ $\beta_{YX \cdot (X-\bar{X})}$
Contextual	2. Psychological (opportunity to learn)—group ability affects instructional practice (amount of instructional time, topics covered, way in which topics are taught), which, in turn, affects individual learning and achievement	$\beta_{Y\bar{X} \cdot X}$ $\beta_{Y\bar{X} \cdot (X-\bar{X})} = \beta_{Y\bar{X}}$
	2. Sociological (peer pressure and social sanction)—group ability affects individual motivation to learn and hence individual learning and achievement	
Frog-Pond	1. Psychological (opportunity to learn)—the student's relative standing within the group affects the allocation of instructional resources and style of instruction provides the student and thereby the student's learning and achievement	$\beta_{Y(X-\bar{X}) \cdot \bar{X}} = \beta_{Y(X-\bar{X})}$ $\beta_{Y(X-\bar{X}) \cdot X}$
	2. Sociological (relative status effects)—relative standing in the group affects individual motivation to learn and thereby individual learning and achievement	

[a]The estimators are the coefficients from equations (3.12) through (3.14) for X_{ij}, $\bar{X}_{i.}$, and $X_{ij} - \bar{X}_{i.}$.

The problems in estimating equation (3.15) have implications for the three models incorporating only two of the three effects. If we, in turn, set β_3, β_1, and β_2 equal to zero, we would obtain equations (3.12), (3.13), and (3.14), respectively. But if this is so, these three specifications of individual, contextual, and frog-pond effects ($\beta_3 = 0$, $\beta_1 = 0$, and $\beta_2 = 0$) are observationally equivalent, and none can be ruled out simply on technical grounds. Thus, the estimators in Table 3-6 do not represent separable effects, and questions about which of the two estimates of each effect is the correct one $(\beta_{YX \cdot \overline{X}}$ or $\beta_{YX \cdot (X-\overline{X})}$ for individual, $\beta_{Y\overline{X} \cdot X}$ or $\beta_{Y\overline{X} \cdot (X-\overline{X})}$ for contextual, and $\beta_{Y(X-\overline{X}) \cdot \overline{X}}$ or $\beta_{Y(X-\overline{X}) \cdot X}$ for frog-pond) become less of an issue.

The interdependency of the estimators from the three effects can be approached from an entirely different perspective. It has been shown (Duncan, Cuzzort, and Duncan, 1961; Cronbach, 1976) that

$$\beta_T = \eta_X^2 \beta_\beta + (1 - \eta_X^2)\beta_W,$$

where β_T is the coefficient from the between student regression of Y_{ij} on X_{ij}, β_β is the coefficient from the weighted (by group size) between group regression of $\overline{Y}_{i.}$ on $\overline{X}_{i.}$, β_W is the coefficient from the pooled within group regression of $Y_{ij} - \overline{Y}_{i.}$ on $X_{ij} - \overline{X}_{i.}$, and η_X^2 is the ratio of the between group variation on X to the total variation on X (the correlation ratio for variable X).

Given the above decomposition of the individual regression into between group and within group regressions, we can show (cf. Burstein, 1977; Firebaugh, 1977; Werts and Linn, 1971) that in equation (3.12),

$$\beta_{YX \cdot \overline{X}} = \beta_W \text{ and } \beta_{Y\overline{X} \cdot X} = \beta_B - \beta_W ; \qquad (3.16)$$

in equation (3.13),

$$\beta_{Y(X-\overline{X}) \cdot X} = \beta_{Y(X-\overline{X})} = \beta_W , \text{ and}$$

$$\beta_{Y\overline{X} \cdot (X-\overline{X})} = \beta_{Y\overline{X}} = \beta_B ; \qquad (3.17)$$

and in equation (3.14),

$$\beta_{YX \cdot (X-\overline{X})} = \beta_B \text{ and}$$

$$\beta_{Y(X-\overline{X}) \cdot X} = \beta_W - \beta_B . \qquad (3.18)$$

Thus, no matter which specification is chosen, the three effects (individual, contextual, and frog-pond) can be shown to be various analytical combinations of two regression coefficients—the between group coefficient, β_B, and the pooled within group coefficient, β_W. As before, we see that what appears to be three substantively interpretable effects are linearly dependent when measured by X_{ij}, $\overline{X}_{i.}$, and $X_{ij} - \overline{X}_{i.}$, and only two coefficients are uniquely estimable.

Empirical Illustration. The interrelations among individual, contextual, and frog-pond effects can be illustrated using data on science achievement of U. S. fourteen year olds from the IEA Six Subjects Survey. The models exhibited in the six columns of Table 3-7 are variations of the general model

$$RSCI = f(RWK, POPCC, GRADE, SCISTUDY),$$

where

RSCI = total raw score on the science achievement test;

RWK = total raw score on the word knowledge test;

POPOCC = student's report of father's occupation;

GRADE = the grade in which the student is enrolled; and

SCISTUDY = student's report of exposure to science.

All coefficients reported in the table are larger than twice their standard errors.

The first three columns of Table 3-7 report the three single level regression analyses—between student (total), between school, and pooled within school. The last three columns present results from models that posit individual and contextual effects of verbal ability (RWK) and socioeconomic background (POPOCC) on achievement (as in equation [3.12]), individual and frog-pond effects (as in equation [3.14]), and contextual and frog-pond effects (as in equation [3.13]), respectively. The sets of coefficients for POPOCC and RWK behave as expected.

In columns (4) through (6), GRADE and SCISTUDY are represented by individual level variables only. This specification accounts for the small differences between the coefficients for GRADE and SCISTUDY in the between student analysis and the corresponding coefficients in the analyses reported in columns (4) through (6). It also explains why the coefficients for the individual, contextual, and frog-pond effects do not correspond exactly to the values suggested by equations (3.16) through (3.18). In column (4), $\hat{b}_{RSCI,RWK}$ = .799 and $\hat{b}_{RSCI,RWK}$ = .799 and $\hat{b}_{RSCI,BRWK}$ = .161. If all variables were included at both the student and school levels, we would expect from equation (3.16) that $\hat{b}_{RSCI,RWK}$ would equal $\hat{b}_{WITHIN SCHOOL}$ = .792 and $\hat{b}_{RSCI,BRWK}$ would equal $\hat{b}_{BETWEEN SCHOOL} - \hat{b}_{WITHIN SCHOOL}$ = 1.018 − .792 = .226. Similarly, in column (5) $\hat{b}_{RSCI,RWK}$ = .960 and $\hat{b}_{RSCI,WRWK}$ = −.161, although from equation (3.17) we expect $\hat{b}_{RSCI,RWK}$ = 1.018 and $\hat{b}_{RSCI,WRWK}$ = − .226; and in column (6) $\hat{b}_{RSCI,BRWK}$ = .960 and $\hat{b}_{RSCI,WRWK}$ = .799 compared with 1.018 and .792 predicted from the application of equation (3.18).

Table 3-7. Illustration of Dependency among Individual (X_{ij}), Frog-Pond ($X_w = X_{ij} - \bar{X}_{i.}$), and Contextual Effects ($\bar{X}_{i.}$) Using Data from the Regression of Science Achievement (RSCI) on Background and School Characteristics for Fourteen Year Olds from the IEA Study (N = 2,537 students).[a]

Variables[b]	Between Student (1)	Between School (2)	Within School (3)	Metric Regression Coefficients[c] Individual and Contextual (4)	Individual and Frog-Pond (5)	Contextual and Frog-Pond (6)
RWK (X_{ij})	.873	—	—	.799	.960	—
BRWK ($\bar{X}_{i.}$)	—	1.018	—	.161	—	.960
WRWK ($X_{ij}-\bar{X}_{i.}$)	—	—	.792	—	-.161	.799
POPOCC (X_{ij})	.580	—	—	.343	1.355	—
BPOPOCC ($\bar{X}_{i.}$)	—	1.357	—	1.012	—	1.355
WPOPOCC ($X_{ij}-\bar{X}_{i.}$)	—	—	.341	—	-1.012	.343
GRADE	1.875	.896	2.351	1.742	1.742	1.742
SCISTUDY	.007	.012	.006	.008	.008	.008

[a]The analyses are run on a slightly different sample than were used for Table 3-2, although both are based on the science study from the IEA Six Subjects Survey.

[b]The variables are a subset of the variables used to construct Table 3-2. The variables names are the same for both tables.

[c]All coefficients presented are significant.

Source: Burstein, Fischer, and Miller, 1978.

Toward a Theoretical Resolution

The results in Table 3-7 reinforce the points made above about the interdependency among individual, contextual, and frog-pond effects as measured—X_{ij}, $\overline{X}_{i.}$, and $X_{ij} - \overline{X}_{i.}$, repsectively. No amount of empirical manipulation of these three quantities can yield three distinct estimates given the linear dependency, and as a result, empirical procedures cannot estimate any two of the effects without estimating the third as well.

The key to the separation and identification of the three effects lies elsewhere. Firebaugh (1977) suggests three methods of breaking the linear dependency:

1. Delete one of the variables on theoretical grounds;
2. Obtain more direct measures of the frog-pond and/or contextual effects; and
3. Use different variables in measuring frog-pond and contextual effects.

All three involve a respecification of equation (3.15) on the basis of theoretical considerations.

Operationally, the first method yields one of the three two regressor specifications already represented by equations (3.12), (3.13), and (3.14). The distinction here is that one arrives at one of these three specifications on theoretical grounds. That is, one is asserting that either individual, frog-pond, or contextual effects do not exist. This type of theoretical resolution of a methodological problem is not uncommon in social science research. For example, the three variable simple causal chain $(X \rightarrow Y \rightarrow Z)$ is observationally equivalent to the spurious causation model (Y is a prior case of X and Z, but X and Z are not directly related). However, this does not imply that these two models cannot be distinguished on theoretical grounds. Similarly, in a given situation, we can justify distinguishing among the two effect models that we have considered on theoretical grounds alone.

The second method places the burden on the investigator to think more carefully about the way in which frog-pond and contextual effects are measured. Going back to our ability-achievement example, we might reconsider what is meant by the effect of the student's relative ability standing on performance. We have already offered two substantive interpretations of frog-pond effects (Table 3-6), one associated with relative allocations of instructional resources due to the student's relative standing, the other based on the student's motivation to achieve as a function of self-perception of relative standing. Another interpretation might be that the teacher's perception of the student's relative standing might affect the teacher's expectations, which, if transmitted to the student, affect performance.

In practice, the three separate substantive interpretations of frog-pond effects can be measured more precisely by alternatives to the $X_{ij} - \overline{X}_{i.}$ measure. For example, the difference between the instructional resources allocated to a student and the resources allocated to the average student in the class is a more direct measure of the frog-pond effect of relative allocation of resources. A student's response to a self-concept of academic ability scale may be a better measure of the frog-pond effect associated with perception of relative academic standing. Finally, the teacher's judgments of the pupil's academic ability more directly capture the frog-pond effect envisioned to operate through teacher perceptions and expectations. Any of these three measures described—the instructional resource measure, student self-concept of academic ability, and teacher perception of academic ability—might be substituted into equation (3.15) for $X_{ij} - \overline{X}_{i.}$ to specify more directly the frog-pond effect and to break the linear dependency. Similarly, we could replace $\overline{X}_{i.}$ or a measure of the contextual effect with more direct measures of the processes that the contextual effect is supposed to represent. Replacement of either $\overline{X}_{i.}$ or $X_{ij} - \overline{X}_{i.}$ requires theoretical support but affords improved opportunities to interpret the process directly affecting individual outcomes.

Finally, method 3 involves the recognition that frog-pond and contextual effects might involve different aspects of the group. Firebaugh cites Alexander and Eckland's (1975; see also Meyer, 1970) argument that, for educational attainment, the SES level of the school determines the school's contextual effect, while the student's relative ability level within the school might determine the frog-pond effect. In this instance, two distinct characteristics (SES and ability) are viewed as antecedents of the two effects of group membership, while in method 2 alternative manifestations of the same underlying characteristic (ability) were suggested.

The shift to direct measurement of the processes believed to determine frog-pond and contextual effects (methods 2 and 3) seems warranted regardless of whether one chooses to delete one of the variables from the model (method 1). And once this shift has been made, contextual and frog-pond effects as operationalized by $\overline{X}_{i.}$ and $X_{ij} - \overline{X}_{i.}$ cease to exist. Instead, the distinctions of contextual and, for that matter, compositional and frog-pond effects from group and structural effects fade away. In some cases, the distinction between the types of group effects and types of individual effects that occur in a group become blurred (cf., e.g., the alternative substantive interpretations of frog-pond effects).

In any event, we are left in the same camp with Hauser (1974) and Firebaugh (1977), although disagreement over terminology persists. Although more proximal than the use of class and school dummy variables, contextual and frog-pond effects as measured by $\overline{X}_{i.}$ and $X_{ij} - \overline{X}_{i.}$ are still too mechanical and are distally related to the sociological or psychological processes that they are intended to represent. Instead, following Firebaugh (1977:14) and, implicitly, Hauser, we conclude that:

1. Analyses involving both individual level and group level effects should be based on careful theory in which both the source and form of group effects are specifically stated.
2. As a result, contextual effects and frog-pond effects should be measured directly.
3. Once direct measures are specified, terminology more adequately describing these measures should be used in place of "contextual" and "frog-pond" designations.

While the first two points reflect substantive matters, the third is in response to a more emotional issue. The languge that one chooses to communicate theory in the social sciences is, in many respects, arbitrary. However, in educational effects research, the terms "contextual" and "frog-pond" are strongly identified with a dispute that is more form that substance. Therefore, in line with Hauser, I suggest that in order to encourage more careful examination of school and classroom processes, investigators drop both the offending practice (the use of $\overline{X}_{i.}$ and $X_{ij} - X_{i.}$ mechanically) and the offending language. More direct measures and language more descriptive of the processes that operate within and between groups are available and should be used.

APPROPRIATE UNITS OF ANALYSIS

When faced with the analysis of multilevel data, many researchers assume that there is only one appropriate unit (pupil, class, school, etc.) and proceed to justify their choice of a unit of analysis and thereby the level at which all analyses are conducted. This attempt to delineate the level at which the research question is addressed is a logical consequence of the problems of cross-level inference discussed earlier. Since models analyzed at different levels rarely yield similar results, investigators assume that the analysis at only one of the levels is correct. Unfortunately, this assumption is often unwarranted.

Competing Arguments about Choice of Units

Traditionally, a variety of competing reasons have been cited as justification for the choice of either students or groups as the appropriate units of analyses in studies of educational effects. Both conceptual and statistical arguments have been voiced in favor of either level or against making a choice. A few of the key arguments about choosing the appropriate unit of analysis can be stated as follows:

Pupils as the Appropriate Unit
1. In education the phenomena to be investigated are pupil outcomes. More specifically, we want to determine the effects of the educational resources that an individual pupil receives and his or her background, and the influence of his or her community setting and peers on the individual pupil's educational outcomes (Averch et al., 1972). Therefore, pupils are the units for which questions must finally be addressed.
2. Pupils react as individuals, and the effects on them should be the focus of educational evaluation (Bloom, in discussion in Wittrock and Wiley, 1970:271 ff.).
3. Effects in the classrooms are an aggregation of effects of environment arrangements on individuals (Glaser, in discussion in Wittrock and Wiley, 1970:271 ff.).
4. In classroom interaction research, most teacher behavior directed at students is directed at individuals rather than at the whole class, and student individual differences affect such teacher behavior. Even teacher behavior directed at the whole class interacts with student individual differences to determine outcomes (Brophy, 1975).
5. Theoretical arguments concerning the effects of educational structure on pupil outcomes are formulated at the pupil level. To analyze the data at the group level is to enhance the likelihood of specification and aggregation bias (Hannon, Freeman, and Meyer, 1976).

Groups (Classes, Schools, etc.) as Units
6. The appropriate unit of study in educational evaluation is the collective—class or school—rather than the individual. The effects of a treatment on the classroom (school) are fundamentally different from the effects of the treatment on the individual within it (Wiley 1970:271 ff.).

7. The sampling unit determines the unit of analysis. If classrooms are the sampling units, they are also the units of analysis (Cline et al., 1974; Cronbach, 1976).
8. The unit of treatment defines the level of analysis. If treatments are administered to intact classrooms (schools), they are the units (Cline et al., 1974; Cronbach, 1976; Glass and Stanley, 1970).
9. The treatments received by pupils and thereby their performance within classrooms (schools) are generally intercorrelated. These dependencies dictate the choice of between class (school) analyses (Glass and Stanley, 1970; Glendening, 1976).
10. Characteristics of the teacher (school) take on the ame value for every pupil in a particular classroom (school). An analysis at the pupil level overemphasizes the amount of information one has about class (school) level variables (Keesling and Wiley, 1974).

Other Considerations

11. The same manifest variables answer different questions at different levels of analysis. Therefore, the research foci should determine the appropriate units of analysis (Burstein, 1976a, 1977, 1978a; Burstein and Miller, 1978; Cronbach, 1976; Haney, 1974).
12. Dependence among observations within classrooms (schools) is a matter of degree rather than existence. Therefore, choosing the group as the unit of analysis simply because students receive instruction together in classrooms (schools) is inappropriate. Approaches that investigate degree of dependency and adjust for the effects of dependency are more appealing than automatic aggregation to the classroom (school) level (Burstein, 1977; Burstein and Knapp, 1975; Glendening, 1976; Webb, 1977).
13. Analyses of class (school) means can mask important between class differences in the within class distributions of outcomes and the relation of outcomes to inputs. Thus, the use of group means as the only unit of analysis is appropriate (Brown and Saks, 1975; Burstein, 1976a, 1977, 1978a; Burstein, Linn, and Capell, 1978; Klitgaard, 1975; Linn and Burstein, 1977; Lohnes, 1972: Wiley, 1970).
14. Overall between student analyses are weighted averages of between class (school) and pooled within class (school) analyses and thus are rarely advisable in educational contexts (Cronbach, 1976).

The points cited above are generally compelling, and disagreements are virtually unresolvable if a choice of either pupil or class or school as the only unit of analysis is required. Moreover, those analysts who resort to theoretical justifications either reject plausible alternative theories or find themselves unable to choose. Picking the appropriate unit on the basis of statistical considerations (sampling, dependence observations) can also leave the choice unresolved because of competing alternatives (Burstein, 1975a, 1978b; Burstein and Smith, 1977; Glendening, 1976; Haney, 1974).

Concerns about units of analysis in the evaluation of Project Follow Through exemplify the dilemma. Haney (1974) cites four general types of considerations: (1) the purpose of the evaluation (questions to be addressed), (2) the evaluation design (nature of treatments, independence of units and treatment effects, appropriate size), (3) statistical considerations (reliability of measures, degrees of freedom, analysis techniques), and (4) practical considerations (missing data, policy research, multiple year comparisons, economy). Haney was unable to choose among units because the purpose of the evaluation dictated the child as the unit but the unit of treatment was the classroom; moreoever, the multiyear character of Follow Through made classrooms impractical as units of analysis.

Cronbach (1976:1.3a–1.19) also considers the units of analysis problem as presented by the Cline et al. (1974) report on Follow Through. Cline et al. had analyzed the data at the individual, class, and school levels but emphasized the school level in their report. Cronbach (1976:1.5) supports this emphasis on the grounds that treatments were assigned to schools and program delivery probably varied from school to school. Thus, Cronbach's choice puts him at odds with Haney (1974), although they both recognize the problems in arriving at a choice.

Thinking of the analysis of multilevel data as a problem in the choice of a unit of analysis is not a very penetrating perception. Phenomena of importance occur at all levels and need to be described and subjected to inference making (Burstein, 1978a; Burstein and Linn, 1976; Burstein, Linn, and Capell, 1978; Cronbach, 1976). Haney's arguments on this issue are succinct and to the point:

> Investigators ought to have a strong bias for studying various properties of the educational system at the level at which they occurs; . . . variation in attributes of interest ought to be studied at those levels (or between those units) at which it does (or is expected to) occur. . . . If the hypotheses are explicitly stated in terms of mathematical models, the impact of shifting levels of analysis from one unit of analysis to another will be much more easily assessed than if they are not. (1974:96–97)

Given the above, an emphasis on the choice of a substantive analytical model rather than on making a choice among competing units of analysis is the more reasonable and tenable position to adopt if an investigator's goal is to learn something about the question one set out to answer. Moreover, the multilevel character of educational data requires analytical models suited to the identification of educational effects at and within each level of the educational system. Thus, it is arguable that analyses of educational data should be conducted at more than a single level and that when questions about the outcomes of groups of individuals are to be addressed, measures in addition to group means require attention. These points are considered in the remainder of the chapter.

Different Questions Addressed and Different Variables Measured at Different Levels

Results from analyses at the group and individual levels often conflict because the analyses bear on different substantive questions (Cronbach, 1976: 1.9; see also Scheuch, 1966, and the papers in Dogan and Rokkan, 1969). The decision about which questions the investigator wants to address remains to be made.

Examples of Group Level Questions. While we have argued that models with individual level outcomes should be the primary method for educational effects research, we can envision situations in which the policy questions of interest warrant a different choice. The California Assessment program and the issue of school finance reform in California provide two illustrative cases. One purpose of the California Assessment Program is to inform school districts about the adequacy of the achievement of the district's schools. The testing program can also provide data to help districts single out "unusually" poor achieving schools for special remedial services. Neither of these uses of the data seems to require the specification of pupil level educational effects models.

The pertinence of school or school district questions to the school finance reform issue is based on similar reasoning. Policymakers can be expected to ask how the reorganization of educational finance in California will equalize resources available to schools and school districts and whether any changes in resource allocations influence educational outcomes at the school and district level. These are clearly questions dealing with educational organizations, and they require the analyst to seek answers at the level at which they are addressed. Hannan, Freeman, and Meyer (1976) present a related example about the influence of administrative intensity on organizational effectiveness.

In citing these examples, we have not forgotten our earlier assertion of the prominent role of individual level data. Each example represents a paradigm shift away from the questions that guided Averch et al. (1972) and that dominate educational effects research. Nonetheless, the question each example addresses has important policy implications. Moreover, manipulation of macrolevel educational conditions in response to these questions may alter the processes operating at the microlevel.

Changes in Variable Meaning. The process of aggregating data across group members can change the meaning of variables that enter a particular regression model at different levels (Burstein, 1975a; Burstein, Fischer, and Miller, 1978; Burstein and Miller, 1978; Cronbach, 1976; Scheuch, 1966, 1969). That is, measured variables in studies of educational effects typically serve as indicators for some latent construct (ability, background quality, educational quality). By aggregating a specific variable over students within schools (classrooms), we can change the latent construct for which the variable serves as a proxy.

An example of the shift in meaning across levels is the variable father's occupation. Father's occupation is perhaps the most frequently used indicator of the home and socioeconomic background of a pupil. At the level of the individual, it conveys the parental investment (nurturance, environmental support for academic achievement) in the child's learning efforts. This investment can directly affect the academic motivation of the child by supplementing or detracting from in-school learning efforts. In this sense, father's occupation and other family background measures represent both a base and a supplement for the educational process.

When aggregated over the pupils that attend a given school, measures of family background describe community characteristics (wealth, urbanism, etc.). Differences among schools in aggregate indexes of background can also reflect variation in social policies governing the organization, content, and administration of education. These social policies can also determine the way in which the distribution of social and economic resources outside the school constrains resource allocation to education.

More concretely, community wealth and attitude toward education affect the type of programs offered, the content emphasis of the school, and the role of the parents in the administration of school programs. Community characteristics can also determine the school's ability to seek better qualified teachers, higher quality materials, and better physical facilities. State and national funding of educational programs also fosters relationships between community characteristics and school organization and resources.

Within schools (classrooms), a pupil's family background can take on a different meaning through its role in the conferral of status (Alexander, Cook, and McDill, 1978; Heyns, 1974; see also the discussion of frog-pond effects above). The student's relative socioeconomic background can affect both teacher and peer behaviors toward the child. Likewise, relative background can cause the student to respond differently out of a sense of relative advantage or disadvantage.

Recent empirical work with data from the IEA studies (Burstein, 1977; Burstein, Fischer, and Miller, 1978; Burstein and Miller, 1978) illustrates the distinct differences in interpretation of family background effects, particularly when one moves from a between school to a within school analysis. In this investigation of science achievement data, between school and corresponding pooled within school educational effects models for fourteen year olds from the United States and Sweden were compared. The effects of family background were substantial, as usual, in the between school analysis of the U. S. data, but much smaller in the same analysis of Swedish data (Table 3–8). In fact, in Sweden $R^2_{\text{Between Students}}$ was larger than $R^2_{\text{Between Schools}}$, which would not occur in analyses of typical U. S. data. In contrast, the effects of family background in the pooled within school analyses for United States were substantially smaller than they were in the between school analyses. In fact, the within school effects for background and ability in the United States were essentially the same as the effects found in the within school of Swedish data.

The results from the between schools analyses were attributed to differences between the countries in the social policies governing the relationship between pupil backgrounds and school resources— the predominance of local control and community determination of resources in the United States versus national control and a policy of uniformity of resources (e.g., curriculum offerings) in Sweden. The within school results suggest that the role of pupil background and ability in the interpersonal allocations of rewards operates similarly within American and Swedish schools. Within school reward mechanisms appear to be resistant to the factors governed by the social policy orientation of the country (e.g., curriculum diversity).

Empirical analyses from two national educational systems were juxtaposed to highlight the potential benefits of considering variables measured at different levels as reflecting different constructs. Whether treating different states or different large school districts in the same fashion will yield equally striking distinctions across levels and across comparison groups within levels remains to be seen.

Table 3-8. Between Student, Between School,[a] and Pooled Within School Regression Analyses of Factors Affecting Science Achievement (RSCI) for Fourteen Year Olds from the IEA Study (N students = 1,806 [U.S.]; 1,675 [Sweden]; N schools = 107 [U.S.]; 93 [Sweden]).

Variable	Between School		Metric Regression Coefficient Pooled Within School		Between Student	
	United States	Sweden	United States	Sweden	United States	Sweden
SEX	−6.620 (3.90)[b]	−3.362+ (1.68)	−3.853* (11.30)	−5.281 (14.18)	−4.157 (11.87)	−5.165 (13.68)
RWK	.876 (6.47)	.569+ (3.24)	.812 (21.53)	.773 (18.36)	.861 (23.22)	.754 (18.02)
POPSOCC	.843 (2.87)	.194+ (.67)	.307* (3.91)	.297 (3.64)	.487 (6.39)	.256 (3.26)
BOKHOM	3.577 (3.37)	1.217+ (.92)	1.233* (5.36)	1.324 (5.04)	1.661 (7.20)	1.324 (4.99)
GRADE	1.390 (1.69)	4.186+ (2.49)	2.291* (5.25)	2.941* (7.25)	1.912 (5.24)	3.083 (7.65)
SCISTUDY	.110 (2.34)	−.149+ (2.32)	.065* (3.90)	−.122* (5.70)	.066 (4.29)	−.125 (6.16)
EXPLORE	.240 (1.50)	.382+ (1.10)	.067* (1.25)	−.099* (1.31)	.130 (2.52)	−.064 (.85)
R^2	72	31	31	34	39	34

[a]The between school analyses are run with each school weighted by the numbers of students. However, all t statistics were adjusted to reflect the number of schools rather than the number of students.

[b]The t statistics are reported in parenthesis.

+Between school and within school coefficients with cross-national differences of at least two standard errors.

*Within country variables for which the between school and within school coefficients differ by at least two standard errors.

Source: Burstein, Fischer, and Miller, 1978.

Dependencies among Observations within Groups

The problem of dependencies (correlations) among observations within groups is endemic to research on hierarchically nested school data and can be especially critical when intact classrooms are investigated. Cronbach and Webb (Cronbach, 1976; Cronbach and Webb, 1975; Webb, 1977) have argued that when intact groups are assigned to instructional treatments, the students in those treatments cannot be considered as independent units. Therefore, the typical analyses based on all individuals pooled across groups can be justifiably criticized.

There are basically two issues associated with dependencies among observations—the effects of dependence on standard statistical analyses and the substantive interpretation of dependence as information on educational processes within groups. In the statistical literature, robustness to within group dependence is of primary interest; the dependence is considered to be a nuisance. For educational data, however, dependence may provide important substantive information. Different kinds and different measures of within group dependence are discussed below.

Dependence and Statistical Analysis. Educational treatments are not administered independently to individuals; individuals within the classroom have shared experiences. This dependence among individuals within the group can be expressed by an intraclass correlation structure. The consequences of ignoring this intraclass structure (i.e., treating individuals as independent by ignoring group membership) are serious (Walsh, 1947; Weibull, 1953).

A thorough discussion of the problem of dependency among observations in the experimental design frame of reference is provided by Glendening (1976). Glendening simulated the effects of violating the assumption of independence within the context of a balanced, two level hierarchically nested design, with subjects nested within classrooms and classrooms nested within treatments. She found that a model with the pupil as the unit or a conditional model where a preliminary test of independence is followed by a choice of the appropriate unit of analysis for testing treatment effects yielded spuriously small error terms and, therefore, led to liberal tests of treatment effects. Glendening concluded that the researcher must choose a priori between the class (dependence) or student (independence) as the unit, but acknowledged the complications of obtaining prior knowledge about independence of response.

The statistical problem considered by Glendening also arises in the regression context. The kinds of dependencies considered so far are reflected in correlations among the residuals within groups. Obviously, such dependencies have serious consequences for the robustness of statistical tests of educational effects.

Dependence as Information on Educational Processes. Undoubtedly, research on must educational phenomena will involve dependent observations. But dependency is not an all or none phenomenon, it is a matter of degree. It is a function of what is being measured (the outcomes) and the "treatments" or "causes" under study. It is also a function of the composition of the groups and the nature of the grouping mechanism (Webb, 1977; also see below).

Rather than assume complete dependency or independency, it seems more reasonable to acknowledge that dependencies exist, but dependency may vary across groups or even among pairs of persons within groups. This line of reasoning shifts the focus to efforts to measure within group dependency directly. In this way, the investigator can adjust standard analyses of treatment effects for actual dependencies among observations and/or assess the antecedents of within group dependencies and the direct effects of dependencies on educational outcomes. In the latter sense, the variation of dependency across groups characterizes within group processes in a convenient metric that can in turn be used to explain educational performance.

We can approach the question of the source and consequences of within group dependency from both theoretical and empirical perspectives, focusing on the class as the group of interest. At a theoretical level, it is important to distinguish between "additive" effects and "proportional" effects (Glendening, 1976). Additive effects are shifts in the level of performance. Thus, between teacher differences (within the same treatment condition) are additive effects that will be assessed as intraclass relationships using standard methods of estimation. However, each child could be taught independently of all others taught by the same teacher. In this case, the estimated intraclass relationship is not a result of interpersonal relationships; instead, it is only an indicator of differing levels of teacher effectiveness.

Proportional effects are changes in the variation within a group (class), making it either more or less heterogeneous than a random collection of independent units. Proportional effects may result from interpersonal interactions. That is, if students were taught independently, they should not tend to increase or decrease in variability except when an additive effect creates a pseudoproportional effect (e.g., by raising one group to a ceiling level on the outcome measure).

In concrete terms, the distinctions between additive and proportional within class dependencies revolve around the uniformity or variability of the effects. If Teacher A taught the entire class how to work a specific type of algebra problem that no student would have been able to answer otherwise, an additive effect for Teacher A has been induced—that is, every student's score is incremented by the same amount. If, instead, some of Teacher A's students had benefited from being taught but others had not (due to inattention, lack of ability to comprehend the instruction, or whatever), there is a proportional effect from being taught by Teacher A. Students were affected differently according to their attention or ability.

Unfortunately, the classical method for estimation of the dependency among observations within groups does not distinguish between additive and proportional effects. Either could be the source of the observed intraclass correlation $\hat{\rho}_I$. Efforts to assess directly the dependency among observations within each class would be of value.

Present methods of characterizing the homogeneity of instruction within classrooms may be insensitive to important educational effects. To portray a class as largely individualized or teacher directed does not convey how classroom structuring and interpersonal dynamics (peer relations, teacher praise, group cohesiveness) interact to form the eudcational treatment received by each student. Better measures of similarity (or dissimilarity) of instruction across students within classrooms need to be developed. Perhaps a measure of within class dependency can capture certain aspects of this element of educational effects.

When carefully measured, within class dependency indexes are surely more proximal descriptors of classroom processes than are designations such as individualized, open, or traditional. The British study of open education by Bennett (1976) would have certainly been less provocative and more informative if it had approached the differences in instructional styles from this perspective.

There is no general method for estimating within group dependency in a naturalistic study. Even the most careful data collection efforts in actual classrooms barely scratch the surface as far as the question of degree of dependency in instruction is concerned. A logical next step might be exploratory studies with empirical data like that collected by the Far West Laboratory (FWL) in the Beginning Teacher Evaluation Study (BTES) (Fisher et al., 1978).

The FWL collected extensive and detailed information on a sample of pupils and their learning conditions and activities from second and fifth grade classrooms. The data include daily teacher logs; allocations of time in specific content areas in reading and mathematics for each sample pupil; observational data on instructional topics, difficulty of material, instructional settings, and learning and instructor moves for the same sample of children for whom the teachers kept logs. Over the school year, there were approximately twenty-two days of observation per classroom.

The FWL reports on instructional time allocations and teacher behaviors (cf., e.g., Dishaw, 1977; Filby and Fisher, 1977) reflect both diversity of practices across classrooms and variation in the homogeneity of practices within classrooms. For example, in fifth grade math instruction, there were classes with high, but uniform average daily time allocated to mathematics (e.g., a mean of sixty-four minutes with a standard deviation of two, classes with low but uniform allocations (e.g., twenty minutes with a standard deviation of two), and classes with allocations that varied across children (e.g., averages of thirty-three and forty-seven minutes with standard deviations of thirteen minutes). Within specific content areas, between class and within class fluctuations in allocated time were also dramatic—from classes with an average of one minute per day on fractions (s.d. = 1) to a class with twenty-three minutes per day (s.d. = 1) to yet another class within twenty-nine minutes per day (s.d. = 22!). The percentage of total time in small group and whole class settings varied from 9 to 51 percent for these classes, while the percentage of total time devoted to substantive teacher behaviors (explanations, academic monitoring, and feedback) varied from 7 to 33 percent. As a group, the types of indicators described from the BTES study and the variation in practices exhibited by the data suggest that this data source is a fruitful point of departure for investigating within class dependencies.

In terms of the consequences of dependencies, there are potential benefits from experimental studies of the effects of learning in group and in individual settings. Webb (1977) compared learning in interacting groups and learning singly, attempting to explain differences as a function of the characteristics of the individual, the group, and the group process. Her group process results provided a key to understanding why some students learned best in interacting groups, whereas others did best learning singly. In general, group members who actively participated in discussions did better than those who did not, and they did at least as well as after individual learning. Whether a pupil actively participated was related to the pupil's ability ranking within the group and to the range of ability in the group. Knowing the abilities of the students in a group, one could predict fairly well who interacted with whom and, consequently, who did best.

The results of this highly structured study suggest that knowledge of group processes in a particular class is crucial for understanding the degree to which students are working together—and therefore crucial for estimating degree of dependence in the class. Webb (1977) suggests that her procedures may be generalized to real teacher taught classrooms, considering the interactions between teachers and students, interactions among students, and characteristics of classmates (abilities, personality variables) and teachers. In the long run, one hopes to be able to predict student performance from a combination of these variables.

CHOICE OF AN APPROPIRATE ANALYTICAL MODEL

In the preceding sections, a case has been made that consideration of the multilevel properties of educational data is both a central and a complex part of the specification of educational effects. To be sure, the complications due to cross-level inference, the identification of group effects on microlevel outcomes, and the determination of appropriate units of analysis are important question. But each should be simply a part of a more fundamental activity—the development of an adequate theory of educational processes and the determination of analytical methods for identifying the effects of such processes.

Thus, as with most social science inquiry, appropriate analyses of multilevel educational data depend on the investigator's ability to (1) identify the questions of interest, (2) elaborate a theory that can provide evidence about these questions, and (3) determine analytical methods suitable for investigating the theory. In the remainder of this chapter, we focus on theoretical consideratinos in determining suitable analytical methods for multilevel educational data and discuss briefly several approaches that may be useful.

Factors Influencing Choice of Analytical Model

Although there are numerous technical considerations involved in the specification of educational effects, the choice among analytical models need not be a methodological decision. In the final analysis, the substantive questions being addressed determine the choice of a model. The types of processes and the types of outcomes under investigation, as well as the type of study, enter into the decision process.

For example, what may be a reasonable analytical model for the effects of instruction or of a program on a short-range outcome (e.g., an achievement test at the end of an instructional unit) loses its salience when generalizations, especially time-dependent ones, are desired (Burstein, 1978a; Wittrock in Wittrock and Wiley, 1970). Nevertheless, instructional psychologists interested in the impact of a well-circumscribed instructional unit should have little difficulty selecting a model.

On the other hand, the sociologist studying school effects, the evaluator investigating program effectiveness, or the stratification theorist focusing on the educational determinants of socioeconomic achievement deal with a more complex educational history. This history cannot be simply described by instruction in a single classroom or, for that matter, in a single school at a given time. Moreover, when the phenomena under study are dynamic rather than static, the required exercise in model specification is much more difficult.

Another distinctly substantive constraint on the specification of analytical models can be found in comparing educational effects research in elementary schools with similar research in secondary schools. In the elementary grades, instruction in a single classroom with a specific teacher and a complement of classmates is the norm. Moreover, at least in the lower grades, effects of such factors as relative status and peer group aspiration are weak if they exist at all. Most of the effects of schooling on the educational performance of grade school children are mediated by the teacher. The degree to which the teacher organizes an instructional program to meet student needs and to motivate participation determines the educational performance of the student over and above the student's entering levels of ability and motivation.

The forces influencing individual educational performance are different in secondary schools. Students receive instruction from several teachers. Thus, performance in one subject (e.g., physics) may be influenced by the quality of instruction in another (e.g., mathematics). Curriculum diversity (the curricular options available to the student) also enters the picture. For example, public-speaking skills cannot be affected by speech classes if such classes are not offered. Peer group influence, extracurricular activities, and school spirit might also affect the performance of high school students.

Clearly, models for analyzing educational effects at the elementary level need to emphasize accurate assessment of the role of the classroom and the teacher and to be sensitive to the dependencies associated with instruction in intact groups. Classroom level and within classroom analyses are likely to be required. In contrast, educational effects models at the secondary level would perhaps include the instructional investments from several courses, measures of curriculum diversity, peer influences, and indexes of school "atmosphere." The dependencies among students associated with specific classes and teachers are probably weak, but school level dependencies may be strong. Students take different sequences of courses during the day, but are constrained by the available offerings and overall climate. School level and pooled within school analyses deserve to be emphasized, although for certain types of outcomes, class level and pooled within class analyses should be conducted.

An endless number of additional examples can be provided, but the point is clear. The problems associated with the analysis of multilevel data vary according to the type of study, the types of outcomes, and the types of processes under investigation. Moreover, much remains to be learned about choosing the appropriate analytical models in some areas (e.g., nonexperimental longitudinal studies of teacher effects).

Decomposition of Educational Effects

It was asserted above that analyses of multilevel data should be conducted at more than a single level. Also, in the substantive discussion of contextual and frog-pond effects, we described processes that may affect group level outcomes, within group outcomes, or both. In this section,[3] a general discussion of the decomposition of educational effects into those between groups and those within groups is presented, and several approaches to analyzing data in this fashion are described briefly. To simplify matters, only a two level (pupils and classes) model is considered, and all equations are expressed in terms of population parameters. Perfect measurement of all variables is also assumed.

Once membership in a specific class is acknowledged (i.e., instruction from a specific teacher), any measure that varies over pupils can be decomposed into its between class (teacher) and within class (teacher) components. That is, the posttest or outcome performance, Y_{ij}, of pupil j in class i ($j = 1, \ldots, n$ persons per class; $i = 1, \ldots, K$ classes; for simplicity, we assume equal-sized classes) can be decomposed into

$$Y_{ij} \quad = \quad \mu_Y \quad + \quad (\mu_{Y_i} - \mu_Y) \quad + \quad (Y_{ij} - \mu_{Y_i}).$$

| individual outcome | grand mean | between class effect for class i | within class effect per person ij |

$$(3.19)$$

If, in addition, we consider the performance level, X_{ij}, of the pupil prior to entering the class (i.e., the pretest or some measure of entering ability on the same scale as Y), the relation of X_{ij} to Y_{ij} is given by

$$Y_{ij} = \mu_Y + \beta_t(X_{ij} - \mu_X) + \epsilon_{1ij},$$

where β_t is the coefficient from the between student (total) regression of Y_{ij} on X_{ij}.

The regression of Y_{ij} on X_{ij} can also be decomposed into between class and within class components. Following Cronbach (1976: 3.1–3.11), this decomposition can be written as

$$Y_{ij} = \mu_Y + \beta_b(\mu_{X_i} - \mu_X) \qquad \text{predicted between class}$$

$$+ (\mu_{Y_i} - \mu_Y) - \beta_b(\mu_{X_i} - \mu_X) \qquad \text{adjusted between class effect}$$

$$+ \beta_w(X_{ij} - \mu_{X_i}) \qquad \text{pooled within class}$$

$$+ (\beta_i - \beta_w)(X_{ij} - \mu_{X_i}) \qquad \text{specific within class}$$

$$+ \epsilon_{2ij}. \qquad \text{specific residual associated with person } ij$$

$$(3.20)$$

In the above equation, β_b is the between class slope from the regression of μ_{Y_i} on μ_{X_i}, β_w is the pooled within class slope from the regression of $Y_{ij} - \mu_{Y_i}$ on $X_{ij} - \mu_{X_i}$ across all classrooms, and β_i is the specific within class slope from the regression of Y_{ij} on X_{ij} within the ith classroom.

Each of the four components of the decomposition reflect the influence of educational processes (between classes, within classes, or both). Possible substantive interpretations of each component are offered below.

Between Class Slopes. The magnitude of β_b, the between class slope, provides an indication of the extent to which initial differences in the mean performance levels in a set of classrooms are maintained, exaggerated, or reduced at a later measurement occasion. If positive, as it typically would be, β_b reflects the tendency for classes with highest mean inputs to have high mean outcomes. A low value of β_b implies little dependence of class mean outcomes on average initial performance. A weak influence of entering characteristics can be the result of a "compensatory effect," whereby instructional resources are allocated between classes in an equalizing or redistributive manner.

Adjusted Between Class Effects. The adjusted between class effects reflect the impact of the specific teacher or class on the mean outcome of its pupils after controlling for the effects of mean inputs on mean outcomes. Included in adjusted class effects are the main effects of the teacher, plus such things as unusual group cohesiveness or disharmony, high or low quality program delivery (e.g., well-structured, individualized instruction), and average error of measurement of Y_{ij} for the class.

In any event, large positive adjusted classroom effects may be an indication of exemplary educational practices. Whatever analysis strategy is employed should generate accurate estimates of this teacher-class effect on mean outcome and perhaps should identify generalizable characteristics of teachers or classes achieving large effects.

Pooled Within Class Slopes. The pooled or common within class slope, β_w, reflects the tendency across all classes for students above the class average on input to do better or worse than the rest of the class on the outcome measure. The interpretation of β_w parallels that of β_b; the former refers to the consistent tendencies in within class processes and the latter deals with corresponding tendencies for class averages.

Estimation of the common within class regression is of value in the study of teacher-class effects. The pooled within class slope, β_w, provides an indication of the overall redistributive properties of classroom instruction for the school population represented in the study. If policymakers and educators are intent on raising the relative performance of youth of low ability and low socioeconomic status through specific instructional practices, β_w reflects the magnitude of the problem they will encounter.

Specific Within Class Slopes. Differences among educational programs in their pooled within class slopes can be given substantive interpretations and can be the basis for the policy decision. The interpretation of slope differences proffered here falls within the domain of aptitutde-treatment interaction (ATI) research (Cronbach, 1976; Cronbach and Webb, 1975; Snow, 1976). The logic of ATI research is built on the substantive significance of differences in within treatment slopes.

We can carry the ATI logic one step farther to the level of the individual classroom. The within class regression of pupil outcome on pupil inputs (denoted by β_i) is likely to vary across classrooms. Cronbach (1976:316) cites as sources of the variation in β_i: (1) sampling variability due to chance and stability problems due to small class sizes when the processes operating in the classes are the same, (2) differences in the selection factors forming the classes, and (3) differences in causal processes going on in the classrooms. This last source encompasses the possibility that some teachers or classes have relatively greater compensatory (redistributive) effects than others.

Variation in the β_i is a potentially important source of information for researchers and policymakers, especially when such information is combined with the adjusted between class effects discussed earlier. Specific within class slopes gain salience in educational research primarily because the β_i are class level indexes that may reflect actual within class processes. The isolation of classroom process variables that are associated with the magnitude of β_i could have considerable policy implications. In a later section on alternative measures of group outcomes, we consider heterogeneous within group slopes along with other indexes of group outcomes and elaborate further our view of how heterogeneous slopes can arise in practice.

Selected Analytical Strategies for Multilevel Data

The above discussion highlights the complexities in specifying educational effects in multilevel educational data. The investigator who conducts only a between group, between student (total), or pooled within group analysis will fail to identify (or will misspecify) certain educational effects—assuming all four types exist.

Several investigators (Burstein and Linn, 1976; Burstein, Linn, and Capell, 1978; Cronbach and Webb, 1975; Hannan and Young, 1976b; Keesling, 1976; Keesling and Wiley, 1974; Young and Erbring, 1976) have suggested approaches for analyzing multilvel data that identify combinations of the components from the decomposition. Some approaches are heuristic or pragmatic, while others are based on strong theories about the educative process. Several of the approaches (Burstein and Linn, 1976; Hannon and Young, 1976b; Keesling, 1976; Young and Erbring, 1976) were first presented at an NIE conference, "Methodology for Aggregating Data in Educational Research." Unfortunately, little is known about these approaches, because only limited additional analytical and empirical work has been conducted. Each approach is briefly described below.

Between Group, Pooled Within Group Analysis (Cronbach, 1976; Cronbach and Webb, 1975). Cronbach (1976:10.3 ff.) asserts that the usual overall between student analysis combines two kinds of relationships—those operating between collectives and those operating among persons within collectives—into a composite that is rarely of substantive interest. In fact, as noted by Cronbach, β_t, the overall between student regression, has been shown by Duncan, Cuzzort, and Duncan (1961) to be a composite of the between group regression, β_b, and the pooled within group regression, β_w. Therefore, Cronbach (1976; Cronbach and Webb, 1975) recommends that the between group effects and individuals within group effects be examined separately.

With a single class level measure, T, a single measure of student input, X, and a single student level outcome measure, Y, Cronbach's strategy would require the inspection of the following two regression equations:

$$\mu_{Y_i} = \mu_Y + \beta_{\overline{Y}\,\overline{X}\cdot T}(\mu_{X_i} - \mu_X) + \beta_{\overline{Y}\,T\cdot\overline{X}}(T_i - \mu_T) + \omega_{1i}; \quad (3.21)$$

$$Y_{ij} = \mu_{Y_i} + \beta_w(X_{ij} - \mu_{X_i}) + \epsilon_{3ij}. \quad (3.22)$$

In the above, $\beta_{\overline{Y}\,\overline{X}\cdot T}$, $\beta_{\overline{Y}\,T\cdot\overline{X}}$, and β_w parallel or equal three of the components in the decomposition (the between class slope, the adjusted class effect, and the pooled within class slope). Cronbach's report does consider specific within group regressions (1976:3.2 ff., 5.5 ff., 8.1 ff., and elsewhere), but mostly indirectly. Cronbach concludes (1976:5.5 ff.) that in Anderson's ATI study, the specific within class regressions do not account for much variance (4.1 percent in the "drill" condition and 6.9 percent for the "meaning" condition). Yet, the portions of outcome variance attributable to adjusted class effects are also small (5 percent for drill and 6.9 percent for meaningful).

Thus, although Cronbach emphasizes the consideration of between group and pooled within group effects, his report clearly recognizes the significance of heterogeneous within group regressions. At the same time, he offers no strategy for a systematic examination of the determinants of differences in within class slopes. In the studies he considered, differences in within class slopes that appeared to be significant were generally traceable to anomalous students (e.g., Cronbach, 1976:5.21–22).

Regression Models for Hierarchical Data (Keesling and Wiley, 1974; Wiley, 1976). Keesling and Wiley (1974) proposed a model for disentangling the effects of variables defined solely at the school level from those defined at the pupil level. (We can talk about classes rather than schools without loss of generality.) The process of disentanglement involved two states: (1) the adjustment of the effects of individual background characteristics on outcome for the effects of the classrooms in which the individuals receive instruction and (2) the adjustment of the effects of classroom characteristics for those of the individuals. The adjusted effect estimates and other by-products of the adjustment process are relevant to our interest in the components of the effects on pupil outcomes.

In the Keesling-Wiley model, the adjusted effects of pupil level variables are found by controlling for all outcome-relevant class variables and for any interactions between class and student variables. If no interactions exist, this adjustment leads to estimates of pooled within class slopes, β_w. Keesling and Wiley's only comment on the effect of significant heterogeneity of regression is to indicate that such a condition would preclude using the same adjustment algorithm for each class.

The second stage of the Keesling and Wiley model uses the adjusted effects of individual level variables, aggregated over pupils within classes, to determine the adjusted effects of class level variables. In practice, they apply equation (3.22) to obtain individual outcome scores—that is,

$$\hat{Y}_{ij} = \mu_{Y_i} + \beta_w (X_{ij} - \mu_{X_i}).$$

Then the predicted mean outcome for each class based on the pooled within class slope is determined:

$$\hat{\mu}_{Y_i} = \mu_Y + \beta_w (\mu_{X_i} - \mu_X).$$

Finally, a model is fitted at the class level regressing the observed mean outcome for each class on class level explanatory variables and the predicted mean outcomes for each class:

$$\mu_{Y_i} = \gamma_0 + \gamma_T T_i + \lambda \hat{\mu}_{Y_i} + \phi_i, \tag{3.23}$$

where γ_T is the adjusted effect of the class level variable T, and λ allows partial removal of additional specification bias due to omission of class level variables that are correlated with the sum of the average individual level effect values represented in $\hat{\mu}_{Y_i}$. If all relevant class level variables are included, $\lambda = 1$.

In this model, γ_T is analogous to the adjusted teacher-classroom effects from a between class analysis in the style of Cronbach. The key distinction between γ_T in equation (3.23) and $\beta_{\overline{Y}_T \cdot \overline{X}}$ in the between class analyses of means from Cronbach is that the means of individual level explanatory variables (the μ_{X_i}) have been multiplied by the constant β_w, the estimated pooled within class slope. Since a linear transformation of the μ_{X_i}s does not affect their relationship to other explanatory variables, for a single class level variable,

$$\gamma_T = \beta_{\overline{Y}_T \cdot \overline{X}}.$$

Thus the Keesling-Wiley analysis provides the same information about adjusted teacher-class effects as Cronbach's does.

The information conveyed in the estimates of λ may be important. It can be shown that for a single class level explanatory variable, T, and a single individual level variable, X,

$$\lambda = \frac{\beta_{\overline{Y}\,\overline{X} \cdot T}}{\beta_w}.$$

But, if it is assumed that within class slopes are homogeneous and that no other class level variables affect the average individual level explanatory variables (the μ_{X_i}), $\lambda = 1$. This implies that for properly specified models,

$$\beta_{\overline{Y}\,\overline{X} \cdot T} = \beta_w.$$

The implication of the last step is that there is no class level relationship of μ_{Y_i} to μ_{X_i} beyond that conveyed by the pooled within class slope. That is, there are no class level effects of aggregate explanatory variables. The above also implies that departures of λ from one indicate the presence of specification error such as the exclusion of a relevant individual level variable or perhaps the presence of heterogeneity of within class slopes.

Empirical work with artificial data (Burstein, Linn, and Capell, 1978) indicates that the value of λ is influenced by systematic relationships between within class slopes, β_i, and teacher-class effects, T_i. If these results hold up under more careful scrutiny, the Keesling-Wiley strategy deserves much more attention that it has received thus far.

Slopes at Outcomes (Burstein, 1976a; Burstein and Linn, 1976; Burstein, Linn, and Capell, 1978). In contrast to Cronbach and to Keesling and Wiley, the examination of slopes as outcomes (Burstein,

1976a; Burstein and Linn, 1976; Burstein, Linn, and Capell, 1978) emphasizes the specific within class slopes. The analysis of the pooled within slope represents the fall-back position in case the analysis of the β_i produces no interpretable antecedents of slope heterogeneity.

The steps in the slopes as outcomes analysis are:

1. For each class, find

$$Y_{ij} = \mu_{Y_i} + \beta_1 (X_{ij} - \mu_{X_i}) + \epsilon_{4ij}.$$

2. Fit a model at the class level with μ_{Y_i} (see equation [3.21] and β_i as outcomes and class level (or higher level) explanatory variables as independent variables. The equation for β_i is given by

$$\beta_i = \theta_o + \theta_T T_i + \theta_X \overline{X} + \omega_{2i}. \tag{3.24}$$

The adjusted teacher-class effects in the slopes as outcomes analysis are $\beta_{\overline{Y}_T \cdot \overline{X}}$ in equation (3.21) and θ_T in equation (3.24). Thus, the adjusted teacher-class effects on class means are the same as in the Cronbach and the Keesling and Wiley analyses. The regression of the within class slopes on teacher-class quality measures presumably identifies antecedents of heterogeneity of within class regressions. That is, θ_T may reflect systematic effects of teacher-class characteristics on slopes. This interpretation of θ_T is directly relevant to an elaboration of the components of teacher-class effects on pupil outcomes.

Pooled Cross-Sections and Time-Series Analysis (Hannan and Young, 1976b). An analytical strategy that has some theoretical appeal for dealing with the problems of dependencies among observations within groups can be found in the econometric literature on pooling cross-sections and time series. Hannan and Young (1976b) discuss the similarities in the problems that arise in analysis of multiwave panel data and multilevel cross-sectional data. In particular, they argue that the application of the logic developed for multiwave panels (Nerlove, 1971; Maddala, 1971) to multilevel analysis problems would clarify issues in current work.

In practice, Hannan and Young (1976b) propose the application of generalized least-squares (GLS) estimation procedures to measure the intraclass correlation among pupil disturbances within classrooms. Their GLS procedures amount to a scheme for weighting pooled within group and between group estimates to provide efficient estimation of the desired parameters in the context of intra-class correlation among persons within groups.

Hannan and Young present neither simulated or empirical data to illustrate their approach in the context of the multilevel analysis problem. Furthermore, their presentation assumes constant ρ (i.e., constant dependency among persons within groups and the same magnitude for all groups). The latter problem may not be serious, since with a priori rules for partitioning the variance-covariance matrix of disturbances, ρ can be varied across classrooms to reflect possible variation in intraclass correlations for different configura-tions (e.g., individualized versus whole group instruction). Obviously, further investigations of the Hannan-Young approach are needed under conditions of presumed constant or variable intraclass corre-lations.

Components of Covariance Analysis (Keesling, 1976, 1978). Keesling (1976), 1978) pointed out that the observed variances and covariances used in the typical between group analysis (e.g., equation [3.21]) are generally combinations of both between group and with-in group components of variance and of covariance. His reasonging is based on the analogies between standard analysis of variance esti-mates of treatment effects and the estimation of group effects in hierarchically nested school data.

Keesling starts from the multivariate random effects model.

$$Y_{ij} = \mu + b_i + e_{ij}$$

($i = 1, \ldots, k$ groups, $j = 1, \ldots, n$ persons within each group of equal size). The covariance matrix for the Y_{ij} can be written as

$$\Sigma_Y = \Sigma_b + \Sigma, \tag{3.25}$$

where Σ_y, Σ_b, and Σ are the population variance-covariance matrixes from the between student, between group, and within group data. If S and S_b are the sample variance-covariance matrixes, maximum likelihood estimators of Σ and Σ_b are given by:

$$\hat{\Sigma} = \frac{1}{k(n-1)} S \tag{3.26}$$

and

$$\hat{\Sigma}_b = \frac{1}{k} \left(\frac{N}{k} S_b - \hat{\Sigma} \right). \tag{3.27}$$

Keesling argues that there may be some interest in specifying different relational models for the between components and the within components of covariance matrix. He also describes analytical techniques from Schmidt (1969) for obtaining separate estimates of the two matrixes.

Of value in their own right, the ideas suggested by Keesling are all the more interesting because of the possibilities of linking work on the analysis of multilevel data to the developments in the analysis of covariance structures (Jöreskog, 1970). Keesling's later paper (1978) provides an example of how such a linkage might proceed.

Multilevel Feedback Model of Contextual (Classroom) Effects (Young and Erbring, 1976). The primary contribution by Young and Erbring to the methodology for analyzing multilevel data is to redirect the arguments on the statistical existence of contextual effects toward questions about how to specify more accurately the model underlying the group level processes. As a result, Young and Erbring expect that spurious interpretations of the statistical results on contextual effects will be reduced.

Young and Erbring assert that even when it is recognized that many contextual effects are spurious, some intrinsic group properties may still remain. They prefer not to define context in statistical terms, but assume that there are real group processes. They suggest starting by specifying the process rather than the effect.

Once specified, the group processes are described by models incorporating endogenous feedback: if performance of one student affects the performance of others, notions such as dyadic linkages, mutual awareness, and face-to-face interaction become relevant. Exogenous variables such as pupil ability and family background feed back into the system through classroom interactions.

According to Young and Erbring, the models required to identify the effects of group process are simultaneous equation systems. The simultaneous nature of the equations, even using reduced forms, poses difficult estimation problems requiring special methods (Mitchell, 1969).

The approaches suggested by Hannan and Young, by Keesling, and by Young and Erbring draw heavily on structural equation methods adapted from econometrics. In general, such approaches require correct specification of models based on strong theories about the substantive processes under investigation and on reliable and valid measures of the variables in the model. Unfortunately, current research on the effects of education is relatively primitive when judged by structural modeling standards.

At the same time, however, further work with these approaches is warranted. Until we have had an opportunity to delineate further the similarities and differences among approaches when applied to large-scale educational investigations, it would be inappropriate to exclude any one approach from consideration solely on the basis of the inability of the educational profession to comprehend it or to put it to immediate use.

Alternative Measures of Group Outcomes

Above, it was suggested that analyses of group means can lead to mistaken impressions about the effects of education on pupil performance. Analytical approaches were described that, in one form or another, were intended to ameloriate the difficulties by taking into account the multilevel character of the data.

At this point we approach the problem from the perspective of alternative measures of group outcomes. Once it is determined that the questions of interest or the statistical considerations warrant analyses of aggregated data, the types of between group effects that one expects to find remain to be specified. In particular, when the purpose is to determine factors affecting pupil performance, analyses of between group (class, school, etc.) means can hide important differences in the within group distribution of pupil outcomes and educational inputs. Different groups can have the same mean performance yet vary on other moments of the groups' distributions (e.g., variances).

A variety of educational theories lend support to the notion that specific instructional practices can affect the within school and within class distribution of pupil performance. Moreover, the use of distributional characteristics in addition to the mean as outcome measures has been demonstrated empirically (Lohnes, 1972; Klitgaard, 1975; Brown and Saks, 1975). In an interesting treatment by Brown and Saks (1975), school district level achievement data for fourth graders from the Michigan Educational Assessment are examined. Weighted district means and standard deviations are the measures of outcome, and separate models are estimated for three community types (cities, suburbs, and rural towns). Three district characteristics (average experience of instructional staff, the ratio of pupils to teachers and professional staff, and the percentage of teachers with masters degrees) are included in the models, along with district level SES and ethnicity measures. Brown and Saks found that only three of the nine coefficients for district effects on mean outcomes were significant, whereas six of the coefficients for effects on standard deviations of outcomes were significant. The use of the district standard deviations was particularly rewarding when looking at suburban areas.

As discussed above, within group slopes of outcome on input can contain important information about substantive educational effects. In classroom research, differences in slopes can arise when the allocation of instructional resources among pupils varies from class to class. The possibility of heterogeneous within class slopes becomes obvious from the diversity of instructional practices that are characterized as either individualized, compensatory, or traditional. All things being equal, we expect that higher ability students make more appropriate instructional decisions and learn at a faster rate than lower ability students in a class that emphasizes individualized instruction with student self-pacing. Regardless of the overall effect on class mean performance, individualization could strengthen the relationship between entering ability and student outcome, thereby exaggerating preexisting differences in pupil skills.

In contrast, another class might emphasize mastery learning, wherein it is expected that most students will master the curriculum content. Or, the teachers might compensate for preexisting differences by investing extra instructional resources in those students with the poorest entering performance. These types of practices may or may not raise the mean performance of the class as a whole. It is likely, however, that such practices would reduce the relationship between entering performance and outcome—that is, such compensatory practices would lead to flatter within class regression of outcome on input.

The types of instructional strategies described above do exist in schools along with what might be called the more traditional pattern—the same instructional program being delivered to all students in the class, with heavy emphasis on whole class activities (lecture, seatwork). While these different types of instructional strategies may start with similar instructional resources, they distribute these resources to individual students in a variety of ways. Thus, it is possible that varying instructional strategies would yield different class mean outcomes, and it is also plausible that different within class slopes would result.

The implications of the scenarios presented above for analysis of educational effects data are straightforward. Instructional practices can be combined with student characteristics and instructional resources to affect the mean outcomes of classrooms or a variety of other distributional properties of outcomes (Brown and Saks, 1975; Burstein, 1976a, 1978a; Burstein, Linn, and Capell, 1978; Linn and Burstein, 1977; Wiley, 1970). In particular, there may be teacher-class effects on the within class regression of outcome on input whether or not there are teacher-class effects on class mean performance. If such slope effects exist, the analysis should take them into account.

Linn and I (Burstein and Linn, 1976; Burstein, Linn, and Capell, 1978) generated hypothetical data to examine the effects of heterogeneous within class slopes on several analytical models for identifying educational effects. It was found that heterogeneous within class slopes can make important differences in identified educational effects when the magnitude of the within class slope is systematically related to class-teacher characteristics. The differences were not swamped by sampling variability in the estimation of slopes; moreover, certain analytical approaches exhibited good properties even in the presence of heterogeneity.

A better test of the potential benefits of within group slopes as outcomes would be empirical evidence that within group slopes are related to school and classroom processes. Results of an analysis of science achievement data on U. S. fourteen year olds in the IEA study (Burstein, 1977, 1978a; Burstein and Miller, 1978) provide evidence of the possible payoff from the slope measure. In this analysis, within school slopes of science achievement on a verbal ability measure (assessed concurrently) were significantly and positively related to school mean responses of pupils on indexes of exposure to science study and of the degree to which pupils reported instructional practices that emphasized exploration (discovery methods of instruction; see Table 3-9.).

The steeper within school slopes with greater opportunities for exposure to instruction and with greater emphasis on individual exploration are consistent with expectations from other research (Bennett, 1976; Sørenson and Hallinan, 1977; Stebbens et al., 1977). They also suggest the need for more fine-grained consideration of slopes as outcomes and for similar investigations with other data sets.

SUMMARY COMMENTS

I have attempted to discuss the major issues about the role of levels of analysis in the specification of educational effects. The key points that either guided or grew out of the study can be summarized as follows:

1. Investigations of educational effects are inherently multilevel. That is, education involves students taught by teachers in class-

Table 3-9. School Level Regressions of Means, Standard Deviations, and Slopes on School Means of Background and Schooling Characteristics for Science Achievement of Fourteen Year Olds (N = 107 Schools).

Independent Variables[a]	Dependent Variables[b]					
	Mean	Unstandardized S.D.	Slope	Mean	Standardized S.C.	Slope
RWK	.957* (7.02)[c]	.134 (1.45)	.912* (4.05)	.452	.154	.440
SEX	-6.955* (4.42)	-2.297* (2.16)	-.566* (2.18)	-.219	-.176	-.182
POPOCC	.752* (2.70)	.197 (1.04)	.002 (.04)	.188	.120	.005
BOKHOM	3.729* (3.78)	1.673* (2.51)	-.024 (.15)	.273	.298	-.018
GRADE	1.062 (1.28)	-.559 (1.00)	-.119 (.87)	.071	-.091	-.082
SCISTUDY	.317* (2.33)	.165 (1.80)	.068* (3.03)	.123	.157	.272
EXPLORE	.351* (2.19)	.265* (2.44)	.073* (2.75)	.112	.206	.238
R^2	.77	.34	.37			

[a]The variables are the same as in Table 3-2 except that RWK and SCISTUDY have been modified.

[b]The overall mean, the between student standard deviation, and the between school standard deviation of RSCI are 34.11, 9.47, and 4.57, respectively, in a weighted analysis (mean = 33.47 and s.d. = 5.00 for between schools unweighted analysis). The mean and standard deviation of the within school slopes are .92 and .49, respectively.

[c]the t statistics are in parenthesis.

* Coefficient exceeds twice its standard error.

Source: Burstein and Miller, 1979.

rooms in schools in school districts. Therefore, attempts to specify educational effects involve analyses of multilevel educational data.

2. Research on problems of cross-level inference has shown that analyses of educational effects at different levels reveal substantial differences across levels for specific models. Different variables enter models at different levels. Aggregation typically inflates the estimated effects of background on outcomes and decreases the likelihood of identifying effective teacher-classroom-school characeristics and practices.

3. Analyses involving both individual level and group level effects (contextual analysis) should be based on careful theory in which the source and form of group effects are specifically stated. Moreover, purported group effects should be measured directly.

4. Phenomena of importance occur at all levels of the educational system, and they need to be described and subjected to inference making. Thus, the focus of an investigation of education effects should be on properly specifying the substantive analytical model(s) rather than on making a choice among competing units of analysis.

5. Choices among analytical strategies for multilevel data are not methodological decisions independent of the substantive questions being addressed. The choices are to a large degree constrained by the type of study that one is conducting and by the types of outcomes (e.g., short term–long term; specific-general; cognitive-affective) and processes under investigation.

6. The major measurement issues that affect the specification of education effects in multilevel data involve the identification of adequate measures of outcomes and of the microprocesses in classrooms and schools. With respect to outcomes, measures of group outcomes besides the mean warrant further attention. Moreover, the measurement of classroom and school processes needs to be more directly associated with the educational experiences of individual children. Thus, efforts to achieve better matches between the actual educational "treatment" and the process measures associated with each student involve disaggregation of data and hence multilevel problems.

In rereading these summaries, I find myself returning to the concerns that opened the chapter. Like any other problem in the specification of educational effects, the role of levels of analysis needs to be approached cautiously and tentatively. Caution is necessary because the complexities are great and the natural inclinations of the analyst are to search for parsimony and generalizability.

The above withstanding, this examination of the role of levels of analyses suggests some topics for further investigation. The direct measurement of processes within classrooms and schools is one such topic. Methods are also needed for incorporating these processes in analytical models that focus on the substantive questions guiding the research and that yield outcomes that are easily interpretable as consequences of educational processes.

NOTES

1. The discussion of different types of grouping draws heavily from Hannan, Nielsen, and Young (1975) and Hannan and Young (1976a).
2. This definition of frog-pond effects is perhaps inconsistent with its original use (Davis, 1966; Meyer, 1970). Some authors interpret the coefficient of X_{ij} in equation (3.12) as the frog-pond effect and never actually carry out the analyses based on equation (3.13). However, the analytical consequences of the choice between equations (3.13) and (3.14) are on the estimate of the context effect (i.e., $\beta_{Y\overline{X} \cdot X} \neq \beta_{Y\overline{X} \cdot (X-\overline{X})}$) rather than on the estimate of the frog-pond effect, (i.e., $\beta_{YX \cdot \overline{X}} = \beta_{Y(X-\overline{X}) \cdot \overline{X}}$). So the choice is inconsequential for the substantive interpretations of frog-pond effects.
3. This discussion draws heavily from Burstein, Linn, and Capell (1978) and related papers.

REFERENCES

Aigner, D. J., and Goldfeld, S. M. 1974. "Estimation and Prediction from Aggregate Data When Aggregates Are Measured More Accurately than Their Components." *Econometrics* 42:113-34.

Alexander, K. L.; M. Cook; and E. L. McDill. 1978. "Curriculum Tracking and Educational Stratification." *American Sociological Review* 43:3-22.

Alexander, K. L., and B. K. Eckland. 1975. "Contextual Effects in the High School Attainment Process." *American Sociological Review* 40:402-16.

Alker, H. R. 1969. "A Typology of Ecological Fallacies." In *Quantitative Ecological Analysis in the Social Sciences*, ed. M. Dogan and S. Rokkan, pp. 66-89. Cambridge, Mass.: M.I.T. Press.

Alwin, D. F. 1976. "Assessing School Effects: Some Identities." *Sociology of Education* 49:294-303.

Averch, H.; S. J. Carroll; T. Donaldson; H. J. Kiesling; and J. Pincus. 1972. *How Effective Is Schooling? A Critical Review and Synthesis of Research Findings.* Santa Monica, Calif.: Rand Corporation.

Baker, E. L. 1976. *Evaluation of the California Early Childhood Education Program.* Vol. 1. Los Angeles: Center for the Study of Evaluation, University of California.

Bartlett, M. S. 1949. "Fitting a Straight Line When Both Variables Are Subject to Error." *Biometrics* 5:207-12.

Bennett, S. N. 1976. *Teaching Styles and Pupil Progress.* Cambridge, Mass.: Harvard University Press.

Berliner, D. C.; L. S. Cahen; N. Filby; C. Fisher; R. Marliave; and J. Moore. 1976. *Proposal for the Phase III B, Beginning Teacher Evaluation Study, July 1, 1976-June 30, 1978.* San Francisco: Far West Laboratory for Educational Research and Development.

Bidwell, C. E., and J. D. Kasarda. 1975. "School District Organization and Student Achievement." *American Sociological Review* 40:55-70.

_____. 1977. "Conceptualizing and Measuring the Effects of Schools and Schooling." Unpublished paper, University of Chicago.

Blalock, H. M. 1964. *Causal Inferences in Nonexperimental Research.* New York: W. W. Norton.

Blalock, H. M.; C. Wells; and L. Carter. 1970. "Statistical Estimation With Random Measurement Error." In *Scoiological Methodology 1970,* ed. E. Borgatta and G. Bohrenstedt, pp. 75-103. San Francisco: Jossey-Bass.

Blau, P. M. 1960. "Structural Effects." *American Sociological Review* 25: 178-93.

Brophy, J. E. 1975. "The Student as the Unit of Analysis." Research Report no. 75-12. Austin: University of Texas.

Brophy, J. E.; B. Biddle; and T. Good. 1975. *Teachers Make a Difference.* New York: Holt, Rinehart & Winston.

Brown, W., and D. H. Saks. 1975. "The Production and Distribution of Cognitive Skills Within Schools." *Journal of Political Economy* 83: 571-93.

Burstein, L. 1974. "Issues Concerning Inferences from Grouped Observations." Paper presented at the Annual Meeting of the American Educational Research Association, Chicago, Illinois, April 15-19.

_____. 1975a. "Data Aggregation in Educational Research: Applications." Paper presented at the Annual Meeting of the American Educational Research Association, Washington, D. C., March 30-April 3.

_____. 1975b. "The Use of Data from Groups for Inferences About Individuals in Educational Research." Ph.D. dissertation, Stanford University.

_____. 1976a. "Assessing the Differences of Between-Group and Individual Regression Coefficients." Paper presented at the Annual Meeting of the American Educational Research Association, San Francisco, April 19-23.

_____. 1976b. "The Choice of Unit of Analysis in the Investigation of School Effects: IEA in New Zealand." *New Zealand Journal of Educational Studies* 11:11-24.

_____. 1977. "Three Key Topics in Regression-Based Analyses of Multilevel Data from Quasi Experiments and Field Studies." Paper presented at the Institute for Research on Teaching, Michigan State University, December 16.

_____. 1978a. "Analyzing Multilevel Educational Data. The Choice of Analytical Model Rather than the Units of Analysis." Paper presented at the Winter Measurement and Methodology Conference, Center for the Study of Evaluation, University of California, Los Angeles, January 5.

_____. 1978b. "Implications from the Beginning Teacher Evaluation Study for the IEA Second Mathematics Study." Paper presented at the Annual Meeting of the American Educational Research Association, Toronto, March 27-31.

———— . 1978c. "Alternative Appraoches for Assessing Differences Between Group- and Individual-Level Regression Coefficients." *Sociological Methods and Research* 7(1): 5-28.

Burstein, L.; K. B. Fischer; and M. D. Miller. 1978. "Social Policy and School Effects: A Cross-National Comparison." Paper presented at the 9th World Congress of Sociology, Uppsala, Sweden, August 13-20.

Burstein, L., and T. Knapp. 1975. "The Unit of Analysis in Educational Research." Technical Report no. 4, Consortium on Methodology for Aggregating Data in Educational Research. Milwaukee: Vasquez Associates.

Bustein, L., and R. L. Linn. 1976. "Detecting the Effects of Education in the Analysis of Multilevel Data: The Problem of Heterogeneous Within-Class Regressions." Paper presented at the Conference on Methodology for Aggregating Data in Educational Reserach, Stanford University, October 23-24.

Burstein, L.; R. L. Linn; and F. Capell. 1978. "Analyzing Multilevel Data in the Presence of Heterogeneous Within-Class Regressions." *Journal of Educational Statistics* 3:347-83.

Burstein, L., and M. D. Miller. 1978. "Alternative Analytical Models for Identifying Educational Effects: Where Are We?" Paper presented at the Annual Meeting of the American Educational Research Association, Toronto, March 27-31.

———— . 1979. "The Use of Within-Group Slopes as Indices of Group Outcomes." Paper presented at the Annual Meeting of the American Educational Research Association, San Francisco, April 8-12.

Burstein, L., and I. D. Smith. 1977. "Choosing the Appropriate Unit for Investigating School Effects." *The Australian Journal of Education* 21:65-79.

Campbell, E. Q., and K. N. Alexander. 1965. "Structural Effects and Interpersonal School Relationships." *American Journal of Sociology* 71:284-89.

Cicirelli, V., et al. 1969. *The Impact of Head Start: An Evaluation of Head Start on Children's Cognitive and Affective Development.* A report presented to the Office of Economic Opportunity pursuant to Contract 889-4536. Westinghouse Learning Corporation, Ohio University. (Distributed by Clearinghouse for Federal Scientific and Technical Information, Springfield, Virginia.)

Cline, M. G.; N. Ames; R. Anderson; R. Bale; T. Ferb; M. Joshi; M. Kane; J. Larson; D. Park; E. Proper; L. Stebbins; and C. Stern. 1974. *Education as Experimentation: Evaluation of the Follow Through Planned Variation Model.* Vols. 1A, 1B. Cambridge, Mass.: ABT Associates.

Coleman, J. S. 1975. "Methods and Results in the IEA Studies of Effects of School on Learning." *Review of Educational Research* 45:355-86.

Coleman, J. S.; E. Q. Campbell; C. J. Hobson; J. McPartland; S. Mood; F. D. Weinfeld; and R. L. York. 1966. *Equality of Educational Opportunity.* Washington, D. C.: Government Printing Office.

Comber, L. C., and J. P. Keeves, 1973. *Science Education in Nineteen Countries, International Studies in Evaluation.* Vol. 1. New York: John Wiley and Sons.

Cramer, J. S. 1964. "Efficient Grouping: Regression and Correlation in Engel Curve Analysis." *Journal of the American Statistical Association* 59:233-50.

Cronbach, L. J. (with the assistance of J. E. Deken and N. Webb). 1976. "Research on Classrooms and Schools: Formulation of Questions, Design, and Analysis." Occasional Paper of the Stanford Evaluation Consortium, Stanford University, Stanford, California, July.

Cronbach, L. J.; D. Rogosa; R. E. Floden; and G. G. Price. 1977. "Analysis of Covariance in Non-Randomized Experiments: Parameters Affecting Bias." Occasional Paper of the Stanford Evaluation Consortium, Stanford University, Stanford, California, August.

Cronbach, L. J., and N. Webb. 1975. "Between-class and Within-class Effects in a Reported Aptitude X Treatment Interaction: Reanalysis of a Study by G. L. Anderson." *Journal of Educational Psychology* 67:717-24.

Davis, J. A. 1966. "The Campus as a Frog Pond: An Application of the Theory of Relative Deprivation to Career Decisions of College Men." *American Journal of Sociology* 72:17-31.

Davis, J. A.; J. L. Spaeth; and C. Huson. 1961. "A Technique for Analyzing the Effects of Group Composition." *American Sociological Review* 26 (April): 215-25.

Dishaw, M. M. 1977. "Descriptions of Allocated Time to Content Areas for the B-C Period." Technical Note IV-2b, Beginning Teacher Evaluation Study. San Francisco: Far West Laboratory for Educational Research and Development.

Dogan, M., and S. Rokkan, eds. 1969. *Quantitative Ecological Analysis in the Social Sciences.* Cambridge, Mass.: M.I.T. Press.

Duncan, O. D.; R. P. Cuzzort; and B. D. Duncan. 1961. *Statistical Geography: Problems in Analyzing Areal Data.* Glencoe, Ill.: Free Press.

Duncan, O. D., and B. Davis. 1953. "An Alternative to Ecological Correlation." *American Sociological Review* 18:665-66.

Farkas, G. 1974. "Specification, Residuals, and Contextual Effects." *Sociological Methods and Research* 2:333-63.

Feige, E. L., and H. W. Watts. 1972. "An Investigation of the Consequences of Partial Aggregation of Micro-Economic Data." *Econometrica* 40:343-60.

Filby, N. N., and C. W. Fisher. 1977. "Description of Patterns of Teaching Behavior Within and Across Classess During the B-C Period." Technical Note IV-3b, Beginning Teacher Evaluation Study. San Francisco: Far West Laboratory for Educational Research and Development.

Firebaugh, G. 1977. "Groups as Contexts and Frog Ponds: Some Neglected Considerations." Unpublished paper, Vanderbilt University.

_____. 1978. "A Rule for Inferring Individual-Level Relationships from Aggregated Data." *American Sociological Review* 4:557-72.

Fisher, C. W.; N. N. Filby; R. S. Marliave; L. S. Cahen; M. M. Dishaw; J. E. Moore; and D. C. Berliner. 1978. "Teaching Behaviors, Academic Learning Time and Student Achievement." Technical Report V-1, Beginning Teacher Evaluation Study. San Francisco: Far West Laboratory for Educational Research and Development.

Gehlke, C., and R. Biehl. 1934. "Certain Effects of Grouping upon the Size of the Correlation Coefficient in Census Tract Material." *Journal of the American Statistical Association Supplement* 29:169-70.

Glass, G. V., and J. C. Stanley. 1970. *Statistical Methods in Education and Psychology.* Englewood Cliffs, N.J.: Prentice-Hall.

Glendening, L. 1976. "The Effects of Correlated Units of Analysis: Choosing the Appropriate Unit." Paper presented at the Annual Meeting of the American Educational Research Association, San Francisco, April 19-23.

Goodman, L. 1953. "Ecological Regression and the Behavior of Individuals." *American Sociological Review* 18:663-64.

———. 1959. "Some Alternatives to Ecological Correlation." *American Journal of Sociology* 64:610-25.

Green, H. A. J. 1964. *Aggregation in Economic Analysis.* Princeton, N. J.: Princeton University Press.

Grunfield, Y., and Z. Griliches, 1960. "Is Aggregation Necessarily Bad?" *Review of Economics and Statistics* 17:1-17.

Haitovsky, Y. 1966. "Unbiased Multiple Regression Coefficients Estimated from One-way Classification Tables When the Cross Classifications are Unknown." *Journal of the American Statistical Association* 61:720-28.

———. 1973. *Regression Estimation from Grouped Observations.* Griffin's Statistical Monographs and Courses, no. 33. New York: Hafner Press.

Haney, W. 1974. "Units of Analysis Issues in the Evaluation of Project Follow Through." Unpublished report, Huron Institute, Cambridge, Massachusetts.

Hannan, M. T. 1971. *Aggregation and Disaggregation in Sociology.* Lexington, Mass.: D. C. Heath.

———. 1976. "Aggregation Gain Reconsidered." Paper Presented at the Annual Meeting of the American Educational Research Association, San Francisco, April 19-23.

Hannan, M. T., and L. Burstein, 1974. "Estimation from Grouped Observations." *American Sociological Review* 39:374-92.

Hannan, M. T.; J. Freeman; and J. W. Meyer. 1976. "Specification Bias Analysis of the Effects of Grouping of Observations in Multiple Regression Models." Paper presented at the Annual Meeting of the American Educational Research Association, Washington, D. C. March 30-April 3.

Hannan, M. T., and A. A. Young. 1976a. "Small Sample Results on Estimation from Grouped Observations." Technical Report no. 24, Consortium on Methodology for Aggregating Data in Educational Reserch. Milwaukee, Wis.: Vasquez Associates.

———. 1976b. "On Certain Similarities in the Analysis of Multi-wave Panels and Multilevel Cross-Sections." Paper presented at the Conference on Methodology for Aggregating Data in Educational Reserach, Stanford University, October 23-24.

Hanushek, E. A. 1972. *Education and Race.* Lexington, Mass.: D. C. Heath.

Hanushek, E. A.; J. Jackson; and J. Kain, 1974. "Model Specification, Use of Aggregate Data, and the Ecological Correlation Fallacy." *Political Methodology* 1:89-107.

Hauser, R. M. 1970. "Context and Consex: A Cautionary Tale." *American Journal of Sociology* 75:645-54.

———. 1971. *Socioeconomic Background and Educational Performance.* Rose Monograph Series, Washington, D. C.: American Sociological Association.

————. 1974. "Contextual Analysis Revisited." *Sociological Methods and Research* 2 (February), 365-75.

Hauser, R. M.; W. H. Sewell; and D. Alwin. 1976. "High School Effects on Achievement." In *Schooling and Achievement in American Society*, ed. W. H. Sewell, R. M. Hauser, and D. L. Featherman, pp. 309-41. New York: Academic Press.

Heyns, B. 1974. "Social Selection and Stratification in Schools." *American Journal of Sociology* 79:1434-51.

Iversen, G. R. 1973. "Recovering Individual Data in the Presence of Group and Individual Effects." *American Journal of Sociology* 79:420-34.

Johnston, J. 1972. *Econometric Methods.* New York: McGraw-Hill.

Joreskog, K. G. 1970. "A General Method for Analysis of Covariance Structures." *Biometrika* 57:239-51.

Karweit, N., and J. Fennessey. 1977. "A Pragmatic Framework for Studying School Effects: Estimation Experiments Using Actual and Simulated Data." A progress report, Center for Social Organization of Schools, Johns Hopkins University, April.

Karweit, N.; J. Fennessey; and D. C. Daiger. 1978. "Examining the Credibility of Offsetting Contextual Effects." Paper presented at the Annual Meeting of the American Educational Research Association, Toronto, March 27-31.

Katzman, M. 1968. "Distribution and Production in a Big City Elementary School System." *Yale Economic Essays* 8:201-56.

Keesling, J. W. 1976. "Components of Variance Models in Multilevel Analysis." Paper presented at the Conference on Methodology for Aggregating Data in Educational Research, Stanford University, October 23-24.

————. 1978. "Some Explorations in Multilevel Analysis." Paper presented at the Annual Meeting of the American Educational Research Association, Toronto, March 27-31.

Keesling, J. W., and D. Wiley. 1974. "Regression Models for Hierarchical Data." Paper presented at the Annual Meeting of the Psychometric Society, Stanford University, March 29.

Kelly, H. H. 1952. "Two Functions of Reference Groups." In *Readings in Social Psychology*, rev. ed., ed. G. E. Swanson, T. M. Newcomb, and E. L. Maccoby, pp. 410-14. New York: Henry Holt.

Kiesling, H. J. 1969. *The Relationship of School Inputs to Public School Performance in New York State.* P-4211. Santa Monica, Calif.: Rand Corporation.

Klitgaard, R. E. 1975. "Going Beyond the Mean in Educational Evaluation." *Public Policy* 23:59-79.

Lazarsfeld, P. F., and H. Menzel. 1961. "On the Relation Between Individual and Collective Properties." In *Complex Organizations: A Sociological Reader*, ed. A. Etzioni, pp. 422-40. New York: Holt, Rinehart & Winston.

Linn, R. L., and L. Burstein. 1977. "Descriptors of Aggregates." Paper presented at the Annual Meeting of the American Educational Research Association, New York, April 4-8.

Lohnes, P. 1972. "Statistical Descriptors of School Classes." *American Educational Research Journal* 9:547-56.

Madansky, A. 1959. "The Fitting of Straight Lines When Both Variables Are Subject to Error." *Journal of the American Statistical Association* 54:173-205.

Maddala, G. S. 1971. "The Use of Variance Components Models in Polling Cross-Sections and Time-Series of Cross-Sections." *Econometrica* 39:359-82.

Maw, C. 1976. "Problems of Data Aggregation and Cross-Level Inference with Categorical Data." Paper presented at the Conference on Methodology for Aggregating Data in Educational Research, Stanford, University, October 23-24.

McDill, E. D., and L. C. Rigsby. 1973. *Structure and Process in Secondary Schools: The Academic Impact of Educational Climates.* Baltimore: Johns Hopkins University Press.

McDonald, F. P., and P. Elias, 1976. "Final Report, Phase II." Beginning Teacher Evaluation Study. Princeton, N.J.: Educational Testing Service.

Menzel, H. 1950. "Comment on Robinson's 'Ecological Correlation and the Behavior of Individuals.' " *American Sociological Review* 15:674.

Merton, R. K., and A. S. Kitt. 1950. "Contributions to the Theory of Reference Group Behavior." In *Studies in the Scope and Methodology of "The American Soldier,"* ed. R. K. Merton and P. F. Lazarsfeld, pp. 40-105. Glencoe, Ill.: Free Press.

Meyer, J. W. 1970. "High School Effects on College Intentions." *American Journal of Sociology* 76:59-70.

Mitchell, E. J. 1969. "Some Econometrics of the Huk Rebellion." *American Political Science Review* 63:1159-73.

Mood, A. M., ed. 1970. *Do Teachers Make a Difference? A Report on Recent Research on Pupil Achievement.* OE-58042. Washington, D. C.: Government Printing Office.

Mosteller, F., and D. P. Moynihan, eds. 1972. *On Equality of Educational Opportunity.* New York: Random House.

Murnane, R. J. 1975. *The Impact of School Resources on the Learning of Inner City Children.* Cambridge, Mass.: Ballinger Publishing Company.

Nelson, J. I. 1972. "High School Context and College Plans: The Impact of Social Structure on Aspirations." *American Sociological Review* 37:143-48.

Nerlove, M. 1971. "Further Evidence on the Estimation of Dynamic Relations from a Time Series of Cross-Sections." *Econometrica* 39:337-49.

Peaker, G. F. 1975. *An Empirical Study of Education in Twenty-One Countries.* International Studies in Evaluation, vol. 8. Stockholm: Almqvist and Wiksell.

Pearson, K. 1896. "Mathematical Contributions to the Theory of Evolution. III. Regression, Heredity and Panmaxia." *Philosophical Transactions of the Royal Society* (series A) 187:253-318.

Pettigrew, T. F. 1967. "Social Evaluation Theory: Convergences and Applications." In *Nebraska Symposium on Motivation,* ed. D. Levine, pp. 241-311. Lincoln: University of Nebraska Press.

Prais, S. J., and J. Aitchison, 1954. "The Grouping of Observations in Regression Analysis." *Revue of International Statistical Institute* 22:1-22.

Robinson, W. S. 1950. "Ecological Correlations and the Behavior of Individuals." *American Sociological Review* 5:351-57.

St. John, N. 1971. "Elementary Classroom as a Frog Pond." *Social Forces* 40:581-95.

Scheuch, E. K. 1966. "Cross-National Comparisons Using Aggregate Data: Some Substantive and Methodological Problems." In *Comparing Nations: The Use of Quantitative Data in Cross-National Research*, ed. R. Merit and S. Rokkan, pp. 131-67. New Haven: Yale University Press.

————. 1969. "Social Context and Individual Behavior." In *Quantitative Ecological Analysis in the Social Sciences*, ed. M. Dogan and S. Rokkan, pp. 133-55. Cambridge, Mass.: M. I. T. Press.

Schmidt, W. C. 1969. "Covariance Structure Analysis of the Multivariate Random Effects Model." Ph.D. dissertation, University of Chicago.

Schwille, J. R. 1975. "Predictors of Between-Student Differences in Civics Education, Cognitive Achievement." In *Civic Education in Ten Countries*, International Studies in Evaluation 6, ed. J. V. Torney, A. N. Oppenheim, and R. F. Farnen, pp. 124-58. New York: John Wiley and Sons.

Shively, W. P. 1969. "Ecological Inferences: The Use of Aggregate Data to Study Individuals." *American Political Science Review* 63:1183-96.

Smith, M. S., and J. S. Bissell. 1970. "Report Analysis: The Impact of Head Start." *Harvard Education Review* 40:51-104.

Snow, R. E. 1976. "Learning and Individual Differences." In *Review of Research in Education, 4*, ed. L. S. Shulman, pp. 243-56. Itasca, Ill.: F. E. Peacock.

Sørenson, A., and M. T. Hallinan. 1977. "A Reconceptualization of School Effects." *Sociology of Education* 50:273-89.

Stebbins, L. B.; R. G. St. Pieree; E. C. Proper; R. B. Andersen; and T. R. Cerva. 1977. *Education as Experimentation: A Planned Variation Model*. Vol. IV-A. *An Evaluation of Project Follow Through*. Cambridge, Mass.: ABT Associates.

Stouffer, S. A.; E. A. Suchman; L. C. DeVinney; S. A. Star; and R. M. Williams. 1949. *The American Soldier: Adjustment during Army Life*. Princeton, N. J.: Princeton University Press.

Summers, A., and B. Wolfe. 1975. "Which School Resources Help Learning? Efficiency and Equity." *Federal Reserve Bank of Philadelphia Business Review*, February.

Theil, H. 1954. *Linear Aggregation in Economic Relations*. Amsterdam: North Holland Publishing Company.

————. 1971. *Principles of Econometrics*. New York: John Wiley and Sons.

Thomas, J. A. 1962. "Efficiency in Education: A Study of the Relationship Between Selected Inputs and Mean Test Scores in a Sample of Senior High Schools." Ph.D. dissertation, Stanford University.

Thorndike, E. L. 1939. "On the Fallacy of Inputing the Correlations Found for Groups to the Individuals or Smaller Groups Composing Them." *American Journal of Psychology* 52:122-24.

Valkonen, T. 1969. "Individual and Structural Effects in Ecological Research." In *Quantitative Ecological Analysis in the Social Sciences*, ed. M. Dogan and S. Rokkan, pp. 53-68. Cambridge, Mass.: M. I. T. Press.

Walberg, H. J., and S. P. Rasher. 1974. "Public School Effectiveness and Equality: New Evidence and Its Implications." *Phi Delta Kappan* 56:3-9.

Wald, A. 1940. "Fitting of Straight Lines if Both Variables are Subject to Error." *Annals of Mathematical Statistics* 11:284-300.

Walker, H. 1928. "A Note on the Correlations of Averages." *Journal of Education and Psychology* 19:636-42.

Walsh, J. E. 1947. "Concerning the Effect of Intraclass Correlation on Certain Significant Tests." *Annals of Mathematical Statistics* 18:88-96.

Webb, N. 1977. "Learning in Individual and Small Group Settings." Ph.D. dissertation, Stanford University.

Weibull, M. 1953. "The Distribution of t- and F-statistics and of Correlations and Regression Coefficients in Stratified Samples from Normal Populations with Different Means." *Skandinavisk Aktuarietidskrift* (Sup.) 36:407-16.

Werts, C. E., and R. L. Linn. 1971. "Considerations When Making Inferences Within the Analysis of Covariance Model." *Educational and Psychological Measurement* 31:407-16.

Wiley, D. E. 1970. "Design and Analysis of Evaluation Studies." In *The Evaluation of Instruction: Issues and Problems*, ed. M. D. Wittrock and D. E. Wiley, pp. 259-69. New York: Holt, Rinehart & Winston.

———. 1976. "Another Hour, Another Day: Quantity of Schooling, a Potent Path for Policy." In *Schooling and Achievement in American Society*, ed. W. H. Sewell, R. M. Hauser, and D. L. Featherman, pp. 225-65. New York: Academic Press.

Wiley, D. E., and R. D. Bock, 1967. "Quasi-Experimentation in Educational Settings: Comment." *School Review* 75:353-66.

Wittrock, M. D., and D. E. Wiley. 1970. *The Evaluation of Instruction: Issues and Problems.* New York: Holt, Rinehart & Winston.

Young, A. A., and L. Erbring. 1976. "Unraveling Classroom Effects: A Multilevel Feedback Model of Contextual Effects." Paper presented at the Conference on Methodology for Aggregating Data in Educational Research, Stanford University, October 23-24.

Yule, G. U., and M. G. Kendall. 1937. *An Introduction to the Theory of Statistics.* 11th ed. London: Griffin.

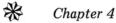 *Chapter 4*

Studying Instruction in the Elementary Classroom

David C. Berliner
The University of Arizona

It is difficult to do research in classrooms. Serious problems confront the social scientist who would study various aspects of educational finance and productivity at the classroom level. Among the problems that may have to be faced are those related to using standardized tests as measures of student achievement, attributing effects to events in the classroom when students' activities outside of school are not recorded, accurately observing certain teacher and student classroom behaviors, etc. A number of the more salient problems for classroom-based research are discussed in the first section of this chapter. Within the usual limits of time and fiscal support allocated to such studies, some of these problems may be insoluble.

Many of the problems noted cast doubt on the profitability of doing traditionally designed large-scale observational studies of instructional processes. A more microanalytical approach, using small samples and dense observation, may be more profitable. Such small but in-depth studies are often called clinical studies. Clinical inquiry in the study of classroom decisionmaking, resource allocation, and the use of technology—various aspects of the study of finance and productivity—has much to recommend it. A more thorough discussion of the clinical attitude and clinical method applied to the study of classroom teaching and learning constitutes the second part of this chapter.

PROBLEMS OF CLASSROOM RESEARCH

Anyone who wishes to study teaching and learning at the classroom level must confront and solve (or at least learn to live with) a few unique problems. Among these are:

191

1. Problems associated with standardized testing;
2. Problems associated with defining the adjunct curriculum;
3. Problems associated with the effects of the home environment on classroom activities;
4. Problems associated with developing multivariate outcomes;
5. Problems associated with defining the unit of analysis for the independent variable;
6. Problems associated with sequencing instruction;
7. Problems associated with recording the difficulty level of the instructional materials;
8. Problems associated with determining rules for access of materials; and
9. Problems associated with generalizability, including:
   a. The stability of teacher behavior,
   b. The stability of student behavior, and
   c. The generalizability of measures of teacher effectiveness.

Problems Associated with Standardized Testing

In studies of how teachers affect students, standardized achievement tests are used extensively as criteria or outcome measures. As a group, these tests are highly reliable instruments. They usually have adequate curriculum content validity and can predict future academic success. However, they do have one overwhelming flaw: they simply may not reflect what was taught in any one teacher's classroom. The tests are designed to be used in all kinds of courses within a curriculum area and therefore cannot be completely sensitive or appropriate for any one teacher's teaching (Gall, 1973). They lack content validity at the classroom level.

Different philosophies of education result in different beliefs about what is important for students to learn. These beliefs, along with the teacher's likes and dislikes for teaching certain areas, result in some interesting differences in the functional curriculum of a class. For example, at the second grade level, as shown in Table 4-1, students in class 13 had an average of 400 minutes each to learn the concepts and operations involved in linear measurement, while students in class 5 had an average of 29 minutes each. In the content areas of fractions and money, class 21 received very little time while class 13 received markedly more. Also from Table 4-1, at the fifth grade level, it can be seen that classroom 11 spends dramatically more time on comprehension activities in reading than do any of the other three fifth grade classes. In classroom 25, silent reading and spelling were emphasized, as can be seen from the dramatically greater allocation of time to those areas in contrast to the mean time each student in classes 1, 3 and 11 received.

Table 4-1. Mean Class Time Allocated to Some Reading and Mathematics Content Areas in Second and Fifth Grade.

Content Area	Class Number			
	Class 5	Class 21	Class 8	Class 13
Mathematics (grade 2)				
Word problems	109	226	416	132
Money	98	9	228	315
Linear measurement	29	130	107	400
Fractions	0	21	63	399
Addition and Subtraction, no regrouping, short form	835	420	1,839	540
	Class 1	Class 3	Class 11	Class 25
Reading (grade 5)				
Comprehension, inference, synthesis	235	252	1,432	306
Identifying main items in reading	153	243	943	326
Silent reading	1,083	724	956	3,640
Spelling	694	847	664	1,415
Creative writing	56	343	98	573

Source: Berliner, 1979. Used by permission.

These rather significant differences in the functional classroom curriculum should, by all we know about learning, result in considerable differences in achievement. If students in these second grade classrooms were tested at the end of the year on linear measurement, you might do well to wager that the students in class 13 would demonstrate better performance than the students in class 5. If these fifth grade classes were part of some end of year statewide testing program where drawing inferences from paragraphs of prose was tested, as it often is, one might well expect that the students in classroom 11 would show superior performance when contrasted to similar students in the other fifth grade classes. Such simple hypotheses have been supported in analyses of these data (Fisher et al., 1978).

The broad spectrum, standardized achievement test may be a social indicator by which state or national policy can be informed. But as long as teachers have the freedom to choose what areas they will emphasize and what materials they will use, these tests can never be used as fair measures of teacher effectiveness. At the classroom level, it simply is not fair to teachers to evaluate their students in areas that they did not cover or emphasize. Thus, between teacher comparisons of effectiveness using standardized tests as outcome measures cannot be defended unless natural variation in choice of content and time allocated to content areas of the curriculum are experimentally controlled.

Problems Associated with Defining the Adjunct Curriculum

When studing the teaching and learning of reading and mathematics, two of the most commonly examined subjects, a good deal of adjunct instruction is ignored. In a lengthy examination of a second grade classroom (Berliner et al., 1978), it was discovered that all work on fractions was introduced at the cooking center. A teaching aide presented this information while preparing recipes. The teacher has decided not to provide any instruction of fractions during the regular mathematics time periods. It was also found that a considerable amount of elementary social studies is taught by allocating time to the silent reading of relevant material. Some of the elementary school science curriculum is also taught this way. The teachers consciously use these other curriculum activities to build upon their reading programs. To study instructional decisions, then, for evidence about the use of classroom technology requires observers to be in the classroom for the entire day, over several days, observing many different activities in order to learn about the adjunct curriculum. Unless this can be done, a good deal of this adjunct academic curriculum will not be observed.

Problems Associated with the Effects of the Home Environment on Classroom Activities

The decisions a teacher makes in classrooms are affected in a number of ways by what happens to students outside school. The carrying out of homework assignments, the amount of parental interest shown, the students' time spent reading comic books and newspapers, and so forth all have ramifications for the classroom. These often unknown out-of-school activities cause peculiar problems for research. For example, the child who reveives extensive guidance at home in reading and mathematics, either through help with homework or through general parental academic concern, may not pay attention to work assignments in school. Such children sometimes find school boring, since much school instruction is geared for the lower and lower-middle ability child (Lundgren, 1972). Special decisions about instruction for these children need to be made. On the other hand, the child who receives no home support as a backup may be getting all his instruction in reading and math in the classroom. If the classroom is not one where engaged time is high, the entire elementary curriculum for a child may total well under one hundred hours per school year of engaged time in academic pursuits (Berliner, 1979). If so, special instructional support systems will be needed. In either case, what happens at home does affect the decisionmaking and instructional activities of teachers in classes. Not to know what goes on in the homes of children is to miss an important part of the forces that shape classroom reality and to which teachers must respond. The teacher's decisions about who will do drill work, who will play mathematics games, and who will help tutor others are affected by the teacher's perception of out-of-school family support for children's learning activities. Thus, classroom resource allocation decisions are sometimes made on the basis of a teacher's perceptions of a student's life at home. The accuracy of these perceptions and the appropriateness of the decisions are often completely unknown.

Problems Associated with Developing Multivariate Outcomes

There are at least two dependent variables in any instructional activity that should be of interest. One of these is the achievement of the learner in the situation. This has been a commonly used measure of instructional outcome. The other, less often examined, is the learner's feelings about the instructional situation. Research workers do not always ask students questions that probe their liking for their teacher or the subject matter. The research worker often overlooks inquiring about the students' enjoyment of their classmates, the degree of threat felt in the class, and whether they would take more courses in that area. Even when such issues are addressed in research studies, the affective set of dependent measures is kept separate from the achievement measures.

A problem in classroom research is to find ways to use multivariate outcomes so that many kinds of achievement and affective responses are used as indicators of the quality of classroom life for a child. The problem is similar to the difficulties in teaching reading. You can instruct so that high comprehension at slow reading rates is achieved, or you can produce low comprehension at high rates of reading. But it is obvious that there must be some optimum multivariate outcome that simultaneously considers both reading comprehension and speed. The same kind of multivariate outcome measures, which simultaneously consider both achievement and affect, are needed for research on teaching. Not to consider simultaneously both what is learned and what is felt about that learning is to fractionate school learning into pieces that do not resemble the student's view of reality.

Problems Associated with Defining the Unit
of Analysis for the Independent Variable

In recent studies of instruction, it appears as if the investigators have had a problem indentifying the unit of analysis for characterizing the independent variable. Is the teacher's question the unit of interest? Is the question, along with the wait time, the unit? Or is the teacher's question, the wait time, and the student's answer the unit that best characterizes the independent variable? And if the latter is most appropriate, does that transaction become part of an episode or strategy of even more complex dimensions and longer duration? Teachers follow strategies of questioning and of discussion. In an inductive lesson, the meaningful unit of analysis may be a one hour or one week episode that is concerned with the conservation of matter. The individual questions, reinforcers, probes, and student responses may be trivial aspects of the overall episode. New conceptions for the units underlying independent variables used in studies of classrooms are needed.

But the problem is not just with picking the appropriate teacher behaviors as independent variables for the study of teaching and learning. There are related and more general problems of defining the unit of analysis for the observation of classrooms. Is the individual student the focus of investigation? Would the observation of the student-teacher dyad be a more appropriate focus? Or would the small group, large group, grade level, or school be the proper focus of study for some questions, some times? There are similar problems to face about the dependent variable. One could study certain classroom processes in relation to one column addition, two column addition, addition and subtraction, or mathematics as outcome measures. The issue is to pick the proper characteristics of the phenomenon of interest in relation to the questions being asked. And this is hard to do. These issues of data collection are very similar to the issues raised by Leigh Burstein in Chapter 3 about choosing the appropriate level of aggregation in data analysis.

Problems Associated with
Sequencing Instruction

A special case of the unit of analysis problem is the problem of sequence in instruction. Teachers give a good deal of thought to how they will sequence instruction. They purposely make decisions about the allocation of time and other resources to implement beliefs about sequence and its relation to achievement. One aspect of sequence is the cycle of activities chosen to promote learning. For example, a short chalk-talk about decoding blends may be given, using modeling and reinforced practice. This activity could be followed by allocating student time to decoding blends in a workbook; then a small group activity on decoding may take place. This might be followed by more decoding of blends in a workbook. This sequence of large group instruction, seatwork, small group work, and seatwork, all concerned with decoding blends, represents a sophisticated, though untested, instructional strategy of the teacher. The strategy provides for an acquisition phase, a testing phase, and a retention phase of instruction.

In addition to the problems generated by the need to study the sequencing of instructional activities over relatively short periods of time, there is also the problem of studying the sequencing of instruction in a curriculum area over relatively long periods. Table 4-2 presents data about the ways different teachers allocated time to the teaching of addition and subtraction to five second grade students over seventeen weeks of instruction. Besides differences in the total time allocated, very different patterns of sequencing are noted in these data. Student 0506 is instructed continuously in the content area. Student 1006, although receiving about 50 percent as much time in this content area as student 0506, also receives instruction throughout most of the time period. On the other hand, students 0702 and 1501 receive instruction for about ten weeks and then receive almost no instruction for the remaining time. Finally, student 0406 has had instructional activities distributed primarily over two blocks of time, with a distinct period of no instruction occurring between instructional periods. From William James's laboratory to today's computer terminals, the issue of massed versus distributed practice has been vigorously studied. In these records of time allocation, reflecting instructional decisions of teachers, we see evidence that the debate is as yet unresolved. Because teachers sequence activities and allocate time in various ways, researchers must learn to follow these patterns to learn how classroom instruction really takes place. Observation instruments that do not pick up sequence in types of activities and in the scheduling of instruction miss important effects attributable to the teacher's instructional decision making.

Problems Associated with Recording the Difficulty Level of the Instructional Materials

It is becoming evident that the level of difficulty of the material for individual students in the classroom must be examined. One reason is that when materials are well matched to the ability level of the student you have a logical indicator of teacher accuracy

Table 4-2.   Time (in minutes) Allocated to Addition and Subtraction (no regrouping) for Five Students over Seventeen Weeks of Instruction.

Week	Student 0506 Raw	Cumulative	Student 0702 Raw	Cumulative	Student 1006 Raw	Cumulative	Student 1501 Raw	Cumulative	Student 0406 Raw	Cumulative
1	30	30	40	40	45	45	60	60	35	35
2	62	92	95	135	20	65	30	90	20	55
3	105	197	0	135	10	75	20	110	80	135
4	105	302	0	135	0	75	50	160	35	170
5	20	322	50	185	20	95	20	180	40	210
6	0	322	20	205	30	125	30	210	0	210
7	5	327	90	295	50	175	30	240	0	210
8	15	342	45	340	40	215	30	270	0	210
9	50	392	10	350	20	235	20	290	10	220
10	30	422	30	380	55	290	10	300	45	265
11	20	442	0	380	25	315	0	300	20	285
12	80	522	0	380	0	315	30	330	15	300
13	38	560	0	380	0	315	0	330	0	300
14	0	560	0	380	0	315	0	330	0	300
15	20	580	0	380	10	325	0	330	5	305
16	30	610	0	380	35	360	0	330	0	305
17	55	665	0	380	4	364	0	330	10	315

Source: Fisher and Cahen, 1978. Used by permission.

in diagnosis and prescription, and diagnostic and prescriptive activities are crucial aspects of individualized programs of instruction. Another reason for this concern with difficulty level is the interpretation of the empirical data from the Beginning Teacher Evaluation Study (Fisher et al., 1978). In that study, using regressions, the percentage of a student's work in activities or materials whose difficulty was judged to be "hard" for a particular student was a consistent negative predictor of achievement. The percentage of material that was judged "easy" for a particular student was a consistent positive predictor of achievement. It is probable that some unknown ratio of easy to medium level difficulty is a strong predictor of achievement in elementary school classrooms.

These findings indicate that those who would observe teaching and learning in classrooms will have to consider the difficulty level of the materials that the student is working with. It will take considerable effort to define "easy," "medium," and "hard" operationally. In addition to extensive observer training, such categorizations will require extensive amounts of observer intuition and judgment.

Problems Associated with Determining Rules for Access to Materials

How certain rules are formulated and enforced in classes affects student access to classroom resources. There are classrooms where, in the first few days of instruction, well over one hundred rules for student behavior are clearly expressed by the teacher (Tikunoff and Ward, 1978). Such rules include many teacher statements about pushing in line and chewing gum in class. But more subtle and therefore more difficult to spot, yet much more important for research in productivity and finance, are the rules for trading in workbooks, for obtaining free time, for access to mathematics and reading games, and so forth. These rules prevent or enhance the chances that certain students will engage in particular activities. The major rules for work in a classroom are developed and codified in the first few days of school, a time when observers are usually asked to stay out of schools. Thus, understanding the rules for behavior in a classroom becomes, in part, a problem in the timing of research. Unless researchers know something about the periodicity of certain events (e.g., rule setting in the first few days, costume design before Halloween, the study of plants in the spring, preparation for testing at the end of school, etc.), they may make mistakes in the timing of their observations. If the timing is wrong, learning about the origins of a classroom's rules may be impossible. Yet without knowledge of the rules and some understanding of their functional significance for teachers, the study of student access to resources will be incomplete.

Problems Associated with Generalizability

Perhaps the biggest problem for those who would study instruction is the problem of the stability of the behaviors of the subjects and events under study. There are three important aspects to this problem that need to be considered—the stability of teacher behavior, the stability of student behavior, and the stability of measures of teacher effectiveness.

The Stability of Teacher Behavior. Before entering a classroom to code teacher behavior in any sensible way, an observer has to be sure of two things: first, that the frequency of the event one is trying to observe is high enough so that at least one instance will occur during the observation period; second, that the behavior to be coded represents the teacher's usual and customary way of behaving. Only if these conditions are met can a teacher's behavior be sensibly characterized by the frequency count or rating scale description obtained in observations of classroom activities.

Many studies relating teacher behavior to student outcome have examined teacher behavior that did not occur frequently. For example, among thirty-two primary grade science teachers, the use of questions calling for identifying relationships, hypothesizing, and testing hypotheses is extremely rare on any given occasion of observation (Moon, 1971). Another case of low frequency events in an important area of teaching has to do with the management skills of teachers. In some communities, classroom management is not difficult. Students are motivated, and parents exert pressure for conformity to school rules, so that traumatic disturbances are very infrequent. In other communities, serious problems exist all day long. Therefore, to observe instances of teacher behavior in the area of classroom management, designers of research must remember to take ecological factors into account. Furthermore, it has been learned that even in settings where management problems usually occur with high frequency, certain teachers are so quick to establish a nondisruptive social system that by the time the observer enters the class, particular kinds of events have been precluded from occurring. This is another example of the problems associated with the timing of research, discussed above.

How then can one study teacher behavior when important variables in the study rarely occur? One answer, of course, is denser observation. Five one hour observations of teacher behavior, which is unusually high for most studies of teaching, may simply not provide all the information an investigator wants. In addition, part of the answer is knowing when and where to observe. For example, the first two weeks of schooling would be important for a study of management skills in inner-city schools, while trying for denser observation later in the year, in other types of schools, might be wasted effort.

The problem of estimating behavioral stability is partly related to the problem of the frequency of occurrence of behavior. When the frequency of a behavior is low, the correlations between the frequency of occurrence for certain events, over occasions (that is, a coefficient of stability for the behavior), will be low. But part of the problem is quite distinct from the frequency issue. Think for a moment about the characteristics you prize in a teacher. Usually, people think of "good" teachers as flexible. Such teachers are expected to change methods, techniques, and styles to suit particular students, curriculum areas, time of day or year, and so forth. That is, our standard of excellence in teaching implies a teacher whose behavior is inherently unstable. Needless to say, that is a problem for an observer who is trying to measure a teacher's customary and usual ways of teaching.

For our study of teaching, we have reviewed teacher stability, over occasions, for a great many variables (Shavelson and Dempsey, 1975). The results are fascinating. On the laughable side are the coefficients of stability from Campbell's (1972) analysis of science teaching at the junior high school level over two occasions. The Flanders Interaction Analysis System was used, and the stability coefficient—that is, the correlation between a teacher's standing on a measure across two occasions—was, for a measure of indirectness in teaching (the i/d ratio), -0.90. On five occasions, Moon (1971) studied thirty-two primary grade science teachers trained in the Science Curriculum Improvement Study. The stability coefficient for the Flanders indirectness measure went all the way up to 0.18; for the frequency of fact or recall questions, the stability coefficient was -0.12; and for amount of teacher talk, only 0.12. In Borg's (1972) study, the behavioral stability of teachers was measured after training in questioning techniques had taken place. The stability of the ratio of higher-order-to-fact questions was 0.07. The rather large number of low and even negative stability coefficients that exist in the literature confirms our belief that the independent variables we often work with in studies of teacher effectiveness are not fair indicators of typical behavior.

We are so eager to capture variables for data analysis with our rating scales and frequency counts that we seem to have forgotten to check whether our methodology is appropriate to the phenomena we are studying.

Of course, there are many exceptions to the trend for teacher behavior to be unstable. We have found ratings of variables over ten occasions that yield high stability coefficients. These include coefficients of 0.92 for teacher warmth, 0.79 for teacher enthusiasm, and 0.83 for teacher sensitivity (Wallen, 1969). We have found frequency counts demonstrating that a global variable composed of all types of reinforcement is reasonably stable over occasions, yielding a stability coefficient of 0.64 (Trinchero, 1974). In the latter study, however, we find considerable evidence pointing to the lack of generalizability of stability coefficients across different teacher populations, curriculum areas, and student populations. For example, the stability coefficient over two occasions for the frequency of positive verbal behavior was 0.04 for English teachers and 0.57 for social studies teachers.

By examining the stability of teachers' behavior, which is used as the independent variable in studies of teacher effectiveness, we conclude that

1. Some teacher behavior that we think important to study occurs infrequently. To study it requires extensive observation in particular settings at appropriate times.
2. Some teacher behavior that we think important to study is unstable over occasions. No practical amount of observation will result in a reliable estimate of a teacher's use of such behavior. Perhaps we need to develop measures of variance instead of measures of central tendency to describe it.
3. Some teacher behavior is stable over occasions. In general, but not always, ratings or high inference variables, rather than frequency counts or low inference variables, are the more stable.
4. Stability coefficients for much teacher behavior will not demonstrate ecological or population validity. Teacher behavior is moderated, as it should be, by the kinds of students and the variety of settings that teachers work in.

Until we know more about what teacher behavior fluctuates, and how and why it fluctuates over time, settings, curricula, and populations, studies relating teaching behavior to student outcomes must remain primitive.

The Stability of Student Behavior. Another problem of generalizability in research on teaching and learning has to do with the stability of the student from day to day. My colleagues and I have recently spent a good deal of time studying the engagement of students in classrooms. Our evidence tells us that day-to-day stability of engagement rates for individual students is nonexistent. Since engaged time in academic pursuits is one reliable predictor of school achievement (Fisher et al., 1978), information about the stability of this behavior becomes important. But we do not know what makes for stable or unstable engagement rates across subject matter areas, grade levels, or even ten minute segments of instruction. Engagement for particular students in particular content areas of the curriculum varies from 0 percent to 100 percent for consecutive ten minute blocks of time. Traditional approaches to inquiry in this area examine mean engagement for a student or a class. This could lead to an estimate that a student or a class is engaged about 70 percent of the time over different tasks and different days. But is is the variance of such behavior, within and across tasks and days, that is most interesting. The reactivity of the variable of engaged time to perceived and actual environmental changes can be understood only by inquiring of the subject involved, by observing, and by employing small-scale interventions in the environment. To study variation in engaged time, a clinical approach with a student or a class may yield information of great value to the teacher and the students.

The Generalizability of Measures of Teacher Effectiveness. To characterize teachers as more or less effective, we need to know whether they maintain their rank ordering on measures of effectiveness over time and over subject matter areas. There are about eight studies of teacher effectiveness over lengthy periods of time (see Shavelson and Dempsey, 1975). The mean of these correlations between teacher effectiveness measured two or more times is about 0.30. This figure is based on data from predominantly primary age children tested with standardized reading and mathematics achievement tests. Brophy's (1973) study presents some interesting data. Residual gain scores over three years were examined for 165 elementary teachers. Of these teachers, 28 percent were consistent in their effects on students three years in a row. Approximately 14 percent were consistently effective in producing higher than predicted reading and math achievement, and 14 percent were consistent in being associated with classes that had scores lower than predicted. On the other hand, 13 percent of the teachers showed linear increases in residual gains over the three years. That is, they appeared to be getting more effective in their teaching. Similarly, 11 percent showed a linear decrease over that time period. They seemed to be getting less effective over time. The remaining 49 percent of the teachers in this sample were inconsistent in the patterning of their residual scores over time.

In a review of short-term studies of teacher effectiveness, ranging across grade levels and all kinds of curriculum areas, moderately stable estimates of teacher effectiveness are obtained when the same content is taught to similar students (e.g., teaching and reteaching an ecology lesson to two samples of urban students). But when different content is taught to two or more groups of similar students the effectiveness measures are not found to be stable. Similarly, when different content is taught to the same students, estimates of effectiveness from occasion to occasion are unstable. Another study of this problem involved about 200 elementary school teachers, each of whom taught a two week, specially designed teaching unit in reading and mathematics. Residual gain scores for each class in each subject matter were calculated. These measures of effectiveness, using different content and the same students, were correlated. From these data we find that measures of effectiveness in the two curriculum areas correlate about 0.30 (Berliner et al., 1976).

It appears that teachers do not, by and large, remain in a stable ordering on measures of teacher effectiveness. If, as we have discussed, the independent variables we typically look at are often unstable and measures of teacher effectiveness also show instability, the possibility of correlating teacher behavior with student achievement to determine effective teaching behavior is very limited.

Summary
Observing in classrooms is difficult. Some of the problems may be insurmountable if traditional research methods, including simple regression and the testing of models using regression approaches, are used. However, there are other forms of inquiry besides those that lead to analyses by regression equations. Many of these other forms of inquiry are clinical in nature and rely upon methods that are more descriptive and less quantitative. When we examine the phenomena to be studied and look at some real classroom problems, the clinical method appears to gain in appeal.

THE PHENOMENON TO BE STUDIED

The core of the phenomenon of interest is the day-to-day interaction between teachers, students, tasks, and materials. This process can be observed and experienced in any local elementary school. However, what we observe in a classroom is the surface structure of the phenomenon, whose deeper structure is rooted in a series of social, political, and economic systems. Indeed, attempts to understand portions of the schooling process in isolation from the rest of the phenomenon have been of very limited utility. Three characteristics of the phenomenon have important consequences for understanding teaching and learning in classrooms.

First, the phenomenon is remarkably complex. The factors affecting school learning must surely number in the thousands. These include presentation variables, management and control structures, physical layout of the classroom, class membership, social milieu within the class, staffing and resource allocation within the school, and so on. The network of influences from these sources interact in a complex manner to produce, or at least moderate, the behavior observable in the classroom. In addition, the inhabitants of each classroom fill a wide variety of roles. Teachers operate as presenters, organizers, providers, and punishers. They are also parents, taxpayers, and employers. Students develop and maintain roles in relation to teachers, principals, and peers. These and other factors attest to the complexity of the teaching-learning process in elementary schools.

Second, the phenomenon is dynamic. The factors that give rise to particular types of behavior during one hour, or one day, do not continue in a steady state for very long. Influences on individual children and teachers, as well as influences on classes and schools, change from minute to minute and from day to day. It is a commonplace to hear a teacher state that "today is just not a typical day." This statement is true, in that the process changes enough from one day to another that few days seem "typical."

Third, the phenomenon is extensive in time. A student is typically grouped with a class of thirty students and one teacher for ten months at a time. Social as well as cognitive skills are developed slowly over relatively long periods. Learning to read and write is achieved over several years. For teachers too, the phenomenon is extended in time. Teachers spend about 900 hours per school year with students. Substantial changes in teacher or student behavior can hardly be seen in a week, let along a day.

The complex, dynamic, and extensive characteristics of the phenomenon have not often been given enough attention. Conventional research often ignores the implications of these characteristics for the study of classroom teaching and learning.

MATCHING METHOD OF INQUIRY WITH
THE PHENOMENON OF INTEREST

A kind of inquiry into the realities of classrooms that is also appropriate for the phenomena under study depends upon methods ordinarily called clinical. Such methods have been undervalued and consequently underutilized in research on teaching and learning in classrooms. Clinical method *qua* method has been neglected as a means of inquiry for a number of reasons. First, clinical work usually takes a longer time than the experimental methods used in educational inquiry. Second, clinical method implies helping (e.g., clinical psychology) and the related belief that knowledge generated while serving to help others is of less worth than knowledge arrived at by other means. Finally, our prestigious journals are loath to publish clinical studies because of their applied nature and suspect methods. For these and other reasons, such studies do not bring professional rewards, and this reduces the incidence of clinical inquiry by researchers.

To promote critical thinking about clinical methods in instructional research, particularly as applied to the study of teaching and learning in classrooms, I will try to distinguish clinical method from other methods, note some unfortunate and inaccurate connotations associated with the method, describe a number of classroom phenomena uniquely suited to study by clinical approaches, and discuss methodological techniques compatible with clinical forms of inquiry.

CLINICAL INQUIRY: AN ATTITUDE
AND A METHOD

What often distinguishes a clinical internist, a clinical neurologist, or a clinical psychologist is the attitude taken in a scientific inquiry. If the approach is that of understanding the individual person or individual classroom for the sake of helping the person or the participants in that classroom to function better, the clinical attitude and consequently the clinical method have been adopted (Watson, 1963). Clinical method in psychology is generally though of as the application of psychological principles and techniques to the problem of the individual. Thus, clinical method encompasses a broad spectrum of ideas and practices. Clinical method in the study of classroom teaching and learning, and in the service of the clinical attitude, is designed to promote the welfare of the individual in classrooms. The clinical instructional researcher, like most clinicians, is a scientist, although not all scientists are clinicians. The basic data are the same for the clinical and nonclinical educational researcher—the behavior and experiences of participants in the educational process. The clinician, however, unlike his nonclinical colleague, is sometimes compelled to do something immediately useful with his observations and hypotheses. That urgency to act may demand reliance upon data of unknown reliability and validity, depend upon subjective interpretations of phenomena, and require the use of intuition by the investigator.

But many educational researchers seem to have forgotten about the clinical attitude and have even more often neglected clinical method. Some reasons for the retreat from the clinical attitude and method have to do, in part, with the connotations associated with the term clinical.

CONNOTATIONS OF THE TERM CLINICAL

Clinical is a word often associated with such terms as idiographic, applied, and qualitative which have a low respectability in the scientific world. It is a word often placed in opposition to such terms as statistical or experimental, which have very high respectability in the scientific world. Because of the company it keeps and the opposition forced upon it, the word clinical has taken on lower class status. But let us examine these terms a little more closely.

Nomothetic and Idiographic Qualities

Because of the concern with individual cases, it is felt that clinical inquiry can never yield the nomothetic generalizations and findings that the scientific endeavor so values. Yet Cronbach (1975), reviewing the findings of traditional educational research, has seriously questioned the generalizability of the findings held in such high repute. Social science research in general, and educational research in particular, he says, are so complex that generalizable findings may elude us forever. Too many variables interact simultaneously for us to be able to study their joint effects, and too many effects change over time. This makes it very difficult to rely on the replication of social science findings in a particular setting at a particular time.

Can clinical information be so much worse? Was the world enriched or impoverished by Freud's insights? Are Erikson's intuitions about developmental crises of no scientific merit? Are the behavioral data from single subject studies of behavior modification of such little worth?

These three powerful concepts and methods in psychology were the result of clinical, not traditional, research approaches. From these examples we learn two things. First, as in the case of Freud and Erikson, clinical inquiry can serve as the basis for theory. In helping an individual person or classroom function better, a clinical psychologist can develop—through observation, interview, record keeping, and anlysis—powerful conceptualizations of human behavior. Some clinical work is concerned with generalizability (e.g., double-blind studies in medical research). However, much of it is idiographic. But regularities in idiographic phenomena can become the basis for nomothetic generalizations. Second, as in the behavior modification studies, we can see how clinical endeavors apply well-respected scientific findings in respectable scientific ways, while helping individuals. The *Journal of Applied Behavioral Analysis* is devoted to such applied, clinical science and does not differ in function from clinical journals of medicine.

I conclude that the difference between nomothetic and idiographic approaches, in terms of their yield of generalizable findings, is not as clear-cut as was once thought. Thus clinical methods, which are necessarily idiographic, need not be downgraded for that reason.

Basic and Applied Research

The word psychology, sociology, anthropology, or economics prefaced by the term educational connotes an applied discipline. Such applied disciplines are concerned, however minimally, with the improvement of education. Implicit in almost all educational research is the clinical attitude and, thus, an applied focus. Should it be necessary, I suppose, we can talk about more and less directly useful research. But to talk of basic and applied research in education is, perhaps, to misunderstand the goal of an applied discipline. Cronbach and Suppes (1969) tried to avoid this problem by talking about decision-oriented and conclusion-oriented research in education. They pointed out that equating basic research with good research and applied research with bad or sloppy research is useless. Research studies differ simply as a function of the different questions they are designed to answer. It should be repeated, over and over again, that good research is a quality that is independent of whether or not a study is directly or indirectly useful in education.

Recently, in the presidential address to the American Educational Research Association, Kerlinger (1977) made the annual plea for more basic research and managed to equate basic research with good research. But others have a different perspective. Jackson and Kiesler

(1977), discussing the same issues, take a much more sophisticated view of the benefits and effects of more or less directly usable research. They conclude, as does Kerlinger, that a proper mix of the two forms of inquiry is needed. But, unlike Kerlinger, they assert that

> ideas that are good . . . are those buttressed by rational and empirical arguments, which are the kind of arguments offered by scientific research and disciplined scholarship. Some knowledge, on the face of it, is closely related to the substantive concerns of educators, some more distantly so. Within broad limits, it is the former to which we would give preference in seeking support for new endeavors. (Jackson and Kiesler, 1977:

And Slavin (1978), taking vociferous exception to Kerlinger's call for more basic research by the National Institute of Education, concludes that "what is needed in education is more, not less, research directed at the improvement of instruction and of the schooling experience for children" (p. 17). That kind of statement represents the clinical attitude.

Ultimately, as a profession, what we want is good research, of whatever degree of applicability. I personally want to see more good research that has a high degree of immediate usefulness.

Quantitative and Qualitative Data

Another unfortunate distinction is found in the association of the term clinical with the term qualitative. It is as if a clinician eschews quantification, when no such supposition need be made. Data are always, in some sense, both quantative and qualitative.

Because of the focus on individual people or classrooms, events that occur just once may be given special weight by a clinician. This appears to be qualitative. Because the clinician is particularly aware of ecological contexts, descriptions of environmental press variables become important. This appears to be qualitative. If compelled to help, the clinician may act before reliable and valid relations are established. Although the clinician may not make public the numerical values of variables, this is not the same as avoiding quantification. In the course of the work, a clinician must do some very rapid and complex quantification. Weights are assigned to events, probabilities are estimated, Bayesian hypotheses are tested, and sophisticated judgments of utilities are computed. This is not always articulated, but it is always present. Scientists must engage in some degree of quantification, but they need not always define their variables in that manner. Scientists should also respond to the qualitative aspects of their variables. It is these qualities that elicit insights and help clarify thinking about complex events, such as *n* way interactions in data. This kind of analysis of data is necessarily more qualitative. In sum, empirical data, which are the fundamental data of clinician and nonclinician alike, are always more or less qualitatively analysed at some point in the study. Thus, the distinction between quantitative and qualitative is one of emphasis in research styles and not a clear dichotomy. The recent distinction between data analysis and statistical analysis made by Tukey (1977) is relevant here.

Clinical versus Statistical Approaches

The work of Meehl (1954) and others on statistical versus clinical prediction in clinical psychology set up an unfair opposition. The solely clinical prediction, if formal tests exist, is as silly as making an estimate of a person's temperature when thermometers exist. If thermometers exist they should be used. If reliable and valid scales and instruments are indicators of conditions, events, and states of people, they too should be used. The *combination* of what has been called clinical intuition and statistical information is what is valued and successful. Either alone has faults.

Clinical versus Experimental

Another opposition is that between clinical and experimental. An experiment, like a test, is nothing more than a controlled observation. Clinical method, while often relying on observations of natural behavior, has always supplemented such observations with tests and has always proposed experiments for the subject of the clinical inquiry. Piaget's methods are a case in point. Although not possessing the clinical attitude (he is not interested in helping anyone improve any thing), his techniques are clearly clinical. He observes, he verbally probes and tests, and he does experiments, often with his own children. Is Piaget a great clinician, a great experimentalist, or simply a great scientist? I think the latter, and thus the clinical versus experimental dichotomy is also found wanting.

Preliminary State of Research or Not

In a science where experiments are possible and where multivariate statistical packages and giant computers are at our beck and call, it is often believed that clinical methods serve as a first stage of inquiry: information obtained from clinical inquiry should lead, ultimately, to hypothesis testing in randomized true experiments. This need not be so. Ethologists, anthropologists, sociologists, economists, and many psychologists are quite happy to make clinical inquiries and to use evidence obtained in such inquiries as the basis for decisions, conclusions, models, and theories. And this is justifiable. Clinical evidence need not always be thought of as the first step in inquiry; it is one of numerous ways of obtaining information that may or may not be subject to further inquiry using other methods. More important than providing variables for regression equations is the verification of clinical insights by other researchers using whatever methodology is appropriate.

Summary

The connotations associated with the term clinical do not, on close examination, appear nearly as negative as might be feared. Clinical work is idiographic, but can serve nomothetic causes; it is more applied than basic, but that is often why one studies educational phenomena; it is concerned with both qualitative and quantitative data, the distinction being less apparent once one examines any empirical data; clinical work is both intuitive and statistical, melding the best of the sensitive human information processor with other kinds of sensitive instrumentation; the clinician may be an experimentalist, but is not usually preoccupied with large samples. Finally, clinicians need not view themselves as providing preliminary data for later experimental work. They can choose to see themselves as providing data and ideas that can stand or fall like any other ideas. All clinical insights are subject to verification in the same way that any other findings or ideas are subject to verification—through independent empirical confirmatory evidence and the consensus of opinions from others in the field.

In my opinion, clinical method need not be held in disdain or disrepute. Clinical methods can be employed to understand particular problems in education, some of which may not be understood using more traditional forms of inquiry. Some educational areas of interest that lend themselves to clinical inquiry are described in the next section.

REALITIES OF CLASSROOMS AND THE NATURE OF INQUIRY

I would like to present briefly a number of problems related to the study of productivity and finance that I find puzzling and interesting. I also believe that the nature of these problems can be illuminated by clinical kinds of inquiry. And, if one chooses to adopt a clinical attitude, some of these problems may be remedied.

Social-Psychological Forces in Decisionmaking at the Classroom Level

In a recent study of cross-age tutoring in the public schools, fifth and sixth grade students designated as slow learners were assigned to help second and third grade students, also designated as slow learners. The older tutors were taught how to diagnose and prescribe and how to prepare lesson plans for their students. The project was administered by the teachers involved and monitored by the evaluation team of the school district. After a few weeks there were some behavioral indications that the program was a success. The older tutors were spending a good deal of time preparing to work with their younger tutees. They were also seeking guidance from the teachers about rules of decoding, problems of word meaning, and other areas of reading that they had had difficulty with previously. No gains or losses in achievement were noted in the case of the younger students, but it was clear to everyone involved that the program was having beneficial effects for the older tutors. The program was cancelled. The teachers did not like it.

Why is it that a seemingly successful program was dropped from the schools? What did teachers notice that made them want to stop the program? Were they embarrassed by the potential positive effects of the study? Were they frightened of losing their jobs because the students might no longer be designated as "slow"? What good is it to teach someone about diagnostic and prescriptive procedures, the use of contingent reinforcement, and the advantages of practice, if the program it is a part of can be stopped because of unknown social-psychological forces at work? Learning more about these forces may help others who choose to innovate understand how acceptance of an innovation occurs. The way one would learn this, I think, is by taking a clinical attitude and adopting clinical methods.

Changing Classroom Activities

In a recent study of four second grade elementary school classrooms, four instructional consultants tried to change classroom processes in order to increase student engaged time in academic pursuits (Berliner et al., 1978). From one diary of the process we learned that the consultant raised the possibility of using goal setting to increase student engagement during independent seatwork.

Some reward, he suggested, such as a free reading period, could be used as an incentive for students to complete their assigned work within a given period of time. (This procedure was called goal setting to ease the shock for teachers, since past experience had revealed that the term "contingency management" set off visceral reactions of great magnitude.) The idea of goal setting was explained to the teacher and put into contexts that she understood, because the suggestion came about after many hours of classroom observation. The teacher responded negatively, saying that she did not like the idea of goal setting. The strategy could never be implemented because it always met with resistance. What good is it, we wondered, to have knowledge of behavior modificaiton procedures and confidence in the power of such approaches, when implementation of that knowledge is sometimes so difficult to achieve?

In another class, the instructional consultant tried to restructure the classroom management procedures. Students were given management cards that told them where they should be at different times during a one hundred minute block of time during each morning. Large clocks were purchased so that students could monitor their time in different activities. The new system was designed to allow some time for the teacher to engage in mathematics instruction with carefully selected small groups of students. This pleased him because there had been very little time for the actual teaching of mathematics concepts under the previous classroom management system. The new procedure seemed to be working well for the teacher and students, but not for the paraprofessional classroom aide, who now had many more responsibilities. Formerly, the aide sat at a desk and checked mathematics computations. Now the aide had to perform four different functions during this one hundred minute time period. Although the teacher was rejuvenated with his newfound time to teach, he eventually switched back to the older management structure because of the aide's unhappiness. We wondered about the nature of the symbiotic relationship between teacher and aide. Who was really in charge? Why did the aide control the type of management system present in the class? Was the teacher, despite verbal expressions of delight, really frightened of teaching? It is possible that it is easier to assign workbook pages than to try to teach mathematics concepts. When the teacher is responsible for instruction, a student's failure to comprehend must be much more of a personal blow than it is when instruction takes place by means of a workbook page.

In another classroom, the consultant taught the teacher how to structure activities. This meant having the teacher give explicit directions and instructions so that all students knew what was expected of them at all times. The number of children not engaged in academic pursuits was high in this class, in part because the teacher assumed that the children knew what workbook pages to be on, which contracts to be in, which listening stations to be at, and so forth. In fact, many of the children did not know what to do or where to be. The teacher was instructed in structuring activities, and frequency counts of structuring moves were made. The teacher's behavior changed in the direction desired, and she acknowledged the obvious increase in engaged time for students in that classroom. Many more students appeared to be doing what she had hoped they would do. The consultant and the teacher both agreed that a very functional modification of her behavior had occurred. Four weeks later it had vanished. What is the nature of the classroom such that obviously effective teacher behavior is dropped from the teacher's repertoire?

There were present in each class forces that resisted change. These forces are far more powerful than those who would be agents of change can imagine. But we are dealing with events no different, I think, from the defense mechanisms that occur during clinical studies of individuals. We can use clinical methods to study these events, to figure out what exactly is happening and why they occur. We might also want to adopt a clinical attitude in order to help teachers make changes in their behavior.

Intentionality in Classroom Studies

A totally different area for research in studying teaching and learning has to do with what educational philosophers (Fenstermacher, 1979) call intentionality. When studying the teacher in the classroom, the research paradigm usually in effect has been smugly behaviorist. From the behavior of the teacher and the behavior of the students, cause and effect relationships are hypothesized. Sometimes these are subject to experimental tests, sometimes they are presented in a correlational form, but always it is the *observable* behavior that is examined. But this need not be so. The powerful perspective about admissible evidence in scientific inquiry allows the everyday ordinary language explanations of persons to be taken seriously as explanations of conduct. "The things that people say about themselves and other people should be taken seriously as reports of data relevant to phenomena that really exist and which are relative to the explanation of behavior" (Harré and Secord, 1972:7). Understanding the intentions of teachers as they work calls for clinical inquiry of a type not ordinarily undertaken. Recent research that comes close to this approach includes that of Shavelson (1976) and of Shulman and Elstein (1975), who studied the decision-making of teachers. Teacher decision making in these studies is described as clinical information processing, and the focus is on "the uniquely human characteristics of thinking and feelings, as well as behaving" (Shulman and Lanier, 1977:49). Such research cannot occur without consideration of the purposes of a teacher in the classroom. These purposes, I think, can be discovered only through clinical interview, clinical probing, and careful descriptions of the behaviors of teachers in classrooms.

On Origins and Pawns

Many of the studies of teaching and learning have, at least implicitly, adopted paradigms in which the teacher is conceived of as an origin, or controlling agent, and the student is thought of as a pawn, or a subject of control. Observation reveals that this is not the state of events in all classroom settings throughout the day. Nor is it an accurate description across classes. Most interesting of all is that it is probably not an accurate description of the same teacher over successive years. For example, the correlational data on teacher effectiveness from year to year reveal low estimates of stability when student achievement is used as the criterion. In part, this is because of the individual makeup of each class. The result is that teacher behavior is not emitted in some consistent fashion year in and year out. Instead, behavior is often elicited from teachers by special student demands. The basic controlling agent for the interaction may not be the teacher. This interplay of origin and pawn role in classrooms becomes very interesting to study, either day by day or year by year. And these roles can appropriately be studied using clinical methods.

On Performance Theories versus
Learning Theories

Teachers do not hold learning theories. Despite what they have been taught, they are smart enough to realize that most learning theory is bunk! Observable performance that is logically or philosophically related to learning outcomes and to personal survival becomes very important in determining classroom life. Teachers decide to engage in this or that activity based on some notions of socially reasonable behavior. They do not determine their activities on the basis of some theory about how to optimize student learning. They keep students engaged because that is good; they give quizzes because that is accepted; they assign silent reading because that is considered good and results in personal rest and so forth. The reasons that teachers have to support certain kinds of performance theories need to be explicated. The relations between a teacher's personal performance theory and more formal and scientifically respectable learning theories might best be studied by experimental methods. But uncovering performance theories and the rationales that support them calls for a clinical inquiry of great sensitivity.

On Understanding More About Puzzling Findings

There are a number of puzzling findings in the literature that pertain to research on productivity and finance. Explication of these findings probably requires clinical work. For example, there are a number of research studies that show a negative correlation between the use of teacher-made materials and student achievement. Heavy use of teacher-made materials is often taken as a sign of motivation by the teacher to do extra work. Logically, this might be an indicator of teacher effectiveness. On the other hand, teacher-made materials may not supplement the curriculum materials that are in use: the special materials may be divergent. In that case, a negative correlation would result. Small-scale investigations of teachers' intents and the correlation of the special materials with the standard curriculum are in order. Small-scale clinical studies will probably be as sensitive to this problem as any other form of inquiry.

There is also a suggestion in the literature that classroom puzzles and games, even if academic in appearance, are negatively related to achievement. Many instructors are using puzzles and games with increasing frequency, thinking that this is a way to keep students motivated in academic areas. What is it about puzzles and games that might relate positively to academic achievement, and what characteristics might be deleterious? As with the problem of teacher-made materials, the relation of puzzles and games to achievement needs to be investigated.

Another interesting finding has to do with the inability of many school districts to implement a program of instruction. The follow-through data are quite clear. Site variance within programs is enormous. Between program variance in instructional behavior and activities was not greater, in general, than the variance within programs when different sites throughout the country were examined. If specially constructed and clearly defined curricula cannot be implemented in any coherent way, many of our national efforts to improve curriculum may be doomed to failure. What is it about site pressures that results in such vastly different implementations of curricula? Which people at a site can enhance or hinder the implementation effort? Who has the power to change a defined curriculum in such a way that implementation of a program is not possible? These questions of influence patterns and change are as appropriately addressed by clinical studies as by other means. Certainly such studies would require sensitivity to political and social pressures within schools.

Summary
The point of this section is that there exists a set of problems in the school for which the clinical attitude is appropriate and for which clinical method may be a preferred mode of inquiry. It is my belief that a skilled observer, interviewing teachers, taking seriously what they say, establishing relationships of trust with them, and testing out hypotheses with them, can do more to illuminate certain educational problems than can dozens of true experimental studies. In no way does what I an saying deny the utility of traditional experimental methods. I am merely saying that for a certain set of questions, clinical methods probably have as much chance of uncovering important relations as do experimental methods.

METHODOLOGY IN CLINICAL STUDY

In the last few years, a number of innovations in methodology have been brought to the fore, and some older methods have regained new respectability. A few of these are mentioned in this section.

Exploratory Data Analyses
There now exist new ways to think about data. Tukey (1977) and others have shown that it is perfectly appropriate to work with subsets of data, throwing out cases, keeping others, and doing some things that the classical statistician never dreamed possible. This is, in a way, massaging complex data so that new insights about the phenomena emerge. The techniques that are gaining popularity generally go by the name of exploratory data analyses. To do exploratory data analysis requires a sensitive clinical touch, as well as an advanced set of methodological skills. The statistician massaging these data must have insight into the variables and into the context within which they occur. As these techniques develop, the melding of clinician and statistician will also take place.

Case Studies

Stake (1978) has upheld the usefulness of the case study method. He writes, "When explanation, propositional knowledge, and law are the aims of an inquiry, the case study will often be at a disadvantage. When the aims are understanding, extension of experience, an increase in conviction in that which is known, the disadvantage disappears" (p. 5). In further discussion he says that

> intentionality and empathy are central to the comprehension of social problems, but so also is information that is holistic and episodic. The discourse of persons struggling to increase their understanding of social matters features and solicits these qualities. And these qualities match nicely the characteristics of the case study. (P. 7)

The case study is one of the oldest techniques in social science. It fell into disrepute as the more statistically minded and the emulators of nonsocial sciences increased. The case study as a social science method is now making a comeback, precisely because it is uniquely suited to certain classroom phenomena. In the classroom we find particularly complex phenomena of an episodic nature, where the intentions of the people in situ must be understood. The case study method, in the hands of people who have received training (and not just those who choose to write), can make an important contribution to furthering knowledge about the realities of the classroom. A related way of studying classrooms combines case studies with connoisseurship and criticism—scholarly activities borrowed from the humanities (Eisner, 1976).

Ethnography

Although there seems to be difficulty in defining what is an ethnography, it is clear that a rich observational record, relatively free from bias, is what is meant by an ethnographic report. These reports are records of behavior in settings. They are discriptive, but can be turned into quantitative data—that is, the frequency of cooperative behavior in clay-modeling settings in early childhood classrooms can be recorded. Ethnographers can pick up that sort of information if one of the variables they are concerned with is cooperative behavior. Just as the ethnographer working with a primitive tribe has a set of concepts to work with, having to do with religion, sexual rites, passing of property, and the like, the ethnographer in the classroom has to learn which variables are important for developing a rich description of the class. Certainly such things as academic focus, cooperation, democratic attitudes, and conformity are of concern to the classroom ethnographer. But in our primitive state of application of ethnographic procedures to classrooms, we do not yet have rich conceptual categories on which to focus. Nevertheless, we can expect ethnographic procedures to be highly useful in case studies of classrooms where clinical work is to be undertaken. The rich descriptive records provided by ethnographers are an excellent basis for discussion and potential change in class-room functioning (see Tikunoff, Berliner, and Rist, 1975; Erickson, 1977; Doyle, 1978).

Graphics and Time Series
In the past few years there has been an increase of $N = 1$ studies (see Kratochwill, 1978). Through the use of graphs as developed by the behavior modification clinicians and with the use of time-series analyses, one can infer the cause and effect relations between environmental events and the behavior of single subjects. These techniques become invaluable tools for the clinical scientist inter-vening in classrooms.

Summary
As this section has demonstrated, there are new or newly accepted methodologies for clinical work. As a paradigm shift takes place, these methods and styles of research will become more prevalent.

CONCLUSION

This chapter was designed to make a case for clinical studies of classroom instruction, specifically so that the Finance and Pro-ductivity Center at the University of Chicago could plan their class-room-based research. First some problems in conducting such research were noted. Then the idea of trying more clinical ap-proaches to research was presented; the term "clinical" was analyzed so that some negative connotations associated with the term might be dispelled; and a description of problems that might be addressed by clinical kinds of inquiry was presented. Finally, it was shown that there are new or newly rediscovered methodologies for doing clinical work that have considerable scientific respectability.

The notion of a clinical approach to the study of instruction has much more to commend it than I realized when I first started doing my classroom research. The clinical approach can help teachers and students, while, perhaps, also promoting generalized knowledge in such fields of psychology, sociology, and economics. I hope others will think seriously about clinical inquiry in the study of classroom teaching, learning, finance, and productivity.

REFERENCES

Berliner, D. C. 1979. "Tempus Educare." In *Research on Teaching*, ed. P. L. Peterson and H. J. Walberg. Berkeley, Calif: McCutchan.

Berliner, D. C.; N. N. Filby; R. S. Marliave; J. E. Moore; and W. J. Tikunoff. 1976. "Experimental Teaching Units and the Identification of a Special Sample of Classrooms for Conduting Research on Teaching." Technical Report 76-12-1, Beginning Teacher Evaluation Study. San Francisco: Far West Laboratory for Educational Research and Development.

Berliner, D. C.; N. N. Filby; R. S. Marliave; and C. P. Weir. 1978. "An Intervention in Classrooms Using the Beginning Teacher Evaluation Study Model of Instruction." Technical Report VI-1, Beginning Teacher Evaluation Study. San Francisco: Far West Laboratory for Educational Research and Development.

Borg, W. R. 1972. "The Minicourse as a Vehicle for Changing Teacher Behavior: A Three-Year Follow-Up." *Journal of Educational Psychology* 63: 572-79.

Brophy, J. E. 1973. "Stability of Teacher Effectiveness." *American Educational Research Journal* 10: 245-52.

Campbell, J. R. 1972. "A Longitudinal Study in the Stability of Teacher's Verbal Behavior." *Science Education* 56 (1): 89-96.

Cronbach, L. J. 1975. "Beyond the Two Disciplines of Scientific Psychology." *American Psychologist* 30: 116-27.

Cronbach, L. J., and P. Suppes, eds. 1969. *Research for Tomorrow's Schools.* New York: Macmillan.

Doyle, W. 1978. "Paradigms for Research on Teacher Effectiveness." In *Review of Research in Education*, 5, ed. L. S. Shulman. Itasca, Ill.: F. E. Peacock.

Eisner, E. W. 1976. "Educational Connoisseurship and Criticism: Their Form and Functions in Educational Evaluations." *Journal of Aesthetic Education* 10 (July-October): 135-50.

Erickson, F. 1977. "Some Approaches to Inquiry in School-Community Ethnography." *Anthropology and Education* 7 (2): 58-69.

Fenstermacher, G. 1979. "A Philosophical Consideration of Research on Teacher Effectiveness." In *Review of Research in Education*, 6, ed. L. S. Shulman. Itasca, Ill.: F. E. Peacock.

Fisher, C. W., and L. S. Cahen. 1978. "An Analysis of Instructional Time in Reading and Mathematics." Paper presented at the Annual Meeting of the American Educational Research Association, Toronto, March 27-31.

Fisher, C. W.; N. N. Filby; R. S. Marliave; L. S. Cahen; M. M. Dishaw; J. E. Moore; and D. C. Berliner. 1978. "Final Report of the Beginning Teacher Evaluation Study." Technical Report V-1, Beginning Teacher Evaluation Study. San Francisco: Far West Laboratory for Educational Research and Development.

Gall, M. D. 1973. "The Problem of 'Student Achievement' in Research on Teacher Effects." Paper presented at the Annual Meeting of the American Educational Research Association, New Orleans, February. Also issued as report A73-2, Far West Laboratory for Educational Research and Development, San Francisco.

Harré, R., and P. Secord. 1972. *The Explanation of Social Behavior.* Oxford: Basil Blackwell.

Jackson, P., and S. B. Kiesler. 1977. "Fundamental Research and Education." *Educational Researcher* 6 (8): 13-18.

Kerlinger, F. N. 1977. "The Influence of Research on Educational Practice." *Educational Researcher* 6 (8): 5-12.

Kratochwill, T. 1978. *Single Subject Research.* New York: Academic Press.

Lundgren, V. P. 1972. *Frame Factors and the Teaching Process.* Stockholm: Almqvist and Wiksell.

Meehl, P. E. 1954. *Clinical vs. Statistical Prediction.* Minneapolis: University of Minnesota Press.

Moon, T. C. 1971. "A Study of Verbal Behavior Patterns in Primary Grade Classrooms during Science Activities." *Journal of Research in Science Teaching* 8: 171-77.

Shavelson, R. J. 1976. "Teacher's Decision Making." In *The Psychology of Teaching Methods*, ed. N. L. Gage. Chicago: National Society for the Study of Education.

Shavelson, R. J., and N. Dempsey. 1975. "Generalizability of Measures of Teacher Effectiveness and Teaching Process." Technical Report 3, Beginning Teacher Evaluation Study. San Francisco: Far West Laboratory for Educational Research and Development.

Shulman, L. S., and A. S. Elstein. 1975. "Studies in Problem Solving, Judgment, and Decision Making: Implications for Educational Research." In *Review of Research in Education*, 3, ed. F. N. Kerlinger, pp. 3-42. Itasca, Ill.: F. E. Peacock.

Shulman, L. S., and J. E. Lanier. 1977. "The Institute for Research on Teaching: An Overview." *Journal of Teacher Education* 28: 44-49.

Slavin, R. E. 1978. "Basic vs. Applied Research: A Response." *Educational Researcher* 7 (2): 15-17.

Stake, R. 1978. "The Case Study Method in Social Inquiry." *Educational Researcher* 7 (2): 5-8.

Tikunoff, W. J.; D. C. Berliner; and R. C. Rist. 1975. "Special Study A: An Ethnographic Study of the Forty Classrooms of the Beginning Teacher Evaluation Study Known Sample." San Francisco: Far West Laboratory for Educational Research and Development.

Tikunoff, W. J., and B. A. Ward. 1978. "Problems in Conducting Naturalistic Research: An Analysis of a Case Study of Classroom Socialization." Paper presented at the Annual Meeting of the American Educational Research Association, Toronto, March 27-31.

Trinchero, R. L. 1974. "Three Technical Skills of Teaching: Their Stability and Effect on Pupil Attitudes and Achievement." Ph.D. dissertation, Stanford University.

Tukey, J. W. 1977. *Exploratory Data Analysis.* Reading, Mass: Addison-Wesley.

Wallen, N. E. 1969. "Sausalito Teacher Education Project." Annual Report, Division of Compensatory Education, Bureau of Professional Development, San Francisco State College. Mimeo.

Watson, R. I. 1963. *The Clinical Method in Psychology*. New York: John Wiley and Sons.

Chapter 5

Determinants of Pupil Opportunity*

Annegret Harnischfeger
*ML-GROUP for Policy Studies
in Education, CEMREL, Inc.*

David E. Wiley
Northwestern University

THE SUBSTRATUM FOR MODEL UNFOLDING

In order to use pupils' learning time and educational resources efficiently and consciously with respect to learning outcomes, we have to analyze classroom processes in ways that will allow directed change based on insight. Research on schooling has to result in more rational and effective allocation of human and material resources—intentionality, inherent to education, and restrictedness of funds make this necessary.

Research on schooling should follow a holistic rather than a particularistic view of the educational process—that is, the teaching-learning process should be seen from the perspective of an educationally engaged citizen or politician who wants to ensure that resource allocation occurs rationally. This calls for the analysis of the relationship of relevant and changeable determinants of school learning to outcomes. Instead of evaluating curricula or modules thereof, instead of investigating the effectiveness of teacher characteristics and teaching strategies, and instead of singling out isolated pupil characteristics such as aptitude or engagement, we have to ask, How can a child's school life be organized so that he will learn most efficiently what he should acquire? This implies a segmentation of the teaching and learning processes without destroying the *Ganzheit* of curricular teaching and learning aspects,

*Prepared for the Educational Finance and Productivity Center, University of Chicago. The second author was affiliated with the University of Chicago and CEMREL, Inc. when this paper was prepared.

and this requires relating resources available and their use to pupils' learning experiences.

The isolation of the study of curriculum from that of instruction, of teaching, of school organization and administration, and of school finance has amputated the practical and conceptual relevance of much of educational research. Also, the research focus on narrow segments of the child's classroom experiences has severely constrained the use of results for change *in praxi*, as we lack a comprehensive description of classroom learning into which these particularistic researches may be integrated. Research that contributes directly to practical education must begin holistically and move toward more differentiated, minute issues of the teaching-learning process. Narrowed, well-defined studies and experiments may help to clarify aspects of classroom learning but are not able to contribute directly to inferences for practical and cost-efficient change.

Many of the particularistic research foci and models developed in splendid isolation might be ultimately integrated into a broad perception of the educational process. We have taken on the task of developing a model that spans levels of generality and, likewise, specificity so as to allow integration.

MODELS OF SCHOOL LEARNING

For the past three years, we have been engaged in the continuing development of a model of school learning (Wiley and Harnischfeger, 1974; Harnischfeger and Wiley, 1975, 1977). This model draws heavily on Carroll's Model of School Learning (1963) but is also influenced by Bloom's "Time and Learning" (1973). The consensus of the three models is simply stated: Pupil's experiences, adequately plumbed by the amount of time spent actively learning, and pupils' characteristics, including their cognitive capabilities, are the sole proximal and distinctive determinants of achievement. Instruction influences active learning directly via the allocation and use of instructional time (opportunity) and indirectly via pupil motivation.

Beyond these simple commonalities, the models differ both in emphasis and in assertion. Carroll focuses on the distinctive role that various cognitive abilities play in school learning, discriminating the task-specific from the general and carefully articulating their relations to quality of instruction. Bloom turns his unrivaled perception of the sequential character of many classroom learning experiences into a strong focus on how performance on one task preconditions success in another. Our model refines the nature of class learning opportunities, articulating their strategic origins and their powerful influences on both the content and degree of educational achievement.

The models' treatments of instruction and its relations to learning are diverse and differ greatly in detail and coverage. In contrast to Bloom and Carroll, we extensively sift teaching decisions and activities, elaborating their consequences via a highly differentiated segmentation of pupil pursuits. One important outcome of this differentiated emphasis is the clarity with which the reasons emerge for the great impacts of learning opportunity on achievement. This winnowing also permits separating those elements of instruction that lead to the content and quantity of pupil opportunity (planning and implementing) from those that lead to the degree of active learning (motivating and monitoring) and from those that influence rate of learning (communicating and presenting).

All three models, although different in focus, attack issues centrally important in educational research, practice, and policy. They provide means to overcome nonintegrative views of the teaching and learning process. Their level of specification allows them to be used in empirical research and to answer questions vital to classroom teaching and learning. In the work reported here, we have used our model to link educational resources to pupils' learning opportunities. We will summarize the parts of the model relevant for this study and then illustrate the resource-opportunity link with an example—a very simplified one, however.

The Harnischfeger-Wiley Model

A gross sketch of the model has six components that fall into three categories (Figure 5-1).

Background. Background includes teacher as well as pupil factors, such as social and home background, age, and sex; teacher preparation and education; pupils' prior achievements, motivation, and aptitudes. It also consists of state, community, district, and school characteristics, such as curricular guidelines, community or district wealth, size of district or school, racial composition. The model only partially specifies and delimits the relevant components and does not detail their causal linkages. Curriculum and institutional factors influence both teacher background—in the form of teacher selection practices, curricular guidelines, and so forth—and pupil background, in that districts differentially attract families of varying types, partially regulate school boundaries, and so on. But a school or district's pupil background composition also

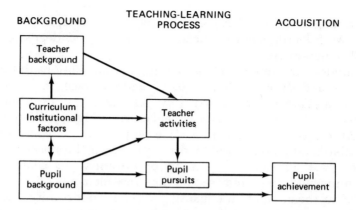

Figure 5-1. Gross determinants of pupil achievement (Harnischfeger and Wiley model).

Source: Harnischfeger and Wiley, 1977. Reprinted with permission from the *Journal of Curriculum Studies.*

influences institutional structures and the curriculum. This can take place not only through parent activities but also through pupil activities as they relate to educational goals and the school's success in meeting them.

Teaching-Learning Process. The teaching-learning process includes the teacher's and the pupil's activities and pursuits, which are the major focus of the model. They are defined, detailed, and timed, and their relationships elaborated. Activities of the teacher are causally relevant only in the way they influence pupil pursuits and, through them, pupil acquisition. The teacher activites themselves are influenced by all three kinds of background factors.

Acquisition. Acquisition represents the outcomes. The model currently considers only pupil achievement. It is specified that there are only two direct determinants of achievement—pupil pursuits and pupil background factors.

Teaching-Learning Process

The Structure of Opportunity. Pupils' activities and their relations to those of the teacher constitute the focus of the model.

Learning Settings and the Segmentation of Instructional Time. The molecular unit in the model is a single activity of a pupil within a *learning setting*—that is, bounded by the context of specific curricular content, a particular grouping (whole class, small group, or individual work), and a characteristic mode of teacher supervision or nonsupervision. Examples include such learning activities or pursuits as seatwork in mathematics, reading group instruction, and whole class instruction in science. Additionally, pupil activities occur in time—that is, they begin and end and consequently have defined durations. The time concept allows the determination, specification, and subdivision of the *quantity of schooling* that particular pupils receive. The total amount of schooling, although only an imperfect indicator of the substance and potency of the educational process, does have strong, causally interpretable relations to achievement (Wiley, 1973); and these relations have potent implications for the societal costs of education (Wiley and Harnischfeger, 1974).

A pupil's total active learning time, devoted to a specific subject matter or content area, *X*, is the time relevant for his *achievement on X*. This will be considerably less than the *nominal quantity of schooling* set by states or districts (Figure 5-2). The nominal quantity of schooling, defined through the lengths of the school year and day, may be cut—for example, by teacher strikes, illnesses, or bad weather conditions. This results in the actual amount of schooling offered to pupils. For an individual pupil, this quantity will be reduced by absences. The resulting time, which is the basis of a pupil's school learning, is the *quantity of schooling* (for a particular pupil, *K*). This quantity is allocated to various curricular areas and consequently to diverse pupil pursuits. For a specified curricular area, this results *in the total time spent in X pursuits (for pupil K,)* which is the key to what and how much *K* learns about subject matter *X*. This amount might be still further reduced by the amount of time that a pupil is not actively engaged in learning.

Teaching Strategy and Time Allocations. Teaching and learning occur in whole class instruction, subgroups, and as individual (seat) work. Teachers employ different grouping and individualization strategies depending on pupil characteristics, subject area, curriculum, resources, and their own preferences. Depending on a teacher's grouping and individualization strategies, pupils receive differential amounts of teacher time which impact on pupil achievement. These strategies also represent an important resource allocation factor, because the teacher, and thus teacher time, is the most expensive resource in education.

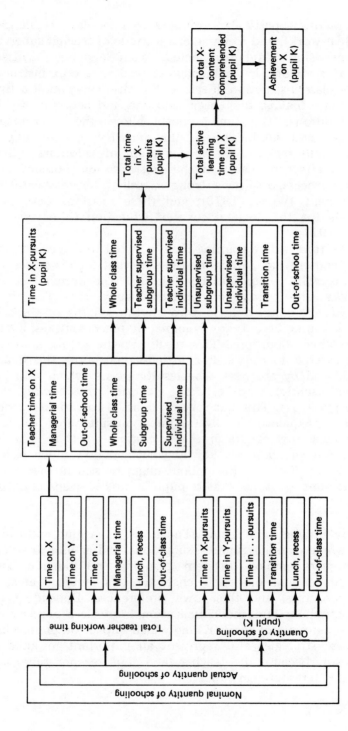

Figure 5-2. Segmentation or instructional time (Harnischfeger and Wiley model).

Source: Harnischfeger and Wiley, 1974. Reprinted with permission from the *Journal of Curriculum Studies.*

Our model stresses an analysis of teacher and pupil time, which are identical only for pure whole class instruction with no pupil absenses. Typically, an unfolding of pupil time reveals differential pupil allocation to learning settings because pupils work in different groupings and receive differential amounts of teacher supervisory or instructional time. The model divides the total time a pupil spends on a subject matter (X) into seven learning-setting categories (see Figure 5-2): (1) whole class pursuits, (2) teacher-supervised subgroup pursuits, (3) teacher-supervised individual pursuits, (4) unsupervised subgroup pursuits, (5) unsupervised individual pursuits, (6) transitions, and (7) out-of-school pursuits.

The time allocations of individual pupils to learning settings in curricular areas allow us to draw a time ledger for pupils' and teachers' total school time and also out-of-class learning or working time. This allows us to study conditions of pupil learning, teacher effectiveness, and resource allocation. The system may be used for summarization and aggregation in several ways: sums by curricular area, grouping category, or type of teacher supervision describe aspects of the structure of learning opportunities open to individual pupils. Aggregations of the complete accounting or its summations over pupils characterize curricular priorities or instructional schemes. Further cumulations for types of pupils or classes with specific attributes would bear upon curricular decisions or assessments of equality of educational opportunity. And as we outline below, these summaries can then be interpreted in terms of pupil achievement, linking school policy and teacher education to educational goals via the model's specification of the teaching-learning process.

Pupil Achievement. We have traced conceptually an individual pupil's quantity of schooling through to a specified curricular area, in a grouping and supervisory surround, stating relevant influences on the way. Another part of the model specifies the proximal causes of achievement in terms of learning time, pupil characteristics, and instruction. However, as this chapter focuses on the relation between resources and pupil opportunity without tracing opportunity through to achievement, we will not explain this part of the model and will instead explore and articulate the origins of learning opportunity. Specifically, this requires analysis of the determination of (differential) pupil exposure to learning settings of various kinds by resource availability and teaching strategy.

RESOURCES, TEACHING STRATEGY,
AND LEARNING OPPORTUNITY

It is obvious that even a pupil who is willing to spend much effort in learning will not acquire knowledge if he is not allowed time to learn; on the other hand, it is common experience that pupils vary enormously in their active learning even when allowed equal amounts of learning time. However, we would assume that, within boundaries, an increase in allocated learning time would increase the amount of active learning time and thus achievement. In other words, if we extend schooling, we expect more achievement. But we could also focus on the relative amounts of time that pupils spend actively learning, and we could increase those amounts of *active* learning time during schooling. We would thus increase achievement by intensifying schooling and the learning experiences within it. Both aspects of school learning and achievement—the extensive and the intensive—are vitally important in allocating resources, and both means are used to increase achievement.

Extensity of educational activities can be simply and importantly quantified as their duration—number of school years, length of school years and school days, subject matter allocations, and individual absence rates. On the other hand, intensity of schooling might be described by the density of teacher-pupil relations, materials, equipment, and other school-related personnel. Thus, small classrooms and those with teacher aides or specialists, plentiful books and curricular materials, and ample equipment may be characterized as educatively intensive, regardless of the total hours of instruction in the school day or year.

As the extent or duration of educational experiences and thus the total amounts of pupils' active learning time increase, the quantities of resources consumed increase concomitantly. As pupils spend more years, months, days, or hours in school, their total quantity of active learning time increases, but so do expenditures for teachers' salaries, books, materials, and school facilities. Intensifying schooling by decreasing class sizes, augmenting the ratio of instructional personnel to pupils, or improving materials and equipment also results in more active learning time, but it likewise consumes additional resources without necessarily augmenting the *amount* of schooling.

There is much controversy over the consequences of such changes for achievement. The controversy is exacerbated because educational research on school effects has not conceptually differentiated extensive from intensive parts of schooling. Investigation has confounded intensive aspects, such as teacher characteristics, with mixtures of extensive and intensive, such as library volumes and staff expenditures, and has ignored or miscategorized the extensive aspect. Consequently, policy decisions concerning extensive or intensive aspects of resource allocations have been formed on dark and slippery grounds.

However, scanning the past decade, we find that additional resources were used mostly to intensify schooling and only relatively small amounts were used to extend it, usually by offering summer school sessions. The largest amounts of additional resources during this time period were provided by the federal government under the Elementary and Secondary Education Act of 1965, intended to overcome educational disadvantages caused by poverty. The resources expended were overwhelmingly used to increase the numbers of teaching personnel per pupil—that is, to decrease class size; to hire more teachers, specialists, and teacher aides; to recruit more volunteers; or to intensify schooling through developing materials meant to be more effective. The reduction of the ratio of pupils to instructional personnel is based on the conviction that the more pupils can interact with teachers, the greater their achievements will be; presumably because these interactions promote additional active learning. Teacher specialists were employed, mostly in reading, on the basis that specific learning problems could be more effectively and efficiently overcome by teachers with special skills for treating a defined problem area.

This increase in classroom resources has no direct effect on pupil achievement, only indirect effects through pupil activities that in elementary school, are primarily determined by the teacher. In this chapter, therefore, we will focus on how the teacher makes use of these resources.

Personnel Resources and Their Relation to Teaching Strategy

In a class with both a teacher and an aide, the teacher can work with a small group while the rest of the class is supervised by the aide. A teacher without additional support personnel, on the other hand, *must* increase pupils' unsupervised time if he or she desires to decrease the size of instructional groups. Thus, the effects on pupils of grouping and individualization decisions strongly depend on the availability of supporting personnel.

Of course, these effects are also dependent on class size. The number of children who regularly attend, along with the time commitments of teaching personnel, determine the normal ratio of children to adults in the classroom. This ratio is the key factor that links instructional strategy to pupil experiences.

To flesh out these notions in a fashion that makes clear the over-all interdependency of teaching strategy, resources, and pupil experiences, we have summarized some data bearing on these issues (Table 5-1).[1] The personnel figures in the table reflect the total time commitments of persons in each teaching category. Thus the 1.11 teachers, if attributed to a single class, could have been one full-time teacher plus a specialist who works with pupils in that classroom for 11 percent of the weekly instructional period.[2] The teacher resources in these classes averaged slightly in excess of one full-time person. This is mostly due to specialists who visited the classroom and provided specific instruction for short periods of time. However, aide resources constituted only about 36 percent of a full-time equivalent. This comes about because about two-thirds of the classes had aides and, on the average, they worked just over half-time. Volunteer efforts were even more severely limited, volun-

Table 5-1. Personnel Resources and Time Distributions to Groupings (thirty-five first grade classes).

| | Average Percentage of Time Spent in Particular Instructional Settings by: | | | | |
	Pupils	Adults	Teachers	Aides	Volunteers
Without pupils or adults	30.85	14.61	8.14	28.32	12.47
Tutorial with 1 pupil	.59	7.85	7.06	8.75	17.37
Tutorial with 2 pupils	.52	3.54	2.06	3.86	16.28
Group size 3–8	10.56	24.83	23.74	29.83	10.81
Group size >8	57.48	49.16	59.00	29.24	43.07
Average number of full-time equivalent personnel for all classes		1.64	1.11	.36	.17
Number of full-time equivalents in classes with such personnel			1.11	.55	.26
Percentage of classes with personnel			100.0	65.7	68.6

Number of classes	= 35
Mean gorup size:	
Small (3–8)	= 6.30
Large (>8)	= 17.33
Average number of enrolled pupils	= 26.07
Average number of attending pupils	= 24.30
Average child-adult ratio	= 14.82
Average length of school day	= 6.04

Source: Devault, Harnischfeger, and Wiley, 1977a.

teers being present only about 17 percent of the time. Again, they were present in only about two-thirds of the classes, while their time commitment, when they were available to pupils, was only about half that of the aides.

These personnel were used to fulfill somewhat differentiated functions. The teachers spent most (59 percent) of their time with large groups and about one-fourth with small ones, devoting relatively small amounts to tutorial instruction and activities not directly instructional. The aides spend much less of their time with large groups (29 percent), somewhat more than the teacher with small groups (30 percent), and considerably more in noninstructional activities (28 percent). The volunteers spend most of their time with children (88 percent), concentrating on individuals and pairs (34 percent), but also with an emphasis on large groups (43 percent). All in all, adults spend almost half their time in large groups, one-quarter in small groups, 11 percent in tutorial or two child settings, and the rest (15 percent) without children.

These allocations probably flow from individual preferences and assessments about the effectiveness of teaching settings, but severe constraints on these decisions follow from restrictions on the personnel resources available. The average number of pupils enrolled in these classes was just over twenty-six, which, given a daily absence rate of about 7 percent, means that teaching personnel deal with twenty-four to twenty-five different pupils during a typical school day. The effective pupil-adult ratio is, therefore, almost fifteen to one. This ratio constrains the average amounts of time that pupils spend in groups of various sizes.

The Determination of Pupil Experiences

Given a teaching strategy and a configuration of classroom resources, a logical question concerns the consequences for pupils: How do these factors influence their educational experiences?

Suppose, for example, that in a class of twenty-five pupils, a teacher and his or her aide spend 10 percent and 25 percent of their time, respectively, tutoring pupils. Since tutorial instruction involves only one pupil at a time, a typical (i.e., average) pupil will be tutored $10/25 = 0.4$ percent of the time by the teacher and $25/25 = 1.0$ percent by the aide. As this example shows, there is a strict defining relation between the adult instructional time available and the grouping context within which it is used, on the one side, and the average amounts of pupil exposure to instruction in that context, on the other.

The relationships between pupil and teaching time allocations for other grouping contexts are as strict and can be generally stated for groups of all sizes.[3] Generally, the proportionate *pupil* time allocation for an instructional context is equal to the product of three factors: (1) the average group size, (2) the personnel intensity ratio (full-time equivalent teaching personnel per pupil), and (3) the proportion of *instructional* time devoted to the context.

To illustrate, suppose that in one classroom, 40 percent of all adult time is spent in small groups of six children. Also, suppose that the class is heavily resourced—for this example we will assume twenty children taught by a teacher, two aides, and a volunteer—so that the adult-child ratio is $4/20 = 0.2$. Then the percentage of pupil time spent in such small groups would be $(40) (6) (0.2) = 48$ percent.

Returning to Table 5-1, it is now clear that although tutorial instruction occupies almost 8 percent of adult time, the pupil-adult ratio of 14.8 implies that pupils will experience such instruction during less than six-tenths of 0.06 percent of their instructional experiences. Similarly, even though one-quarter of adult time is devoted to small group instruction, the average group size of six pupils strictly determines that pupils will spend only about 10.5 percent of their time in such groups. Also, limited resources constrain teaching personnel to use large group instruction extensively if children are not to be left on their own for most of their school day. As adults spend almost half their time with large groups, the typical size of such groups must be extreme (over seventeen pupils) in order to hold the average pupil time in such settings down to less than 60 percent. And even this picture leaves pupils unsupervised over 30 percent of the time.

It is difficult to see how a revision of the teaching strategy could materially improve the situation. If one- and two-pupil settings were entirely eliminated and their time allocations added to small group instruction, unsupervised time would decrease by only about 4 percent. The resource constraints in these classrooms strongly influence pupils' educational experiences.

Thus, since group sizes and the proportion of teaching time devoted to them are determined by teaching strategy and since the personnel ratio indexes the intensity of the resources allocated, instructional strategy and resource intensity strictly determine the situational framework of the child's educational experiences.

TRACING PERSONNEL RESOURCES TO
THE PUPIL: AN EXAMPLE

School administrations allocate a defined amount of instructional resources to elementary school classes or groups of pupils. These resources consist minimally of a teacher, a classroom, curricular material, and equipment such as furniture and perhaps a piano or overhead projector; but these resources might be augmented by time commitments of other personnel such as aides, volunteers, or specialists, as well as by special resources for field trips. The classroom teacher, whose teaching time is the major resource, controls to a large degree the allocation of these additional resources. The teacher groups pupils; allots curricular materials and assigns tasks; parcels out his or her time to the whole class, groups, and individual pupils; allocates the working times of aides or volunteers, if available, to groups and individuals or to materials preparation; plans field trips; and prepares instructional materials, such as work sheets and the like. Thus, the major portion of educational resources are directly allocated to pupils through a teacher's teaching strategies and their implementation.

A teacher interacting with a pupil has assigned that pupil a part of his or her time, and the school district has devoted a part of its monetary resources to that child via the teacher's salary. A teacher devoting more time to some pupils than to others has, in effect, differentially allocated resources. In the example below, we attempt to trace this resource allocation from school district budgetary decisions through to the dollar value of resources received by individual pupils.

In order to accomplish this, logically we must:

- Divide the school district expenditures between those that are used to purchase items and services that directly affect the pupil (e.g., materials, teacher time) and those used for indirect services (administrative time, janitorial services);
- Follow those expenditures down to school and classroom;
- Differentiate teacher time with respect to the amount used for managerial tasks;
- Follow a teacher's grouping and individualization strategy;
- Assess resource allocations with respect to teacher and aide time, as well as materials, down to the level of the individual pupil in a classroom;
- Disentangle teacher time from pupil time;

- Trace individual pupils' actual instructional time over the school day in all areas taught; and
- Estimate the dollar expenditure per individual (not average) pupil in a classroom.

In this chapter we will accomplish only some of these tasks, and this will be done by means of an extremely simplified example. However, we hope that this first attempt at tracing school district and classroom resources to individual pupils' learning opportunities will open a new avenue for evaluation and accountability.

We have constructed our example so that (personnel) dollar resources are followed down to individual pupils. We have invented an elementary school district containing two schools, twelve classes, and 300 pupils. We have linked the data for this hypothetical school district to real time allocation data from two first grade classes.[4]

Organization, structure, and personnel expenditure for the example district are very simple (Table 5-2). The elementary school district has only 300 pupils, who are enrolled in two equal size schools in grades 1 to 6. Each school has six classes, one in each grade level. These classes have average enrollments of twenty-five pupils and are staffed by classroom teachers paid an average of $15,000 per year. The instructional staff also includes two specialist teachers working out of the central office. Teachers are supported by a curriculum coordinator, as well as by administrative personnel and other staff at both schools and in the central office. The total proportion of the personnel budget devoted to direct instruction is 53.6 percent (Table 5-3); 5.8 percent is devoted to instructional support, and 40.6 percent is devoted to administrative, clerical, custodial, and health services.

Our example district is rather wealthy. This becomes more obvious when we translate the expenditure into per pupil personnel expenditure (Table 5-4). On the average, the school district spends $1,321 of personnel expenditure per pupil. More than half of that is going to direct instruction. A pupil's classroom teacher costs, on the average, 45.4 percent of all personnel expenditures. But classroom teachers' salaries vary according to the degrees they hold and their experience. Thus, some classes have more "expensive" teachers than others. And within classes, some pupils are likely to receive more teacher time than others, depending on their attendance and their teacher's teaching strategies.

If we now trace costs to the two example classrooms,[5] then we assume, to simplify, that the district's twelve classes share equally all personnel expenditures for administrative and noninstructional

Table 5-2. A Small Elementary School District and Its Personnel Expenditure.

I. *Demographic characteristics*

Enrollment:	300 pupils
Number of schools:	2
Grade span:	1-6
Number of classes:	12 (1 per grade in each school)
Average class size:	25

II. *Personnel Expenditure*
Central Office Staff
Administrative and noninstructional support staff:

1 Superintendent	$ 28,000	
1 Business manager	24,000	
1 Administrative intern	10,000	
1 Nurse	14,000	
1 Secretary	9,000	
		$ 85,000

Instructional support staff:

1 Curriculum coordinator	$ 23,000	
		$ 23,000

Specialist teachers:

1 Specialist in reading/language	$ 18,000	
1 Specialist in art	14,500	
		$ 32,500

School personnel
Administrative and noninstructional support staff:

2 Principals @ $22,000	$ 44,000	
2 Secretaries @ $7,500	15,000	
2 Custodians @ $8,500	17,000	
		$ 76,000

Teaching staff:

12 Classroom teachers @ $15,000 (average)	$ 180,000	
		$ 180,000
District's total personnel expenditure		$ 396,500

as well as districtwide instructional support staff. These costs bind 46.4 percent of total personnel expenditures, or $613 per pupil. However, district classes vary in classroom teacher salaries as well as in specialist teacher allocations. Our classrooms do not share the specialist teachers. These pupils consequently do not receive any of the average $108 per pupil for specialist instruction. On the other hand, the teachers of our example classes (grade 1 classes) receive far above the district's average teacher salary because of their long teaching experience. Thus, the average per pupil expenditure for classroom teacher time in these two classrooms is higher than

Table 5-3. Personnel Expenditure for Instructional and Other Staff.

			Percent of Total Expenditure
Personnel expenditure for direct instruction			
Specialist teachers	$ 32.500		
Classroom teachers	180,000		
		$212,500	53.6
Personnel expenditure for instructional support			
	$ 23,000		
		$ 23,000	5.8
Personnel expenditure for administrative and			
noninstructional support staff			
Central office	$ 85,000		
Schools	76,000		
		$161,000	40.6
District's total personnel expenditure			
		$396,500	100.0

the district average (Table 5-5). Thus, although the classes do not receive any specialist time, the per pupil expenditure for direct instruction is 10 percent higher in class 1 and 6 percent higher in class 2 than the district average. We want to keep these district

Table 5-4. Per Pupil Expenditure for Instructional and Other Staff.

	Dollars per Pupil		Percent of Total Expenditure	
Personnel expenditure for direct instruction				
Specialist teachers	108		8.2	
Classroom teachers	600		45.4	
		708		53.6
Personnel expenditure for instructional support	77		5.8	
		77		5.8
Personnel expenditure for administrative and noninstructional support staff				
Central office	283		21.4	
Schools	253		19.2	
		536		40.6
District's per pupil total personnel expenditure		1,321		100.0

Table 5-5. Per (Enrolled) Pupil Staff Expenditure for Example Classes.

	Class 1	Percent of Total	Class 2	Percent of Total
Class Size (Enrollment)	27		28	
Personnel expenditure for direct instruction				
Specialist teachers	0		0	
Classroom teachers ($21,000)	778		750	
	778	55.9	750	55.0
Other personnel expenditure	613	44.1	613	45.0
Total per pupil personnel expenditure	1,391	100.0	1,363	100.0

and classroom level averages in mind when we now trace instructional costs to individual pupils in these two classes. In order to do this, we analyze the amounts of teacher time that individual pupils receive and attach dollar figures to them.

In school 1, the day is five hours and twenty minutes long. School 2 has a longer day: six hours and five minutes (Figure 5-3). This discrepancy results from the fact that the pupils in school 2 go home for lunch while those in school 1 have lunch in school. Lunch time for school 1 is accordingly shorter. The scheduled times for instruction are more uniform—four hours and thirty minutes versus four hours and twenty-five minutes. However, scheduled instructional time is not necessarily equal to actual instructional time (Table 5-6).

The class in the first school used about thirty-two minutes more than the scheduled time for breaks (lunch, recess, and toilet), cutting actual instructional time down to 238 minutes. The class in the second school actually extended the school day by 3 minutes and used 2 minutes less than the scheduled lunch time to extend instruction by 5 minutes beyond the 265 minute schedule. From these and other data, it became clear that school 1 has unrealistically scheduled too little time for breaks.

Teachers and pupils used the available instructional times quite differently (Table 5-7). The first teacher devoted ninety-four minutes (40 percent) to pupil contact and seventy-two minutes (30 percent) both to monitoring seatwork and for classroom management and transitions between activities. The second teacher, on the other hand, spent 175 minutes (65 percent) of the time directly teaching pupils. This is 86 percent more pupil contact time than the first teacher spent, a result that came about because of closer

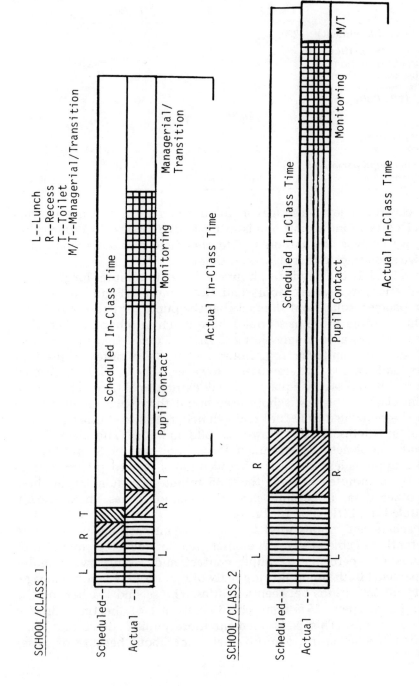

Figure 5-3. The school day in school/class 1 and school/class 2.

Table 5-6. Scheduled and Actual Activity Durations (in minutes).

	School/Class 1			School/Class 2		
	Actual (A)	*Scheduled (S)*	*Discrepancy (A–S)*	*Actual (A)*	*Scheduled (S)*	*Discrepancy (A–S)*
Total School Day	320	320	0	368	365	3
Total Break Time	82	50	32	98	100	–2
Lunch	44	25	19	58	60	–2
Recess	17	15	2	40	40	0
Toilet	21	10	11	0	0	0
Total In Class Time	238	270	–32	270	265	5

Table 5-7.   Teacher and Pupil Time.

	School/Class 1		School/Class 2	
	Minutes	*Percent of Total In Class Time*	*Minutes*	*Percent of Total In Class Time*
Teacher				
Pupil contact	94	39.5	175	64.8
Monitoring	72	30.3	70	25.9
Managerial-transitional	72	30.3	25	9.3
Average Pupil				
Teacher contact	31	13.0	124	45.9
Seatwork	117	49.2	128	47.4
Managerial-transitional	90	37.8	18	6.7
Total In Class Time	238	100.0	270	100.0

correspondence between scheduled and actual break time and less time spent in management tasks and transitions.

In addition, because of differences in teaching strategy—that is, time allocations to supervised group settings with varying numbers of participants—this 80 percent difference in teacher time translates to almost a fourfold difference (31 versus 114 minutes) in teacher contact time for pupils. Thus even though pupils spent similar amounts of time in seatwork (117 versus 128 minutes or about 50 percent of their time), time on actual instructional tasks (including seatwork) was 64 percent greater in class 2 than it was in class 1 (242 versus 148 minutes).

The two teachers followed quite different grouping and individualization strategies (Table 5-8). In class 2, a third of the time is spent in whole class instruction as compared with only 6 percent or 7 percent in class 1, depending on whether we focus on teacher or average pupil time. The teachers used subgroup instruction to about the same extent.[6] But the teacher in class 1 spent considerably more time tutoring and monitoring, which resulted in, relatively, much more average seatwork time for that class.

But within each class pupils receive differential amounts of their teacher's time. We have, thus, found the pupil who had the least contact with the teacher and the one who had the most (Table 5-9). We will compare these extreme figures with the average time that pupils and teacher interact. Teacher-pupil contact time is defined as the ratio of total time allocation to group size, assuming that teacher time, as an educational resource, is allocated equally among group members. This is surely in error, but the general effect of this specification should be to reduce rather than increase estimated variations in resource allocations.

In class 1, the pupil who receives minimum teacher time spends ten minutes in whole class instruction and receives six minutes

Table 5-8. Teachers' Grouping and Individualization Strategies.

	Teacher Time		Mean Pupil Time	
Type of Instruction	Minutes	Percent of Total	Minutes	Percent of Total
School/Class 1				
Whole class	10	6	10	7
Subgroup	58	35	19	13
Tutorial	26	16	1	1
Monitoring	72	43	—	—
Seatwork	—	—	117	79
Total time	168	100	148	100
School/Class 2				
Whole class	82	33	82	32
Subgroup	86	36	42	17
Tutorial	7	3	a	b
Monitorial	70	28	—	—
Seatwork	—	—	128	51
Total time	245	100	252	100

[a]Less than 0.5 minutes.

[b]Less than 0.5 percent.

of teacher instruction in a subgroup. That is, over the whole school day, this pupil spends sixteen minutes in settings where the teacher is instructing and spends all the other instructional time in seatwork. If we take group size into account and dilute the teacher-pupil contact time proportionately by the size of the group, then this pupil received, on the day of observation, a teacher resource equivalent of two and one-half minutes, only a little more than half the average pupil resource allocation, which amounted to four and one-half minutes. However, the pupil with maximum teacher contact time received six minutes, more than double the amount of the pupil with minimum teacher contact. This difference is due to more subgroup instruction for the "maximum pupil," since all pupils share equally the whole class instruction, and that pupil did not receive any tutoring.

The picture in class 2 is quite similar, in relative terms. The minimum pupil received a little more than half the teacher contact time of the "average pupil," and the "maximum pupil" received more than twice that of the "minimum pupil." However, the time allocation in minutes is considerably greater in class 2 than in class 1, because the teacher, on the whole, spends considerably more time in direct pupil instruction. It is apparent that teaching strategy seriously affects teacher-pupil contact time for the class as a whole as well as for individual pupils.

Table 5-9.   Minimum, Average per Pupil, and Maximum In Class Teacher Contact Times and Teacher Resource Allocations (in minutes).

	Whole Class	Subgroup[a] A	Subgroup[a] B	Subgroup[a] C	Tutorial	Total Teacher Contact
Class 1						
Pupil with minimum teacher contact time						
Group size	21	3	—	—	—	—
Total pupil time allocation	10	6	—	—	—	16
Teacher resource allocation per pupil	.5	2.0	—	—	—	2.5
Average teacher contact time per pupil						
Group size	21	7	6	—	1	—
Total pupil time allocation	10	13	6	—	1	31[b]
Teacher resource allocation per pupil	.5	1.9	.9	—	1.2	4.5
Pupil with maximum teacher contact time						
Group size	21	7	6	—	—	—
Total pupil time allocation	10	16	19	—	—	35
Teacher resource allocation per pupil	.5	2.3	3.2	—	—	6.0
Class 2						
Pupil with minimum teacher contact time						
Group size	22	16	—	—	—	—
Total pupil time allocation	82	8	—	—	—	90
Teacher time allocation per pupil	3.7	.5	—	—	—	4.2
Average teacher contact time per pupil						
Group size	22	7	16	10[c]	1	—
Total pupil time allocation	82	26	6	—	[d]	124
Teacher resource allocation per pupil	3.7	3.6	.4	—	.3	8.0
Pupil with maximum teacher contact time						
Group size	22	10	6	16	—	—
Total pupil teacher allocation	82	17	31	8	—	138
Teacher resource allocation per pupil	3.7	1.7	5.2	.5	—	11.1

[a]The subgroup labels (A, B, C) are arbitrary and designate distinctive subgroup experiences in each class.

[b]Does not sum because of rounding.

[c]This time allocation, accounted here as subgroup, is actually for pullout instruction.

[d]Less than one-half minute.

In order to complete our resource flow exposition, we will now translate teacher time allocations to pupils into dollar figures. Aside from the assumption that our observations are typical, this will be done by specifying that teacher salaries are paid only for the typical 180 day school year and only for the scheduled instructional time. We will determine the teacher cost bound in direct teacher-pupil interaction. The importance of the argument resides in the relationships of per pupil teacher cost compared within and between classrooms and in the relationship of teacher cost bound in direct teacher-pupil contact as compared with costs bound in seatwork and in managerial and monitoring activities. Both of these relationships are heavily influenced by teaching strategies.

We have stated earlier that the per pupil teacher costs in our example classrooms were higher than the district average because the teachers of these classes have considerably greater teaching experience than the district's teachers on the average. This is of course also reflected in a teacher's per minute cost (Table 5-10).[7] We will now analyze how much of these costs are bound in direct teacher-pupil contact time.

On the average, pupils in class 1 receive less than half of the teacher resources (45 percent) in direct teacher contact, while pupils in class 2 receive, on the average, 85 percent of teacher resources in direct instruction. If we assume that direct teacher instruction has more impact on pupil learning than seatwork does, we would like to redirect the teaching strategy used in class 1.

If we go to the individual pupil level and from there to the extremes, we find that pupils in class 1 can receive as little as one-fourth of an average pupil's teacher cost in direct teacher contact while others might receive up to 60 percent of such resources in that form. The range is even more pronounced in class 2, where pupils might receive between 44 and 117 percent of average per pupil teacher resources in direct instruction. It is important to note that the pupil with the smallest direct teacher resource allocation in class 2 receives about as much as the average pupil in class 1.

This differential in teacher resource allocation to pupils is a consequence of the classroom teacher's teaching strategies. It is not an outflow of curricular differences, since both first grade classrooms were working with very similar content emphases, using, for example, identical reading materials. Which strategy can be considered more effective? We have not traced the teachers' instruction through to pupil achievement, but, in general, it is justifiable to believe that more teacher-pupil contact results in

Table 5-10. Classroom Teacher Cost and Resource Allocation to Direct Teacher-Pupil Contact.

Classroom Teacher Cost

	Length of School Day	Cost Per Minute	Cost Per Year (180 days)
District average	4 hrs. 30 mins.	$ .31	$15,000
Class 1 average	4 hrs. 30 mins.	.43	21,000
Class 2 average	4 hrs. 25 mins.	.44	21,000

Per Pupil Classroom Teacher Cost

	Number of Pupils	Teacher Salary	Per Pupil Teacher Cost Per Year
District average	300	$180,000	$600
Class 1 average	27	21,000	778
Class 2 average	28	21,000	750

Cost of Direct Teacher-Pupil Contact

	Contact Time (in minutes)	Time Per Year (in minutes)	Cost Per Year	Percent per Year Average per Pupil Teacher Cost
Class 1				
Minimum pupil	2.5	450	$194	25
Average pupil	4.5	810	348	45
Maximum pupil	6.0	1,080	464	60
Class 2				
Minimum pupil	4.2	756	333	44
Average pupil	8.0	1,440	634	85
Maximum pupil	11.1	1,998	879	117

more learning. This has been the basic rationale for smaller class sizes and pull-out programs. Thus if this assumption holds, the teacher in class 1 does not allocate her time as effectively as the teacher in class 2.

RESOURCE LIMITS AND PUPIL OPPORTUNITY

In a very simplified fashion, we have analyzed the powerful role played by personnel resources in constraining and delimiting the instructional decisions made by teachers. These constraints determine the average resource allocation per pupil and limit the forms that these allocations can take. They force teachers into trade-offs between intense contact with few pupils accompanied by large amounts of unsupervised time for many, on the one hand, and large group instruction for all, on the other. Tracing these resources to individual pupils has highlighted the vast variations in educational oppoutunity accompanying these resource-constrained instructional decisions.

Surely, teaching resources are scarce, but additionally, some pupils get many more than others. We cannot but conclude that, within elementary classrooms, the teacher is the major cause of these large differences in pupil opportunity and use of resources. These findings are fundamentally disturbing to us. Some classrooms seem to be on the verge of being expensive depositories, while others actually serve to provide education. The reasons why some pupils might actually receive very little teacher instruction must be exposed.

Our concern for pupil learning, especially for pupils who live in circumstances that do not support school type learning, makes it necessary to open the classroom door if we are to improve education. Teacher education and continuing teacher training will be hampered if the actual classroom processes continue to be locked behind that door.

APPENDIX A: RESOURCE AND GROUPING PROFILES FOR FOLLOW-THROUGH EVALUATION CLASSES—DESCRIPTION OF VARIABLES

The time distributions reported here show the percentage of time that teachers, aides, volunteers, and pupils spend in each group setting. Instructional groupings include tutorial instruction with one or two pupils, group instruction with three to eight pupils, and group instruction with more than eight pupils. The amount of time that adults spend without children or that pupils spend in unsupervised activities (without adults) is also reported.

The time percentages were calculated against the base of the total number of observations made in a class, site, or curriculum. If, for example, sixty observations were made in a particular class, perhaps one teacher was observed during fifty-four of these, while two teachers were observed in the remaining six. This would result in sixty-six teacher "occurrences" and an estimated full-time equivalent teacher staff of 66/60 = 1.10. If thirty-three of these "occurrences" were in small groups, the corresponding teacher time allocation was estimated as 33/66 or 50 percent. Full-time equivalences for aides and volunteers were estimated by computations parallel to those for the teacher staff and the corresponding time distribution estimated in a manner similar to that for teacher time allocations.

The "number of pupils" was calculated in a manner similar to that used to obtain the full-time equivalent personnel values. Thus, the "occurrences" of pupils were divided by the "number of observations" to yield the number of pupils who were present in the classroom at the times when observations were made. Note that this figure corresponds to attendance rather than to enrollment. The pupil time allocations to grouping settings were also estimated from the "occurrences" of pupils in groups of various sizes. (See Appendix B for a discussion of the logic of these procedures.) Ratios of the pupil figure and those for the adults formed the "pupil-adult ratios." These values are based on those reported in SRI (1974).

We have also reported means of the actual "enrollment," "attendance," and "class duration" values recorded by the classroom observers at the beginning of each day of observation.

APPENDIX B: CONVERSION OF INSTRUCTIONAL TO PUPIL TIME

The amount of teaching time devoted to a particular grouping context in which an adult participates, τ, can be summarized as the product of three factors: (1) The number of instructional personnel in the classroom, π; (2) the proportion of teaching time devoted to the specific context, γ; and (3) the daily duration of instruction, δ—that is, $\tau = \pi \gamma \delta$. The aggregate daily time that pupils are exposed to instruction in that grouping context, α, is then equal to the product of the group size, κ, and the instructional time offered, τ—namely, $\alpha = \kappa \tau$. As the average pupil in a class of size N is proportionately exposed to only one part out of N of the aggregate time, the average daily pupil exposure time in a grouping context is θ $(= \alpha/N) = \kappa \tau /N$. As the daily exposure time can also be written as the product of the proportionate pupil exposure time in the context, λ, and the daily duration of instruction, δ— that is, as $\theta = \lambda \delta$—this implies that

$$\lambda\delta = \theta = \kappa \gamma /N$$

$$= \kappa\ (\pi\gamma\delta)/N$$

$$=\left(\frac{\pi}{N}\right) (\kappa\gamma)\ \delta,$$

that is, that

$$\lambda = \left(\frac{\pi}{N}\right)\kappa\gamma.$$

That is, the proportion of pupil time spent in a grouping context equals the product of (1) the personnel intensity ratio, π/N, (2) the group size, and (3) the proportion of instructional time devoted to that context.

If we write the intensity ratio as ρ and index the supervised grouping contexts with the size of the group, then

$$\lambda_k = K\rho\gamma_k .$$

If we index unsupervised time for pupils and time without children for adults with 0, then

$$\sum_{K=0}^{N} \lambda_k = 1 \tag{5.1}$$

$$= \sum_{K=1}^{N} K\rho\gamma_k = \rho \sum_{K=1}^{N} K\gamma_k$$

$$= \rho \sum_{K=0}^{N} K\gamma_k \tag{5.2}$$

$$= \rho\mu, \text{ and}$$

$$\lambda_0 = 1 - \sum_{K=1}^{N} \lambda_k = 1 - \rho\mu, \tag{5.3}$$

where μ is the mean group size.

We can compute the proportion of pupil time in a range of group sizes (say l_1, to l_2) as

$$\sum_{K=l_1}^{l_2} \lambda_k = \sum_{K=l_1}^{l_2} K\rho\gamma_k = \rho \sum_{K=l_1}^{l_2} K\gamma_k.$$

The ratio of pupil to teaching time in this range is

$$\frac{\sum\limits_{K=l_1}^{l_2} K\gamma_k}{\sum\limits_{K=l_1}^{l_2} \gamma_k} = \mu(l_1, l_2),$$

the mean group size for groups having between l_1 and l_2 pupils. Therefore, denoting

$$\sum_{K=l_1}^{l_2} \lambda_k \text{ by } \lambda(l_1, l_2), \text{ and}$$

$$\sum_{K=l_1}^{l_2} \gamma_k \text{ by } \gamma(l_1, l_2), \text{ then}$$

$$\lambda(l_1, l_2) = \rho\,[\mu(l_1, l_2)]\,[\gamma(l_1, l_2)]. \tag{5.4}$$

This average result holds for any contextual partitioning of instructional and pupil time, which can be described by group size distributions, not merely those defined by group sizes.

APPENDIX C: TWO SAMPLE FIRST GRADE CLASSROOMS

A Monday in Mrs. Sitner's First Grade Class

School. The school serves grades K–8. It has a teaching staff of about forty-five and an enrollment of about 900 pupils, all of whom are black. The school received ESEA Title I funds during the observation year, since 44.7 percent of its pupils come from low income families. The principal estimated that about 70 percent of the pupils live in single parent families. The school operates on a "closed campus" basis—that is, instruction begins at 9:10

A.M., and pupils remain in the building with their teachers until dismissal at 14:30 P.M. All pupils receive a free lunch at school, and about half of the pupils arrive early to participate in a free breakfast program. The school building is very old and in poor condition.

Teacher. Mrs. Sitner has been teaching at this school for seventeen years.

Class. Enrollment in fall thirty-one, now twenty-seven. During the school year (observations were performed in May), twelve pupils have transferred out and eight have transferred into the class. One pupil (16), although enrolled, attended school for only one day (November 3) and then returned on March 15. He had not been ill. The class is the one with the lowest achievers out of three first grade classes in this school.

Absence. On Mondays and Fridays typically five to six pupils are absent, on Tuesday, Wednesdays, and Thursdays typically two to three.

Aide Support. An aide is allocated to the class for one hour per day. However, the teacher cannot count on the aide for a specific time.

Curricular Material. Reading—Distar (SRA).

Grouping. Teacher groups only for reading instruction. She has three groups for Distar reading.

Weekly Schedule.

Gym	Wednesdays	13:00 – 13:45
Music	Thursdays	12:15 – 13:00
Enrichment	Fridays	13:00 – 14:30

Enrichment includes Spanish, sewing, art, French, dancing, embroidery. Interest groups are formed.

Daily Schedule.

Recess	10:30 – 10:45
Lunch	11:00 – 11:25

2 toilet breaks approximately 5 minutes long

Classroom Atmosphere. Classroom is disorderly. Pupils are unusually quiet and lethargic.

A Monday in Mrs. Sitner's First Grade Class

9:10   Bell. Teacher collects money for field trip.

9:15   Seatwork, materials are passed out (paper). Writing assignment: copy from blackboard words and story. If finished they should work on mathematics problems, also on blackboard.

9:23   Reading Group I (GI) is called to the reading area (9 pupils, highest group).

9:28   Start GI read aloud whole group. Distar program: "A dog was in the park. . . . I live on a ship . . ." Stories 130, 131, 132 (preparation).

9:38   End of GI. Pupils return to their seats.

9:40   Reading Group II (GII) is called (3 pupils, middle group).

9:42   Start GII read aloud whole group. Story 103.

9:48   End of GII. Pupils return to their seats.

9:49   Reading Group III (GIII) is called (7 pupils, lowest group).

9:50   Start GIII. Sounding words out.

10:06   End of GIII. Pupils return to their seats. Two pupils (3) and (11) usually GII were not called for reading. They sleep in their seats.

10:08   Toilet recess. Girls line up; boys line up.

10:17   Back from toilet recess. Teacher handles some administrative issue with woman who entered the class. One girl complains of neckaches.

10:19   Teacher checks writing seatwork and gives individual help.

10:30   Recess.

10:47   Back from recess; pupils rest.

10:59   Whole class. Read on blackboard days of the week and story writing on blackboard. Story: Today is Monday, May 16, 1977. It is a warm day. The sun is shining. The flowers are blooming. The leaves on the trees are green.

11:00   Lunch. Girls line up; boys line up.

11:44   Back from lunch. Whole class seatwork: number copying and story copying off blackboard. Teacher checks and helps individual pupils.

11:51   Pupils (3) and (11) are called. Reading. They were absent over a longer time and receive individual reading instruction.

11:53   Start reading (3) and (11).
12:00   End of reading (3) and (11).
12:05   Pupils line up at teacher's desk to deliver their mathematics seatwork. Teacher corrects it.
12:24   End of mathematics correcting.
12:25   Physical exercises, whole class.
12:26   End of exercises. Teacher collects pupils' written work while pupils stay in their seats.
12:31   GI gets books "Pets and People." Read silently as seatwork.
12:35   GII and (3) (GII) and (10) (GIII). Seatwork sentence completion.
12:45   (16) and (GII) worksheet for seatwork. Task: detect differences in words and underline.
12:50   Worksheet 3 is given to GII: 2, 3, 8, and 13; and GIII: 10, 14. These six pupils sit down on special table with worksheet and teacher. Task: describe pictures.
13:10   End of work with worksheet 3.
13:12   GI is called. GI starts reading in reading book ("Pets and People") about "Gus, the dog."
13:22   End of GI.
13:23   Toilet recess. Girls in line; boys in line.
13:35   Back from toilet recess.
13:37   Whole class seatwork. Teacher checks some pupils' work.
13:45   Whole class. Teacher hands out permission forms for field trip. Pupils have to write in room number (111). Leave: 9:00. Day: Wednesday (is copied from blackboard). Date: May 25, 1977. Place: Lincoln Park. Lunch: at school. Cost: $1.00.
14:12   End of form writing. Teacher collects work from pupils and fills out form for one pupil. Also checks again on who already paid for field trip.
14:24   Whole class, clean up desks.
14:30   End of school day.

A Thursday in Miss Hernandez's First Grade Class

School. The school is a branch elementary school that serves only grades K-3, with an enrollment of 670 pupils and about twenty-five teachers. Approximately 95 percent of the pupils are Spanish, and 35-40 percent speak minimal English when they enter kindergarten. The pupils' families are primarily blue collar workers, with relatively few families on welfare. This school operates on an "open campus"

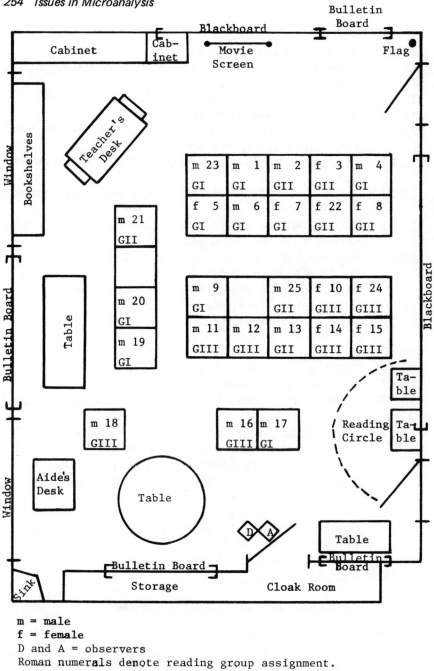

m = male
f = female
D and A = observers
Roman numerals denote reading group assignment.
All pupils are black.

Figure 5-4. Mrs. Sitner's Classroom, First Grade (5/16/77, 5/17/77).

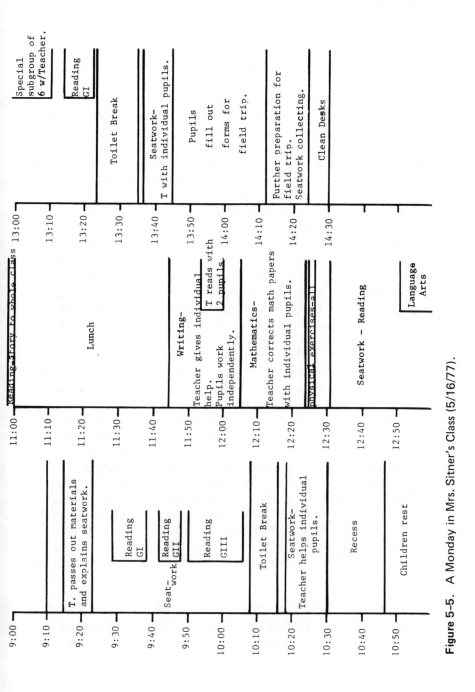

Figure 5-5. A Monday in Mrs. Sitner's Class (5/16/77).

basis; instruction is scheduled from 9:10 A.M. to 15:15 P.M., with a lunch break from noon until 13:00. About half of the children go home for lunch. A continuous first through third grade bilingual program is provided for some pupils. The school was built in 1973 and is completely carpeted and air conditioned.

Teacher. Spanish, twenty years experience (four to five years at this school). Has always taught in inner city.

Class. Enrollment: twenty-eight, but only twenty-five attend regularly. One has dropped out, one has moved to Texas, and one is in Mexico. Only one pupil has officially transferred during the school year (observations were performed in June). Pupils were chosen for this class because all of them were speaking only Spanish at the beginning of school in September. Most children had not gone to kindergarten. Pupils thus range widely in ability, but teacher says this is not a problem, that they are "compatible." She feels that, because of their language difficulty, the brighter ones haven't "discovered their potential" yet. Next year three eight year olds will go to a second-third grade class. Pupil (23) will repeat first grade; the rest will be split between low and middle second grade. Three pupils should be in second grade (pupils 2, 9, 24) and were in bilingual classes before this year. Pupil (2) has been labeled minimal LD, but teacher disagrees. Pupil (23) has a congenital arm injury—cannot move right arm freely from shoulder. Doctors say the arm needs to be broken and reset, and parents may allow this over the summer. His right hand seems to be dominant, but he has been trying to write with his left. Teacher has special assignments for him for most of the day—he has spent most of the year working with manipulables, has just started writing and working on cutting and pasting. He reads quite well, is in RGIII. Next year he will repeat first grade, as he must learn to write before going on. Teacher reports that two pupils come into her class for reading instruction. Pupil (28) is from second grade—present on both days of observation. Other pupil is from third grade. Teacher says he "doesn't need to be here," reads well in Spanish, but his teacher wants him to come to her class. He did not come in on either observation day—I don't know if he was absent or didn't come in for some other reason.

Pull-out Instruction. Two groups go out three times per week for Distar language with language teacher. About half the class is involved—there is no set schedule for these classes. Teacher says

Distar language program is good for these pupils because it "makes it easy to start talking." Pupils' parents come in to talk to the teacher, but they don't get very involved. Teacher says this is a cultural difference: "School is the teacher's domain." All but four pupils qualify for free lunch. A few families are on welfare, but usually because they have such large families.

Absence. On days of observation: Wednesday, no pupil absent; Thursday, three pupils (3, 18, 26) absent.

Aide Support. Teacher has no aide support. Says she could have had someone for two forty-minute periods per week, but it is not worth it. Teachers decided to give up their aides to allow them to work in the kindergarten language program.

Curricular Materials. *Reading:* Distar—they just follow the program. Reading skill cards—work on skills in order of difficulty. *Mathematics:* follows skill cards. Teacher makes or collects own material. Three groups. Reading and mathematics take most of the time. Teacher also tries to do music and social studies, but this is "very incidental." At beginning of year, taught more, then retaught lesson in Spanish. Teacher feels that Distar is excellent for these children becuase it is so phonetic. Can teach sounds from the very beginning whether pupils speak English or not. All pupils in this class are reading, and this is unusual. Also, Spanish is a very phonetic language, so parents can understand the Distar program better. Says the program may be too slow "for some children in the suburbs."

Grouping. Teacher groups for reading and mathematics instruction. She has three groups for Distar reading and three mathematics groups. At the beginning of the school year, teacher had two reading and two writing groups, because some pupils needed more instruction in Spanish than others.

Weekly Schedule.

Library	Mondays	9:00 – 9:40
Gym	Wednesdays	11:15 – 11:55
Language Arts	Fridays	9:40 – 10:20

Daily Schedule. Teacher says she has a set schedule—normally does all reading in the morning. But observation days showed considerable variation.

	Recess	10:40 – 11:00
		13:55 – 14:15
	Lunch	12:00 – 13:00

Classroom Atmosphere. Very neat and orderly. Decorated with displays of pupils' work and teaching aids (letters and words that stick on the blackboard, charts, pictures, etc.). Very relaxed and friendly atmosphere. Teacher can joke with pupils, but is also firm and consistent. Gives very explicit directions. Appears to keep well informed about each individual's activities and gives individual attention very effectively, checking on work or speaking to individuals briefly but frequently. Teacher uses Spanish for two reasons: (1) to make sure pupils catch on and (2) for general cultural enrichment.

Table 5–11. Miss Hernandez's Classroom Roster.

Pupil Number	Sex	Reading Group[a]	Mathematics Group[b]
1	f	I	1
2	m	I	1
3	m	II	2
—	—	—	—
5	m	I	1
6	f	III	3
7	f	II	2
8	f	II	2
9	f	I	1
10	m	III	3
11	m	I	1
12	f	II	2
13	m	I	1
14	f	I	1
15	m	I	1
—	—	—	—
17	f	II	2
18	m	I	1
19	m	II	2
20	m	I	2
21	m	II	1
22	m	II & III	1
23	m	III	3
24	m	I & II	1
25	f	II	1
26	m	II	1
27	m	I	1

[a]Red = I; White = II; Blue = III.

[b]Jets = 1; Boats = 2; Trains = 3.

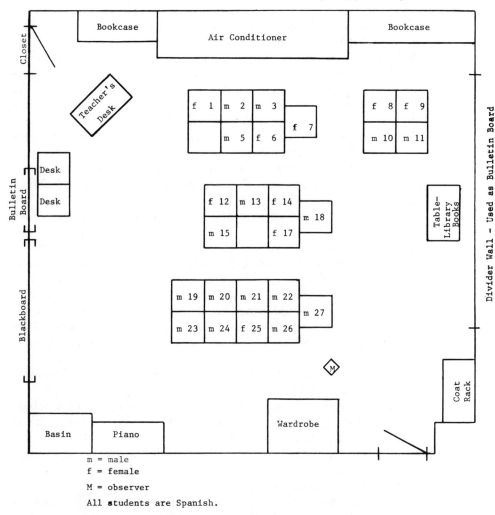

m = male
f = female
M = observer
All students are Spanish.

Figure 5-6. Miss Hernandez's Classroom, First Grade (6/8/77, 6/7/77).

A Thursday in Miss Hernandez's First Grade Class

9:00   Pupils come in, talk to teacher and each other. Teacher speaks to (1) about moving his desk.

9:10   Pledge and "America." Pupils hang up sweaters.

9:13   Pupils sit at front of room. Teacher talks about weather in spring. Someone asks what scientists are. Teacher says "men who study weather, etc." Teacher has a pupil find the first day of summer on calendar to show the class. They talk about weather in summer. Teacher shows summer months on a list of months (written in both English and Spanish). Teacher asks how many pupils are going to Mexico for vacation. About 10 raise their hands.

9:25 Asks if any students are going to move during the summer.

9:26 Goes over work on board: plurals. Teacher points to picture (3 glasses), students say "three glasses." For morning work, pupils are to fold paper into 8 boxes, then, e.g., draw 3 glasses, write "glasses."

9:32 Goes over blends, especially "sh" and "ch." Teacher says, "We people who speak Spanish have lots of trouble with these sounds. We think everything is 'sh.'"

9:36 Children line up. Teacher gives them picture of objects (e.g., a shell). They place the pictures underneath the sign for the correct blend (e.g., "sh"), then check each other.

9:47 End of exercise on blends. Teacher explains worksheet on word endings. On the back is a map showing water and land masses in the world. Teacher says to color water blue, land brown. Teacher calls 7 children's names. Says they did very good work. They stand. Teacher calls names of children who didn't hand in papers. They go to desks and look for papers, then come to teacher's desk.

9:51 Pupils return to their desks, begin seatwork assignments.

9:52 Teacher gives worksheets to (23).

9:53 Children whose names were called earlier go to teacher's desk (pupils 2, 8, 10, 13, 22, 24). Teacher talks to them about their work.

9:56 Pupils return to their seats. Teacher moves several pupil's desks.

9:58 End of desk moving.

10:00 Teacher checks (23)'s work; circulates, checking on others; speaks to (17) in Spanish.

10:04 Teacher calls "White Stars" (RGII: 4 boys, 5 girls).

10:05 RGII starts, works on sounds.

10:14 RGII reads story. Pupils at desk are all working on assignments.

10:27 Pupil (1) is lying down, head on desk. (27) raises his hand, has finished work. Teacher signals to him to draw on the back of his paper. (23) whispers to (20) for help, no response.

10:36 RGII ends. Teacher checks on (23). Asks to see (1) and (2), looks at their work until 10:39. Talks to (25) while they get their papers.

10:38   (19) goes to speech ([18] is supposed to, but is absent).

10:39   All pupils put things away.

10:40   Leave for recess.

11:01   Return from recess. Teacher calls "Blue Stars" (RGIII).

11:02   Sends (10) and (23) to get (28) from 2nd grade for reading.

11:03   Only (6) is in RGIII; she reads sounds.

11:04   (22) comes to RGIII, reads sounds. Teacher says, "That's beautiful. You can paint instead of reading with us." Teacher reminds "White Stars" to work on their take-homes. (23) returns, they can't find (28)'s classroom. Teacher sends (9) with them.

11:06   (19) returns from speech.

11:07   RGIII pupils return. RGIII starts (pupils 6, 10, 23, and 28). (20) is reading a book.

11:15   (2) and (11) are also reading books now. Teacher says, "I'm going to listen to some of you read these next week." (They are really reading, not just turning pages.)

11:30   Visitor comes in (a former teacher) to show her baby to the class.

11:36   Pupil (9) calls teacher, she checks on painters. (23) goes to seat. (28) leaves. Teacher goes over take-home with (6) and (10).

11:37   (6) and (1) go to seats. Teacher calls "Red Stars" (RGI).

11:39   Someone comes in with a message, talks to teacher. Teacher asks (9) to "be teacher," pupils start work on sounds.

11:40   Teacher returns to RGI.

11:44   RGI starts on story.

11:56   RGI dismissed. Pupils put work away.

11:57   Line up, leave for lunch.

12:55   Pupils return from lunch.

13:02   Teacher talks about morning work. Goes over alphabetizing. Gives papers back to (10) and (19) to be corrected. Asks class, "Minus is the same as?" "Take away."

13:05   Gets painters to join class (forgot earlier). Goes over plural papers. Many pupils didn't put a word in each box. Teacher returns papers that aren't complete (most of the class).

13:08   Pupils correct papers. Red Stars (RGI) work on take-homes. Teacher puts on record of a song they have been learning, works at her desk.

13:11   Gives (23) a writing paper.

13:15   Hands back take-homes to be corrected.

13:17   Puts on a record brought to school by (8); says, "In a few minutes we'll begin our spelling."

13:19   Teacher circulates, checks (23)'s work. Asks (23), "Did you do that writing paper? Let's see it." He goes to get it, erases part and starts over. Teacher forgets to come back to look at it.

13:23   Take out spelling materials. Teacher says, "Some people are going to be in trouble because they put their spelling paper with yesterday's work. If you don't have it, you just can't do spelling today." Three pupils don't have papers (6, 22, 24).

13:25   Teacher dictates—for example, "His dad is sad." (22) takes out a piece of paper. Teacher says, "There's a smart boy. He's going to write on a plain piece of paper. I'll let you do that." (24) takes out paper too. After a while, teacher tells (6) to get out paper.

13:28   Looks at (23)'s writing; says, "Those are fine; those you have to do a little better."

13:30   Teacher writes sentences on board to check.

13:32   Checks (23)'s work.

13:34   Put spelling away, sit in front on the floor.

13:35   Teacher explains next step on paintings: filling in the details. Teacher talks about details (eyes, hair, buttons, etc.); shows different kinds of shirts and sweaters worn by girls and boys; discusses shoes, socks, and so on.

13:47   End of detail discussion.

13:48   Teacher plays record of a story (in Spanish). Shows pictures to go with story. Listen to song on other side of record.

13:51   Pupils return to their seats. Teacher passes out story worksheets, tells pupils she will make a book of all their stories.

13:53   Class does worksheet of rhyming words on back of story sheet.

13:55   Bell, pupils line up for recess.

14:15   Pupils return from recess, begin stories. Some pupils ask her to put words on board—she writes "children," "school," but for some words, says, "that's easy" and doesn't put them on board. Teacher helps with words by showing pupils how to sound them out.

14:28   Teacher talks to (23) about his work, says he did cut-and-paste worksheet "perfectly." Looks at coloring paper.

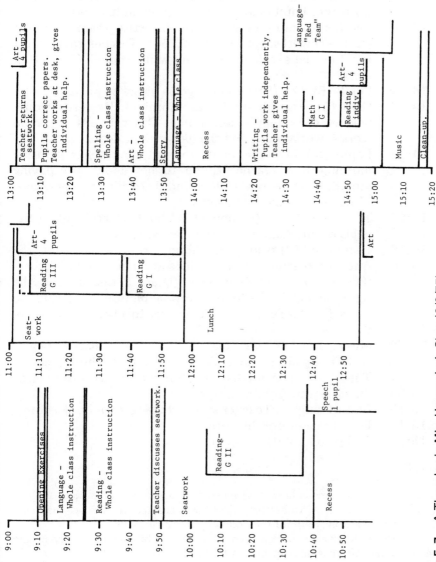

Figure 5-7. A Thursday in Miss Hernandez's Class (6/9/77).

14:29   Language teacher comes to get "Red team" for language. Office calls. Pupil (8)'s mother is there to pick her up. She leaves at 2:30.

14:31   Teacher calls Jets (Math Group I); calls (7); says to try this exercise. (12) wants to try too; teacher says she can if she knows the numbers to 100, tells (6) to try it too. Pupil (10) is the only pupil at his desk.

14:36   Teacher dictates numbers; pupils write them in boxes on their worksheets (e.g., 92, 54). Teacher says, "Just for fun, let's see if you can write these" (110, 105, etc.).

14:44   Pupils (6), (7), (9), and (15) go to closet to paint.

14:48   Calls (5) (was absent in the morning). He reads aloud, teacher gives him a take-home. Other pupils work on stories, worksheets, and the like at their desks.

14:52   Pupil (25) says she wants to read for teacher. (During morning RG, teacher spoke to her about not paying attention.) She reads aloud until 14:55. Teacher says, "You've redeemed yourself."

14:57   Teacher talks to (6) and (15) about an accident in the paint room. Painters return to seats.

14:59   Listens to (13) read from a library book.

15:00   Another teacher comes in to show her a pupil's work. (On a worksheet that said "Draw a ring around the right answer," the pupil drew a picture of a ring on one's finger. Teacher explains this to class, shows them the paper.)

15:02   Music. Teacher plays piano; pupils sing. Teacher begins with a Spanish song. Then lets pupils choose songs. They choose about half English and half Spanish songs.

15:06   Pupils return from language.

15:15   End of singing. Teacher says to take reading books home.

15:16   Pupils clean floor, line up.

15:18   End of school day.

NOTES

1. These data were collected as part of an evaluation of project Follow-Through (Stallings and Kaskowitz, 1974) and characterize classes that constituted a comparison group for the Follow-Through curricula.

2. Formal definitions of the various indices exhibited in the table and their rationales are given in Appendix A to this chapter.

3. A discussion and derivation of these relations is given in Appendix B to this chapter.

4. These data were collected as a part of a larger study that has been reported elsewhere (DeVault, Harnischfeger, and Wiley, 1977b).

5. All classroom-specific data are taken from two actual classrooms, described elsewhere (DeVault, Harnischfeger, and Wiley, 1977b); the base observational records are presented in Appendix C to this chapter.

6. Subgroup instruction was mostly in reading.

7. This cost is calculated in the following way: teacher yearly salary/(Length of school year · length of school day).

REFERENCES

Bloom, B.S. 1973. "Time and Learning." Thorndike Address delivered at the 81st Annual Convention of the American Psychological Association, Montreal.

Carroll, J.B. 1963. "A Model of School Learning." *Teachers College Record* 64 (May): 723-33.

DeVault, M.L.; A. Harnischfeger; and D.E. Wiley. 1977a. *Curricula, Personnel Resources, and Grouping Strategies.* Chicago: ML-GROUP for Policy Studies in Education, CEMREL.

———. 1977b. *Schooling and Learning Opportunity.* Interim Report, Project no. 6-0646, Grant no. NIE-G-77-0004. Chicago: ML-GROUP for Policy Studies in Education, CEMREL.

Harnischfeger, A., and D.E. Wiley. 1975. "Teaching-Learning Processes in Elementary School: A Synoptic View." Studies of Educative Processes no. 9, Department of Education, University of Chicago. Revised as "The Teaching-Learning Process in Elementary Schools: A Synoptic View." *Curriculum Inquiry* 6 (1976): 5-43. Also in American Educational Research Association, *Reading in Educational Research, Educational Organization and Administration,* ed. D.A. Erickson, pp. 195-236. San Francisco: McCutchan, 1976.

———. 1977. "Conceptual Issues in Models of School Learning." Studies of Educative Processes no. 10, ML-GROUP for Policy Studies in Education, CEMREL. Rpt. as "Kernkonzepte des Schullernens." *Zeitschrift für Entwicklungspsychologie und Pädagogische Psychologies* IX: 207-28. Also in *Journal of Curriculum Studies* 10, no. 3 (1978): 215-31.

Stallings, J.A., and D.H. Kaskowitz. 1974. *Follow-Through Classroom Observation Evaluation—1972/73.* Menlo Park, Calif.: Stanford Research Institute.

Stanford Research Institute (SRI). 1974. *Annex to Follow-Through Classroom Observation Report—1972/73.* Menlo Park, Calif.: Stanford Research Institute.

Wiley, D.E. 1973. "Another Hour, Another Day: Quantity of Schooling, a Potent Path for Policy." Studies of Educative Processes no. 3, Department of Education, University of Chicago. Rpt. in *Schooling and Achievement in American Society,* ed. W.H. Sewell, R.M. Hauser, and D.L. Featherman, pp. 225-65. New York: Academic Press, 1976. And in *Evaluation Studies Review Annual,* vol. 2, edited by M. Guttentag, pp. 434-76. Beverly Hills, Calif.: Sage Publications, 1977.

Wiley, D.E., and A. Harnischfeger. 1974. "Explosion of a Myth: Quantity of Schooling and Exposure to Instruction, Major Educational Vehicles." Studies of Educative Processes no. 8, Department of Education, University of Chicago. Rpt. in *Educational Researcher* 3 (4): 7-12.

Index

✳

About the Editors

Robert Dreeben is a sociologist and professor in the Department of Education at the University of Chicago. His major interests lie in the analysis of large-scale organizations, particularly educational organizations, and his most recent work has been concerned with the sociological analysis of classroom instruction and educational effects. His earlier work includes *On What Is Learned In School* and *The Nature of Teaching* as well as many articles.

J. Alan Thomas is William C. Reavis professor of Educational administration in the Department of Education, University of Chicago. After completing his Ph.D. in educational administration and school finance at Stanford University, he participated in several school finance studies and authored *School Finance and Educational Opportunity in Michigan.* His interests in resource allocation resulted in the book *The Productive School* and in more recent work, including a report to the National Institute of Education entitled, "Resource Allocation in Classrooms."